Complete
Indonesian

Christopher Byrnes and
Eva Nyimas

The publisher has used its best endeavours to ensure that the URLs for external websites referred to in this book are correct and active at the time of going to press. However, the publisher and the author have no responsibility for the websites and can make no guarantee that a site will remain live or that the content will remain relevant, decent or appropriate.

For UK order enquiries: please contact Bookpoint Ltd, 130 Milton Park, Abingdon, Oxon, OX14 4SB. *Telephone:* +44 (0) 1235 827720. *Fax:* +44 (0) 1235 400454. Lines are open 09.00–17.00, Monday to Saturday, with a 24-hour message answering service. Details about our titles and how to order are available at www.teachyourself.co.uk

For USA order enquiries: please contact McGraw-Hill Customer Services, PO Box 545, Blacklick, OH 43004-0545, USA. *Telephone:* 1-800-722-4726. *Fax:* 1-614-755-5645.

For Canada order enquiries: please contact McGraw-Hill Ryerson Ltd, 300 Water St, Whitby, Ontario, L1N 9B6, Canada. *Telephone:* 905 430 5000. *Fax:* 905 430 5020.

Long renowned as the authoritative source for self-guided learning – with more than 50 million copies sold worldwide – the *Teach Yourself* series includes over 500 titles in the fields of languages, crafts, hobbies, business, computing and education.

The *Teach Yourself* name is a registered trade mark of Hodder Headline.

British Library Cataloguing in Publication Data: a catalogue record for this title is available from the British Library.

Library of Congress Catalog Card Number: on file.

Previously published as Teach Yourself Indonesian.

First published in UK 2003 by Hodder Education, 338 Euston Road, London, NW1 3BH.

First published in US 2003 by The McGraw-Hill Companies, Inc.

This edition first published 2010.

Typeset by MPS Limited, a Macmillan Company.

Printed in Great Britain for Hodder Education, a division of Hodder Headline, an Hachette Livre UK Company, 338 Euston Road, London, NW1 3BH, by Cox & Wyman Ltd, Reading, Berkshire.

Hodder Headline's policy is to use papers that are natural, renewable and recyclable products and made from wood grown in sustainable forests. The logging and manufacturing processes are expected to conform to the environmental regulations of the country of origin.

Impression number	10 9 8 7 6 5 4 3 2 1
Year	2016 2015 2014 2013 2012 2011 2010

Contents

Acknowledgements

We are grateful to the staff at Teach Yourself books for their diligence and patience and John Pride for his expertise and input for this edition.

Credits

Front cover: © Sergey Skleznev/Alamy

Back cover and pack: © Jakub Semeniuk/iStockphoto.com,
© Royalty-Free/Corbis, © agencyby/iStockphoto.com, © Andy
Cook/iStockphoto.com, © Christopher Ewing/iStockphoto.com,
© zebicho – Fotolia.com, © Geoffrey Holman/iStockphoto.com,
© Photodisc/Getty Images, © James C. Pruitt/iStockphoto.com,
© Mohamed Saber – Fotolia.com

Pack: © Stockbyte/Getty Images

Meet the authors

Christopher Byrnes is a language scholar and teacher. He is an avid language learner, who has studied over a dozen languages. He continues to study new ones while adding to his knowledge of those already learned. He holds a modern languages honours degree and teaching qualifications in MFL (Modern Foreign Languages) and TESOL (Teaching English as a Second or Other Language).

He is the author of several books on teaching and learning languages including *Complete Malay*, also published by Hodder Headline.

With over 25 years learning languages, both formally and through self-study, and over 10 years teaching them at every level from infants to adults, Christopher Byrnes has packed all this experience into this course.

Eva Nyimas is a native of Sumatera. She used to teach languages and tourism at the LIBMI school in Jakarta and she has also taught privately to both adults and children. In addition to Indonesian, she speaks Malay and is proficient in several local languages including Palembangese, Sundanese and Javanese. She also collaborated on *Complete Malay*, published by Hodder Headline. She is dedicated to teaching people about the language and cultures of Indonesia.

For more information and resources for learning Indonesian visit the authors' dedicated website at http://www.speakbahasaindonesia.com

Only got a minute?

Indonesian is spoken by 200 million people in South East Asia and in Indonesian communities all over the world. Indonesian is a form of the Malay language, **Bahasa Melayu**. In fact, to a great extent both languages are mutually intelligible, with some differences in pronunciation and word usage. If you study one, you get the other almost for free! In this volume we are going to focus on the Indonesian form, known as **Bahasa Indonesia** since 1828. The Malaysian form has officially been known as **Bahasa Malaysia** since the decree of 1971.

Where the two varieties differ most is in vocabulary. The Malaysian form has borrowed significantly from English, due to prolonged colonization by the British, whereas the Indonesian has adopted many Dutch words through centuries of Dutch colonization. For example, *Strawberry* in Malay is **Strawberi**, immediately recognizable to English speakers, whereas Indonesian has adopted the Dutch **arbei**.

In addition, some words with similar origins have evolved to have different meanings. For example, in Indonesian **pejabat** means *a functionary* or *an official,* whereas in Malay it means *office*; *a post office* in Malaysia is **pejabat pos**, yet in Indonesia thanks to Dutch influence it is **kantor pos**.

Bahasa Indonesia also includes words borrowed from its colourful array of indigenous languages, especially from Javanese. Indonesian has also been influenced by Arabic, Persian, Chinese and Sanskrit due to its being at the centre of the spice trade for centuries. So while Indonesian is certainly a form of Malay, it is also a language in its own right.

Bahasa Melayu, in both its forms, is the most important language in South East Asia by sheer force of numbers of speakers. It is a language well worth learning for anyone with an interest in SE Asia, for business, and tourism.

If you learn either of these forms of the language, you will cope well with the other, discounting some differences in pronunciation and vocabulary.

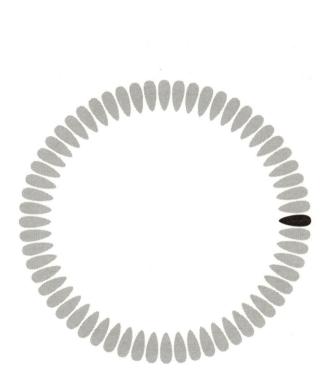

5 Only got five minutes?

You should read through the **Only got a minute?** section before reading this.

Bahasa Melayu, in both its forms, is the most important language in South East Asia by sheer force of numbers of speakers. It is a language well worth learning for anyone with an interest in SE Asia, not just for business, but also for tourism. If you are a student of either one of these forms of the language, you get the other one almost for free, discounting some differences in pronunciation and the borrowings from either English or Dutch.

Indonesian spelling is easy to master because it is very regular. Once you learn how the sounds relate to the written word, which is a quick task in itself, you will be able to read Indonesian easily. There is only one sound that poses any significant challenge to English speakers, and then only when it appears in certain positions in a word. This is represented by **ng**. This sound is the 'twangy' sound found in **orang**, where it poses little difficulty for English speakers. However, it also occurs initially in some words, and in the middle of others, where it must still retain its sound: in the word **jangan**, for example. Indonesians also trill their **r** sounds, but apart from that, the rest of the pronunciation is straightforward, as is the spelling system, which is almost completely regular.

In contrast with English and other European languages, much of the way Indonesian is understood, relies on context rather than on the actual words used. Redundant words, in relation to context, are often left out of sentences when the context is understood. For example, a typical Indonesian greeting, **Mau ke mana?** which means *Where are you going?*, contains neither the word for *you* nor the word for *going*, whose omission is unthinkable in English. However, in Indonesian this is commonplace, especially when the verb *to go* is implicit.

If you've ever struggled with the complicated verb endings and tense forms of a language like French, or the formidable noun cases of German, then you're going to find Indonesian to be a pleasant surprise...

There are no tenses in Indonesian. That is to say, there are no lexically expressed tenses, nor do Indonesian verbs change to express person. This means that a verb, such as **pergi**, *to go*, does not change its form to express *I go*, *he goes*, *we went*, *they will go* etc. The pronouns alone tell you who is doing the action expressed by the verb.

Of course language needs to express present, past and future events, because these concepts exist as very real parts of our life experience. So how does Indonesian do this?

Points in time are simply expressed by stating when an action is supposed to take place. For example, **Saya makan nasi goreng setiap hari** means *I eat nasi goreng every day*. **Saya** means *I*, **makan** means *eat* and **setiap hari** means *every day*. There, the present tense is conveyed by the context. If I said, **Saya makan nasi goreng kemarin**, where **kemarin** means *yesterday*, the verb is automatically sent into the past. So the meaning automatically translates as *I ate nasi goreng yesterday*.

Where a time expression is not appropriate, Indonesian uses what we call tense markers. These are words that, when used before the verb, convey the idea of tense. **Sedang** means *now* in Indonesian, but placing it before a verb conveys the idea of what we call a continuous tense in English. For example, **Saya sedang makan gado-gado**. *I am eating gado-gado*. Replace **sedang** with **sudah**, which literally means *already*, and you've got *I ate gado-gado*. **Akan** expresses the future tense, so **Saya akan makan gado-gado** means *I will eat gado-gado*.

10 Only got ten minutes?

Before reading this, you should already have read the **Only got a minute?** and **Only got five minutes?** sections.

Indonesian shares the same concept of counting with many East Asian languages. Objects are counted according to the category they fall into; according to their inherent characteristics, rather than just by number. Chinese does this; Japanese does this and Indonesian does this too!

For example, people are counted as **orang**. So *two teachers* (*teacher*, **guru**) is expressed as **dua orang guru**.

Animals are counted in tails (**ekor**) – whether they have one or not: **dua ekor kucing**, *two cats* (*two tails of cat*, if you will). We count cattle in heads, after all, which is a hint at a concept that is commonplace in Indonesian).

Flat objects, such as *paper* (**kertas**), are counted using **helai**... **Lima** (5) **helai kertas**, *five sheets of paper*, and so on...

There is a range of these counting words, depending on the characteristics of the object concerned. However, they can be omitted without rendering what you are saying inaccurate.

From an English speaker's point of view, Indonesian vocabulary can be very literal, which can aid in learning considerably, once a certain amount of the raw vocabulary has been internalised.

Take the following, for example: *doctor* in Indonesian is **dokter**. The word for *tooth* or *teeth* (Indonesian doesn't bother about complicated plurals like English ones!) is **gigi**, so Indonesian expresses *dentist* as *a tooth doctor*, **dokter gigi**. Using this logic, if I tell you that *animal* in Indonesian is **hewan**, what do you think **dokter hewan** refers to?

If you said *veterinary surgeon* or *vet*, then you are already adapting to a way of thinking that will serve you well throughout your study of Indonesian.

In keeping with the animal theme, for the young of animals, we have all sorts of completely unrelated words in English, i.e. *dog/puppy*, *cat/kitten* and *hen/chick*. Indonesian thinks literally, and expresses each of these using the word for *child* in each case: **panjing**, *dog*, **anak anjing**, *puppy*; **kucing**, *cat*, **anak kucing**, *kitten* and **ayam**, *hen*, **anak ayam**, *chick*.

Some more examples: **rumah**, *house*, **sakit**, *sick*, so **rumah sakit** means *hospital*; **kebun**, *garden*, **binatang** (another word for) *animal*, so an 'animal garden' refers to a *zoo*. Finally, *abroad* in Indonesian is expressed as **luar negeri: luar**, *outside*, **negeri**, *country*.

Indonesian vocabulary is built extensively around root words, or as we refer to them in *Complete Indonesian*, word bases. These root words, once they have affixes attached to them, take on a different but associated meaning. Affixes are 'bits' that are attached to words to create new words, much as we use *re-* in English. In application, when you attach *re-* to *build*, you get *rebuild*, which means *to build again*. When you encounter *re-* again, in such words as *redraw*, you know instinctively that the *re-*, in this instance, means *to draw again*. So it is with Indonesian words, only more so! The way in which Indonesian is built up is far more predictable than it would be in English, if you were learning it as a foreign language. This makes Indonesian particularly transparent, when you know how to look at it in a certain way.

While you could learn vocabulary words as you come across them, without paying any particular attention to the root, or base word, if you do incorporate them into your study, they will help you to gain a deeper, and more rapid, mastery of the language than you might otherwise have had.

Although new words cannot be formed arbitrarily simply by attaching affixes, knowing the function of such affixes can greatly accelerate the learner's ability to assimilate the language. Let's take a look at some affixes, and how they affect vocabulary, just to get a feel for what this is all about:

pe- (a prefix), i.e. added to the beginning of a verb, creates a noun that means the 'doer' of the action. **Main** means *to play*, **pemain** means *player*.

Using **main** again, the addition of **-an** creates a noun from the verb, so we get **mainan**, which means *toy*.

ber- added to nouns creates related verbs with a range of meanings. It can simply make a verb of what the noun is expressing: **gerak**, *movement*; **bergerak**, *to move*. **Ber-** added to words indicating clothes means *to wear* (whatever the item is). **Topi** is a *hat*; **bertopi**, *to wear a hat*.

Words may also include a combination of affixes. For example, **sehat** means *healthy* in Indonesian. To create the noun *health*, Indonesian surrounds this adjective with **ke-** (a prefix) and **-an** (a suffix), giving us **kesehatan**. Many adjectives are changed into nouns in this way.

Ke- and **-an**, attached to a noun can create an extended meaning of that noun. For instance, **bangsa** means *nation*; **kebangsaan** means *nationality*.

Similarly, **per-** and **-an** can be attached to certain nouns to create an extended meaning. For example, **kebun** means *house*; **perkebunan** means *plantation*.

In *Complete Indonesian*, we will introduce the most common affixes, step-by-step, in word-building sections, alongside your learning of conversational Indonesian.

Introduction

Welcome to this brand new edition of *Complete Indonesian*. This fresh approach to learning the language is based on dialogues in the conversational Indonesian of the capital, Jakarta.

We developed this course with three considerations in mind. Our main goal was to produce a course that would give the reader an introduction to real, everyday Indonesian, even when this meant omitting certain archaic forms and other forms that are falling into disuse. This is a somewhat bold approach, as we have opted, at every step of the way, to teach you the language that is actually used in Indonesia today. We began with the premise that you want to learn to speak and understand the language as it is really used, rather than the textbook-style Indonesian that you might find elsewhere.

Second, we have endeavoured to make the language as easy to learn as possible by focusing on the vocabulary and structure that you will really need. Specific terminology has only been included where absolutely necessary. Indonesian is rare among foreign languages in that it is a lot less complicated than others you might have learnt, so why complicate matters?

Third, we have chosen to concentrate on language that is functional and, above all, useful. To achieve the goal of presenting authentic situational language, we have built the course around a series of dialogues that reflect the way Indonesians speak and use language naturally.

By the end of the course you will be able to function with confidence in Indonesian on a variety of topics and situations, and, most of all, you will understand and be understood.

Although the scope of a course such as this is necessarily limited, it does provide a solid grounding in the language that you can use as a base for more advanced study. In the last unit, several suggestions are given to help you develop your skills further.

Structure of the course

Each unit (apart from Unit 1), contains two dialogues based around situations that you will most likely find yourself in either travelling or on business in Indonesia. The first dialogue in each unit deals with the language you will require for handling certain situations such as booking a hotel room or talking about your family. The Part One dialogue is centred around Ken Knight, a businessman from New Zealand with an Indonesian wife and a son and daughter who arrive later. The Part Two dialogue carries on the theme of the unit, consolidating what you already know and building on the knowledge gained in Part One, often taking similar situations and adding the sorts of complication you are more likely to need to deal with in real life. In Part Two we meet Mark Spencer, a student from Leeds who has flown to Indonesia to meet his e-pal, Reza, for the first time.

The two sets of characters carry out a further function in the course: the language in Part One tends to be rather formal, which is the sort of language you will be using if you are on business or if you want to carry out tasks such as booking hotel rooms and asking for information. The interactions between the characters in Part Two mean that we can introduce you to the more informal, chatty language you are likely to want to use among friends. That is not to say that it is slang. It is very good, natural, conversational Indonesian.

Part Two of Unit 17 is intended as a brief introduction to Indonesian street language, i.e. slang.

Each unit is split into two. **Part One** begins with a **dialogue** followed by **vocabulary** and a natural **translation** of the dialogue.

Following this, there is a section of language notes called **How the language works 1**. This section introduces you to various important features of language structure and usage. Many of these sections include some exercises so that you can practise the specific point that section of the language notes refers to. Part One ends with an exercise section that focuses on the receptive skills of reading and listening and includes exercises that ask you to put what you have learnt in Part One to the test.

Part Two follows the same format: **dialogue, translation, vocabulary** and **How the language works 2**. However, the final exercise section concentrates on the so-called *production* skills, that is, writing and speaking, and features mainly communicative exercises that are designed to develop your functional ability in the topic area of each unit. This section requires you to look at both parts of the unit to complete the exercises. The final exercise in this section simulates a situational conversation that you will be able to take part in if you have the recording or another speaker to practise with. In this exercise, you should complete the part indicated in English and then check your answer in the key before using the recording for fluency practice. There may be more than one way of conveying the information in each of the utterances for you to take part in, but we have chosen just one version that either uses language structures and vocabulary you have encountered in the unit or indicates in full a new form to be used.

Complete Indonesian is not an instant solution to your immediate communication needs, in the way that a phrase book is. Nor was it ever intended to be. The goal of *Complete Indonesian* is to make you an autonomous and accurate speaker of the language in the most rapid and efficient way possible. This is best carried out by focusing on presenting the structure of the language in a logical sequence, with each unit building upon the last. For this reason, and to preserve the natural quality of the dialogues, the order in which vocabulary is presented has been deemed secondary to the all-important structure. It is on completing the course that you will find yourself armed with all the tools you need to function accurately and independently in Indonesian.

Learning a language is not just about the words you use, but the way you react and respond to people and situations and even your body language. It is essential that you are aware of possible problems that may arise from a lack of knowledge about a foreign culture. Each unit also introduces you to certain areas of Indonesian culture and behaviour that you need to be aware of to function effectively; background information on topics of interest, travel information and even the occasional language tip!

How to use the course

Start with the pronunciation guide and work through it until you are sure that you are familiar with it. Some letters represent values in Indonesian different from what you might expect in English, so you need to be sure that you are not embarking on the course with bad habits that may go unchecked and that will be very difficult to eradicate later. If, however, you have the recording, you can move on to the language units after only a brief run through the pronunciation guide as you will be hearing correct pronunciation of the dialogues from the outset.

As not all people like to learn in the same way, we suggest two equally effective methods of approaching a unit:

1 Listen to (or read) the dialogue first without concerning yourself with the *meaning*. This is likely to be the first time that you are being exposed to the language taught in a particular unit, so you should concentrate on the sounds of the words and intonation rather than meaning at this early stage.

2 Alternatively, if you are the type of person who prefers to know what the dialogue means as you listen to it, you could go straight to the vocabulary sections before you even look at the dialogue and learn the words and phrases first. Then you can see how the words and phrases fit into the dialogue to create interaction and meaning.

Listen to the dialogue again several times so that you understand what is going on. You should be starting to get a feel for the language with this repeated listening.

Then move on to the **How the language works** section and study the language notes one by one. If there is an exercise, complete it and check your understanding by referring to the key before moving on.

It is a good idea to listen to the dialogue again several times, now that you know how the language points covered in the language section relate to the meaning in the text. It is recommended that you start to use the recording to repeat the dialogue at this stage, in order to build speaking skills. When you have finished the unit, you should go over it again and practise speaking the parts in the dialogues as much as possible. For best results make sure you have fully understood and mastered all the points in the language sections, and that you can speak all the parts of the dialogues as quickly as the native speakers on the recording, if not faster!

Throughout each unit, we have added more vocabulary for you to acquire in the various exercises and activities. In addition, in some units we have also varied the range of language expression on a certain topic to help you broaden your language ability. For example, in some exercises, you are expected to use what you have learnt in the unit to construct a conversation that might be on the same theme as the unit topic, but might require you to adapt the language to a different context. Sometimes we have introduced another way of expressing something that is different from a phrase or word used earlier. These alternatives are all, of course, in current use.

The first six units give you the basic sentence patterns and lay the foundation for the language so it is recommended that you master these fully before moving on in the course. If you can, work through these units again to reinforce your learning.

Learning tips

DOS

▶ Give yourself time for what you have studied to become part of your repertoire. A language is not a series of facts, it is a skill and a habit that needs to be learnt. Practice makes it a habit.

▶ Play the recording as much as possible. This could be while you are exercising, doing the washing up, driving to work and even at a low volume while you sleep! Do not make the mistake of thinking that passive listening alone will do the work for you. It will not. It will, however, create an environment which will allow your mind to become fully attuned to your new target language, in the same way it would if you were living in the country.

▶ When you listen to the dialogues after you understand the meaning, listen again several times with your eyes closed and try to imagine the 'action' that might accompany the conversation as you listen.

▶ Learn the dialogues by heart, to the extent that you know exactly what is coming next and so that you can respond in place of either speaker when you play the dialogue.

▶ Master each unit in its entirety before moving on and keep revising it so that the language stays fresh in your mind. For each new unit you progress onto, it is a good idea to go back two or three units and revise them fully too.

▶ If something does not make immediate sense come back to it a day later. Remember that, when you are learning a language, you are exposing your mind to a new way to relate to concepts and ideas. It can take a little time for your brain to begin to accept this, but you can be sure that it will if you persevere.

▶ Study or practise the language every day. If you cannot find time for active learning of new language try and spend time playing the recording or going over language that you have already studied.

▶ Go over what you have learnt during the day just before sleeping.

▶ Become as interested in the country and culture of Indonesia as you possibly can. Find as many reasons as possible why learning Indonesian is important and enjoyable to you!

DON'TS

▶ Do not try to learn too much at once, especially in the early stages. Language learning, and learning in general, becomes a habit that you can develop. The more you learn, the more you are capable of learning, so allow yourself to develop the art of acquiring a language over time.

▶ Do not underestimate the value of revision. Learning a language is a cumulative task. You will find that, as you cover later units, when you return to a unit that you completed earlier, you have a deeper sense of knowing and understanding as more parts of the language already learnt as phrases fall into place.

▶ Do not be disheartened if results do not appear immediately. When you have finished a unit, do not be irritated if you do not have that information at your fingertips straightaway. You will find that as you progress through the language, things that you have learnt before start to become available to you and make more sense later! Allow time for the new information to 'gel' in your mind and become part of your linguistic repertoire.

▶ Do not feel that you have to start speaking the language straightaway, if you do not want to. Some language courses emphasize speaking and using the language from the very outset. It is up to you, of course, whether you do this. An effective strategy is to spend time learning to understand the language in the unit without speaking and then go over the unit or even a few units afterwards. If you have the time to do this, you may find it beneficial, as you are mimicking what you did when you learnt your first language. You spent months listening to the language around you before you ever started to speak it! The process of understanding and then using is built into the course to a certain extent.

▶ Above all, do not cram learn! Cram learning the night before an exam in which you have to produce factual information may result in your being able to retain facts in your short term memory long enough to pass, but if you have tried it, you will know that in a matter of days most of the information is lost. Language learning is a skill that needs to be developed over time. Do not try to rush through the course, for the same reason.

We hope that you will enjoy working through this course and enjoying the interaction with Indonesians that learning this wonderful language will give you! **Selamat belajar!**

Christopher Byrnes and Eva Nyimas

Pronunciation guide

🔊 **CD1, TR 1, 1:27**

You will be happy to know that Indonesian pronunciation is very regular. With one or two exceptions what you see is what you say.

The guide we give here will help you to pronounce Indonesian in an acceptable way. It must be stressed, however, that all a written explanation of these sounds can provide is an *approximation* of the real sounds. There is simply no substitute for hearing foreign sounds produced by native speakers so if you do not have access to a native Indonesian, then you would benefit greatly from hearing real Indonesian sounds from the recording that accompanies this book.

Modern Indonesian spelling is much more regular than English spelling. With very few exceptions, separate letters or certain combinations always have the same pronunciation. As far as possible, we have deliberately chosen useful, high-frequency words to illustrate the pronunciation of the sound within the word for this pronunciation guide.

Vowel sounds

🔊 **CD1, TR 1, 2:12**

All vowel sounds are to be pronounced short:

a tiga *three*   like *a* in *far*

e has two distinct sounds, one is pronounced like the *a* sound in *again*. This is, by far, the more common *e* sound in Indonesian.

e empat *four*   terus *immediately*

The other is pronounced like the *e* in *egg*. In texts produced for native speakers this é is not distinguished from the other e sound. This can make it difficult for a beginner to know where these é sounds are. It is surprising that most textbooks and dictionaries, even those intended for foreign learners of the language, do not point this out, especially as it occurs in some very common words!

> é meréka *they*   énak *delicious*

Throughout this course an acute accent has been used to indicate this second sound. Note, however, that it is only used as a guide for learners of Indonesian as a foreign language so you should <u>never</u> use it in your own writing. Note further that this accent does <u>not</u> mark stress in a word, as it does in some languages.

i lima *five*	like the *i* in *Capri*
o tolong *please*	like *o* in *hot* but with lips more rounded
u satu *one*	like the *oo* sound in *cool* but short
aa saat *moment*	pronounced as two separate *a* sounds rather like the two *a* sounds in the phrase *sa(t) at* with the *t* missing! If you are British, imagine how a Cockney might say this.
ai sampai *until*	like *ie* in *tie*
au haus *thirsty*	like the *ou* in *house*

Consonant sounds

◀) **CD1, TR 1, 3:11**

The following consonants are pronounced as in English:

- **b** baru *new*
- **d** dua *two*
- **f** foto *photo*

g	gigi *teeth*	always as a hard *g* as in *got*
h	habis *finish*	
j	rajin *diligent*	
k	keras *hard*	
l	delapan *eight*	
m	sembilan *nine*	
n	enam *six*	
p	sepuluh *ten*	
s	siapa? *who?*	
t	tempat *place*	
v	végétarian *vegetarian*	
w	warna *colour*	
y	ya *yes*	
z	zébra *zebra*	

These consonants are pronounced differently from English:

c cari *look for*	like *ch* in *chop*
h sekolah *school*	at the end of a word, it is pronounced as a puff of air
tujuh *seven*	
k tidak *no*	at the end of a word, it is not pronounced
r tidur *to sleep*	r is always rolled
kh khusus *special*	like the *ch* in the Scottish word *loch*
ng senang *happy*	like the *ng* in lo*ng* but not pronounced as far as the final g sound. It can occur at the beginning of words and is still required to be pronounced as indicated above
bangun *to wake up*	
ny kenyang *full (of food)*	like the *ne* sound in the word *new*
ngg menggosok *to brush*	like the *ng* in lo*ng* but this time as the full sound
sy isyarat *sign*	like the *sh* in *shin*
asyik *fantastic!*	

Stress

◀) **CD1, TR 1, 7:14**

Although stress may differ depending on where you are in Indonesia, as an English speaker, you will probably find it more natural to follow the pattern of stressing words on the penultimate syllable.

se**ko**lah
member**sih**kan

In 1972 Indonesian underwent spelling reforms that gave us the written language as it looks today. In some cases, such as place names, the old spelling has endured. For example, **Java** is sometimes written as **Jawa** although this does not affect the pronunciation. Where such discrepancies occur within the course, they are pointed out and the correct pronunciation is indicated.

Pronunciation practice!

◀) **CD1, TR 1, 7:30**

If possible, listen to these two Indonesian children's nursery rhymes and repeat after the native speakers. Repeat them until you can say (or sing!) them fluently and without hesitation.

We have included a translation, just for information, but do not worry about trying to make sense of them at this early stage. They are just for pronunciation practice.

Satu, dua, tiga, empat, lima, enam, tujuh, delapan.
Siapa rajin ke sekolah.
Cari ilmu sampai dapat.
Sungguh senang.

Amat senang.
Bangun pagi-pagi sungguh senang.

Bangun tidur ku terus mandi.
Tidak lupa menggosok gigi.
Habis mandi ku tolong ibu.
Membersihkan tempat tidur ku.

One, two, three, four, five, six, seven, eight,
Who is keen to go to school.
To look for knowledge until he gets
Really happy
Very happy
I get up early in the morning really happy.

Having got up I take a bath straightaway
I don't forget to brush my teeth
After taking a bath I help mother
To make my bed.

Exercise 1

Although you will meet all these words in the course, any words that you can learn now will give you a head start! Look at the clues and fill in the crossword on the next page, saying each word out loud as you write it in.

Across
4 colour
5 two
8 school
9 happy
12 they
14 no
15 nine
17 special
19 place

Down
1 six
2 one
3 seven
5 eight
6 fantastic
7 please
10 four
11 five
13 thirsty
16 new
18 ten
20 delicious
21 three

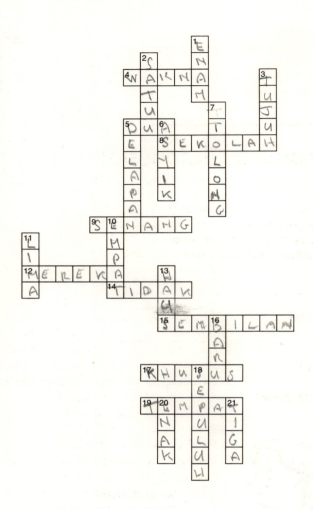

XXX

1

Welcome to Indonesia!

In this unit you will learn how to
- *greet people*
- *introduce yourself and others*
- *say where you come from*

PART ONE

Dialogue

🔊 **CD1, TR 2, 0:03**

Selamat siang!
Nama saya Ken Knight.
Saya berasal dari Sélandia Baru.

Selamat siang!
Nama saya Jamilah Knight.
Saya berasal dari Indonesia.

Selamat siang!
Saya Mark.
Saya dari Inggeris.

Selamat siang!
Saya Réza.
Saya dari Indonesia.

Insight

We have marked the **é** on the name **Réza** for this unit only to show how it is pronounced. In further units we have omitted the accent on the name.

nama saya *my name is*
nama *name*
saya *I am*
Saya berasal dari *I am from*
dari *from*
Sélandia Baru *New Zealand*
Inggeris *England*
Indonesia *Indonesia*
Selamat pagi! *Good morning!*
Selamat siang! *Good afternoon!/Good day!*
Selamat soré! *Good afternoon!*
Selamat malam! *Good evening!*

How the language works 1

1 Unlike English, there is no multipurpose word like *Hello!* in Indonesian. Instead the greetings for the specific time of the day are used: **Selamat pagi** in the morning, **selamat siang** which would correspond to *good day* in older style English, **selamat soré** which is used between 2 and 6 p.m., and **selamat malam** which is used throughout the evening and night.

2 You do not need to use words for *am*, *are*, *is* in Indonesian. So **saya** can mean both *I* and *I am*. Compare the following sentences in English and Indonesian:

I am Reza.
Saya Réza.

I am from England.
Saya dari Inggeris.

EXERCISE 1

See if you can make these sentences.

a I am John. I am from America.
b I am Kylie. I am from Australia.
c I am Suzie. I am from Canada.

Amérika *America*
Kanada *Canada*
Australia *Australia*

3 To give your name in Indonesian you can use **nama saya** + your name or you can just use **saya ...**, *I am* ... **Saya** is far more natural and, consequently, more frequently used, especially in the spoken language, than **nama saya**. We do the same in English. Consider how much more likely you are to say *I am John*, for example, than *My name is John*.

The same thing applies to **saya dari...** and **saya berasal dari...** when you want to say where you are from. The latter form is considered to be more formal and less natural than **saya dari...** In writing, however, it would be better style to use **saya berasal dari...**

Understanding Indonesian

EXERCISE 2

◀) **CD1, TR 2, 2:08**

First familiarize yourself with the new vocabulary.

pengusaha mahasiswa pelancong penari Bali

pengusaha *businessman*
mahasiswa *student (at college or university)*
pelancong *tourist*
penari Bali *Balinese dancer*

If you are not using the recording turn to the **Listening transcripts** section and treat this as a reading exercise. You will hear these people introduce themselves in the order indicated by the number next to their names. Listen to what each person says and link the person's name, the part of Indonesia he/she is from and, finally, the other piece of information about that person.

Insight

Here's an extra clue for the following exercise: some Indonesian words have different forms depending on whether they refer to men or women. **Mahasiswa** is specifically *a male student; a female university student* is **mahasiswi**.

Muhammad (1)   Sutrisno (2)   Tuti (3)   Endang (4)

Sumatra

Kalimantan

Sulawesi

Irian Jaya

Java

Bali

pengusaha   mahasiswa   pelancong   penari Bali

EXERCISE 3

True or false?

When you have completed the listening exercise try the following true/false test.

a Muhammad is a student from Sumatra.
b Endang is a student from Java.
c Tuti is a dancer from Bali.
d Sutrisno is a tourist from Bali.

PART TWO

Dialogue

Mr Knight, a businessman from New Zealand, has arrived at Soekarno International Airport in Jakarta. He has come to Jakarta on business. His Indonesian wife, Jamilah, will be joining him later. Two men from the CITRA company have come to meet him.

CD1, TR 2, 3:05

Bapak Anton	Maaf! Apakah anda Bapak Knight?
Bapak Knight	Ya, betul.
Bapak Anton	Selamat datang di Jakarta. Kami dari perusahaan CITRA. Kenalkan, saya Anton dan ini Bapak Bambang.
(They shake hands.)	
Bapak Bambang	Senang berkenalan dengan anda.
Bapak Knight	Senang berkenalan dengan anda juga.

maaf! *excuse me, I am sorry*
apakah anda? *are you?*
bapak *Mr*
ya *yes*
betul *that's correct*
selamat datang *welcome*
di *in*
selamat datang di *welcome to*
kami *we*
dari *from*
perusahaan *company*
Kenalkan, saya *Allow me to introduce myself. I'm…*
dan *and*
ini *this/this is*
senang *happy*

QUICK VOCAB

dengan *with*
Senang berkenalan dengan anda. *Pleased to meet you.*
juga *too, also*
Senang berkenalan dengan anda juga. *Pleased to meet you too.*

Insight

In the early stages of learning Indonesian, do not worry about a word like **dengan** in the vocabulary above. The Indonesian phrase needs **dengan** whereas the English phrase does not. Just concentrate on learning the phrase for now.

TRANSLATION

Mr Anton	Excuse me! Are you Mr Knight?
Mr Knight	Yes, that's correct.
Mr Anton	Welcome to Jakarta. We are from the CITRA company. Pleased to meet you. I'm Anton and this is Mr Bambang.
Mr Bambang	Pleased to meet you.
Mr Knight	Pleased to meet you too.

How the language works 2

1 To introduce yourself to someone in Indonesian use **Kenalkan, saya** + your name.

Insight

Kenalkan, saya ... is the common colloquial variant of the expression. In hyper-correct Indonesian it would be **perkenalkan saya ...**

When you pronounce this expression, note that there is a pause between **kenalkan** and **saya**, marked by the comma in writing. Listen for this on the recording if you have it.

1 To introduce someone else, simply use the word **ini** which means *this (is)…:*

Ini Peter Robinson.   *This is Peter Robinson.*

2 When you welcome someone to a place in Indonesian you say *welcome in* rather than *to* as in English. For example,

Selamat datang di Bandung, *Welcome to Bandung.*

EXERCISE 4

How would you welcome someone to the following places in Indonesian?

a Sydney
b Washington
c London
d Your home town.

2 In this unit you have come across the words **saya**, *I*, **anda**, *you* and **dia**, *he/she*. Words such as these that can be used instead of repeating a person's name are known as *personal pronouns*. Here are the formal personal pronouns in Indonesian:

saya	*I*
anda	*you*
saudara	*you*
dia	*he/she*
kami/kita	*we*
meréka	*they*

They are called *formal* personal pronouns because you should use them in a situation where you are not familiar with the speaker or where you would be expected to maintain a respectful tone to whomever you are addressing.

There are two words for *you* and two words for *we*. **Saudara** and **anda** can be used interchangeably. The words for *we*, however, have specific meanings and usage depending on the situation. **Kita** is used when you are including the person or people you are speaking to in what you say. **Kami** is used when you mean *us but not you*. For instance, imagine you are at a party with your spouse. When it comes time for you both to leave you announce your departure by saying *We must be leaving now*. You would use **kami** in Indonesian. If you used **kita** it would mean that you expect everybody else to leave with you! Obviously, it would not be taken literally. It is just an illustration, but it is worth bearing in mind the distinction when you are speaking Indonesian as you may unintentionally find yourself altering the meaning of what you want to say otherwise.

Insight

Learnt the words, but can't remember the difference? Try this! Take the **ka** of **kami** as the first syllable in the name **KA**ren (it helps enormously if you have a friend called Karen) and the **mi** as **ME** in English. Think of **kami** as 'Karen and me, i.e. *we*, *but not you*'. **Kita** is the other one.

3 In Part One, you saw that you do not need to use words for *am/are/is* in Indonesian. You may also have noticed that you do not need to use a word for *a* (*an*) or *the* either. You just say *I from England* or *I businessman*, etc. Compare these English and Indonesian sentences:

I am a businessman.
Saya pengusaha.

This is a book.
Ini buku.

In a sentence such as *That is tobacco*, where there would be no *a* in English anyway, the pattern is the same:

That is tobacco.
Itu tembakau.

EXERCISE 5

Put these sentences into Indonesian.

a This is a dictionary.
b He is a businessman.
c That is coffee.
d This is a shop.
e She is a teacher.
f This is water.

QUICK VOCAB

buku *book*
tembakau *tobacco*
kamus *dictionary*
kopi *coffee*
toko *shop*
guru *teacher*
air *water*
nasi *rice*

4 There are two types of question – ones that require an explanation and ones that simply require the answer *yes* or *no*. One way to form a yes/no question in Indonesian is by using **apakah**. In English, we change the word order, for example to turn the statement *This is a book* into a question we say *Is this a book?* To form the question in Indonesian simply take the statement and add **apakah** to the beginning:

Ini buku.	*This is a book.*
Apakah ini buku?	*Is this a book?*

Similarly:

Anda pengusaha.	*You are a businessman.*
Apakah anda pengusaha?	*Are you a businessman?*
Itu nasi.	*That is rice.*
Apakah itu nasi?	*Is that rice?*

EXERCISE 6

See if you can form **apakah**-type questions using the statement you made in Indonesian in Exercise 5. For example:

a (This is a dictionary.) **Ini kamus. Apakah ini kamus?**

Using Indonesian

EXERCISE 7

Look at the dialogue between two people. Can you unscramble it so that it makes sense? Then translate it.

Ya betul.
Senang berkenalan dengan anda juga.
Selamat datang di Inggeris. Kenalkan, saya Robert Davies.
Maaf... Apakah anda Bapak Pranoto dari Indonesia?
Ya betul. Senang berkenalan dengan anda.
Apakah anda dari perusahaan BRITIMPORT?

EXERCISE 8

Over to you!

Imagine that you (**A**) are from a company called ANGLOTRANS. As the only Indonesian speaker at your firm you have been sent to the airport to meet an Indonesian lady (**B**) called Mrs Nasution (Ibu Nasution). You see a lady waiting who might just be Mrs Nasution. Write out the dialogue replacing the English in brackets with suitable Indonesian phrases you have learnt in this unit.

A	*Excuse me. Are you Mrs Nasution?*
B	Ya betul.
A	*I'm from the ANGLOTRANS company. I'm (your name).*
B	Senang berkenalan dengan anda.
A	*I'm pleased to meet you too.*

Insight

It's normal if you found the Over to you! exercise hard-going to begin with! It is expected that you will have to listen, and interact with it several times to be able to do it perfectly. Trust us on this one. The Over to you! exercises are designed to stretch you linguistically, and the only way to do that is to push you slightly beyond your comfort zone, so do persevere with them!

Shaking hands

Young Indonesians and those who are used to contact with foreigners will probably greet you with a western-style handshake and a slight forward bow.

Out of respect, young Indonesians may kiss the hand of their older relatives.

In certain areas, you may encounter a traditional Indonesian style handshake. The hands are clasped together as though in prayer and held, fingers pointing upwards, just above the nose. The hands are brought down until they are horizontal and at a level between the chest and the waist. The fingers of the hands only interlock with the other person's in a sort of clasping motion, but with the fingers still held straight and together and then the hands are withdrawn to the starting position, above the nose.

This is the Javanese way. The Sundanese start the handshake with the hands in the lower position and then bring them up to the nose. This has given rise to a certain amount of humour among Indonesians. They say that a Javanese and a Sundanese can never shake hands as their hands will never meet!

TEST YOURSELF

1 How would you greet someone at 1 p.m.?

2 How would you greet someone at 9.30 a.m.?

3 How would you give your name in Indonesian?

4 How would you introduce yourself in Indonesian?

5 How would you say *I'm from Java*?

6 How would you say *Welcome to England*?

7 **Kami** or **kita**? Which one do you use to include everyone in what you say?

8 How would you introduce Mrs Walters to someone in Indonesian?

9 What word can you add to the beginning of a statement to form a question?

10 If someone said **Senang berkenalan dengan anda** to you, how would you respond?

At the airport

In this unit you will learn how to
- *use less formal yes/no questions*
- *show possession*

PART ONE

Dialogue

Having met at the airport, Ken, Bambang and Anton continue their conversation.

Bambang	Mobil kami sudah menunggu di luar.
Anton	Apakah ini kopor-kopor anda? Mari saya bantu.
Bambang	Anda berbicara bahasa Indonesia dengan baik sekali.
Ken	Terima kasih. Saya coba tetapi saya hanya berbicara sedikit.
Bambang	Tidak apa-apa. Sedikit-sedikit, lama-lama menjadi bukit.

mobil *car*
sudah *already*
menunggu *waits, to wait*
di luar *outside*

kopor-kopor *luggage*
mari *let, allow*
bantu *help, to help*
mari saya bantu *let me help*
berbicara *speak, to speak*
bahasa *language*
bahasa Indonesia *Indonesian (language)*
baik *well, good*
sekali *very*
dengan baik sekali *very well*
terima kasih *thank you*
coba *try, to try*
tetapi *but*
hanya *only*
sedikit *a little*
tidak apa-apa *that's all right/no problem*
Indonesian proverb: **Sedikit-sedikit lama-lama menjadi bukit.**
 Take it one step at a time.

Insight

Kopor-kopor means *luggage*, whereas **kopor** on its own means *suitcase*.

TRANSLATION

Bambang	Our car is already waiting outside.
Anton	Is this your luggage? Let me help you.
Bambang	You speak Indonesian very well.
Ken	Thank you. I try, but I only speak it a little.
Bambang	That's all right. Take it one step at a time.

How the language works 1

1 To express thanks in Indonesian use the phrase **terima kasih**. Adding **banyak** which means *many* or *much* gives you **terima kasih banyak**, *thank you very much*.

To respond with *don't mention it*, use **terima kasih kembali** (often shortened to just **kembali**) or **sama-sama**.

2 **Mobil kami**, *our car*, **kopor-kopor anda**, *your luggage*. The same words that are used for the personal pronouns are also used to show ownership or possession. Take careful note of the position. When they are used to show possession, they are placed *after* the noun they refer to. It is important to be aware that, as these words are the same, meaning depends exclusively on position. When they are placed before the noun they refer to, they have a different meaning, as was discussed in Unit 1.

Study the following:

guru anda	*your teacher*
teman saya	*my friend*
buku dia	*his book* or *her book*

Insight

If the word order seems awkward, think of it as a *teacher of you, a friend of me* etc.

EXERCISE 1

How would you say:

a her photo
b their present
c my watch
d our picture?

foto *photo*
jam tangan *watch*
hadiah *present*
gambar *picture*

The **kita/kami** distinction applies here too. Bambang uses **mobil kami** in the dialogue because in Indonesian he is obliged to convey the idea that the car that is waiting is from the company he and Anton work for and not the one Ken works for.

3 Mari means *let* or *allow*. It is used to form expressions like **Mari saya bantu**, *Let me help*, or, more commonly with **kita** in making an invitation **Mari kita pergi** *Let's go!* (i.e. *Let us go.*)

> ### Insight
> **Saya** means *me* as well as *I*, as in the expression above. We'll meet this formally later in the course.

 pergi *to go*

EXERCISE 2

Can you write these sentences?

a Let's speak Indonesian!
b Let's go to Bandung!
c Let's wait outside!

4 Verbs are often described as the *action words* of a language, such as *run*, *speak*, *take* and *try*, although they do not necessarily have to indicate action to be verbs. *Be* and *have* are also verbs.

In English, verbs change their form to indicate tense (i.e. whether they refer to the present, past or future) and sometimes to indicate the person who is performing the action. For example, we say *I speak* and *they speak* but *he speaks* and *she speaks*. In Indonesian, the same form of the verb is used no matter which tense or person is being expressed. Thus, **berbicara** may mean *speak*, *speaks*, *spoke*, *speaking*, *to speak* etc.

Note that in the vocabulary sections in the text and at the back of the book the *to* form (such as *to run*) is used to indicate a verb.

Understanding Indonesian

EXERCISE 3

True or false?

Read these statements in Indonesian based on the dialogue in Part One and say whether each is true or false.

a Mobil Ken menunggu di luar.
b Anton membantu Ken.
c Kopor-kopor Ken di luar.
d Ken berbicara bahasa Indonesia dengan baik sekali.

membantu *to help/helps*

EXERCISE 4

Fill in the gaps in the sentences below with the verbs in the vocabulary section, concentrating on the meaning of the Indonesian only. Then match up the sentences in Indonesian with the correct English version.

Dia sudah _____ **surat.**	*She teaches Indonesian.*
Meréka sedang _____ **koran.**	*We are watching TV.*
Dia _____ **bahasa Indonesia.**	*He has written a letter.*
Saya sedang _____ **téh.**	*They are reading a newspaper.*
Kami sedang _____ **TV.**	*I am drinking tea.*

Insight

Words like **sudah** (*already*) and **sedang** (*now*) are how Indonesian conveys the idea of tense. They will be fully explained later, but if you need to know now, **sudah** makes a past tense and **sedang** a continuous one.

membaca *to read*
mengajar *to teach*
menulis *to write*
menonton *to watch*
minum *to drink*
surat *letter*
koran *newspaper*
TV *TV (pronounced as in English)*

> ## Insight
> **Menonton** is the strictly correct form you should use in writing; however, colloquially Indonesians shorten this word to **nonton**.

PART TWO

Dialogue

Mark Spencer, a student from the UK, arrives at Soekarno-Hatta Airport in Jakarta to meet his long-standing e-pal Reza for the first time. He passes customs without a hitch but there is no sign of Reza! Looking like a lost tourist, Mark is approached by several private taxi drivers offering their services.

Supir taksi 1	Taksi, Pak?
Mark	Tidak, terima kasih.
Supir taksi 2	Bapak perlu taksi?
Mark	Tidak, terima kasih.
Supir taksi 3	Mau ke mana, Pak?
Mark	Saya sedang menunggu seseorang.
Supir taksi 4	Saya bisa mengantar Bapak ke hotél. Mau pergi ke mana?

> *(Presently, a young lady approaches Mark and says...)*
>
> **Reza**   Maaf, kamu Mark? Maaf saya terlambat. Saya terjebak macet.
>
> **Mark**   Ya. Apa kamu Reza?
>
> **Reza**   Betul. Senang bertemu dengan kamu.
>
> **Mark**   Saya juga.
>
> **Reza**   Apa ini semua kopor-kopor kamu? Mari saya bantu.

supir taksi *taxi driver*
Tidak, terima kasih *no, thank you*
perlu *need*
taksi *taxi*
mau *to want*
ke mana *where to?*
Mau ke mana, Pak? *Where do you want to go, Sir?*
sedang *now*
sedang menunggu *am waiting (for)*
seseorang *someone*
bisa (verb) *can/to be able to*
mengantar *to take (someone somewhere)*
ke *to*
hotél *hotel*
Mau pergi ke mana? *Where do you want to go?*
kamu *you (informal)*
maaf *sorry*
terlambat *late*
Maaf, saya terlambat. *I'm sorry I'm late.*
terjebak *trapped/stuck*
macet *jammed*
Saya terjebak macet. *I was stuck in traffic.*
bertemu *to meet*
Senang bertemu dengan kamu. *Pleased to meet you.*
saya juga *me too*
semua *all (this)*
Mari saya bantu. *Let me help.*

QUICK VOCAB

TRANSLATION

Taxi driver 1	Taxi, Sir?
Mark	No, thank you.
Taxi driver 2	Does Sir need a taxi?
Mark	No, thank you.
Taxi driver 3	Where do you want (to go), Sir?
Mark	I am waiting for someone.
Taxi driver 4	I can take you to a hotel (Sir). Where do you want to go?
Reza	Excuse me, are you Mark? I'm sorry I'm late. I was stuck in traffic.
Mark	Yes. Are you Reza?
Reza	That's correct. Pleased to meet you.
Mark	Me too.
Reza	Is this all your baggage? Let me help.

How the language works 2

1 In the dialogue, **bapak** is used to mean *you*. **Bapak perlu taksi?** Used in this way, **bapak** can be likened to the older style, hyper-polite English, *Does Sir require a taxi?* although its usage is still commonplace in Indonesia. Any title or a name can be used to mean *you*. Therefore, if you say, for example, **Apakah Tuti dari Bali?** this could mean *Is Tuti from Bali?* but if you were addressing Tuti directly, the meaning would be *Are you from Bali, (Tuti)?*

2 In addition to the formal pronouns, there is an informal pronoun **kamu** that is widely used between friends. Note, however, that it should only be used with people with whom you are on very familiar terms, or with people who are the same age or younger.

It would be highly inappropriate to use **kamu** in a business environment or when you are unfamiliar with the speaker. If in doubt use **anda** or **saudara**.

Kamu behaves just like most of the formal pronouns in that it can be placed after a noun to indicate possession.

Thus:

Kamu cantik.   *You are beautiful.*
kucing kamu   *your cat*

However, when it is used to show possession it may be shortened to -**mu**. When shortened in this way it is *added onto* the word it refers to:

kucingmu   *your cat*
rokok kamu → rokokmu   *your cigarette*

cantik *beautiful*
kucing *cat*
rokok *cigarette*

EXERCISE 5

Use -**mu** to make the following phrases:

a your camera
b your spectacles
c your key
d your passport

kaméra *camera*
kacamata *spectacles*
kunci *key*
paspor *passport*

3 In Unit 1, we saw that **maaf** can mean *excuse me*. It can also be used to express apology for something in the following way:

Maaf, saya terlambat.   *I'm sorry I'm late.*

4 In Unit 1, you were introduced to **apakah** as a means of forming a yes/no question. As in the dialogue, you can make the same type of question just by placing **apa** at the beginning of the statement. In this case, **apa** is simply the shortened form of **apakah**:

Apakah dia sedang menunggu seseorang?
Apa dia sedang menunggu seseorang?   *Is she waiting for someone?*

EXERCISE 6

Use **apa** to ask the following questions:

a Is this all your (use **kamu**) luggage?
b Are they waiting outside?
c Is he stuck in traffic?
d Are we (use **kami**) late?

Whereas **apakah** may be considered to be highly formal, **apa** tends to be less so. As we shall see later on in the course, it is the **-kah** that gives the question a more formal tone.

5 Did you notice that not all the questions in the dialogue are formed with **apa** or **apakah**? In informal style, these may be omitted when forming a question and, as Indonesian tends towards brevity and simplicity, this is often the case, especially in the spoken language. So another way to form a yes/no question is simply to take the statement and add a rising intonation at the end; that alone forms the question.

Look at the following examples and, ideally, follow along with the recording, if you have it, as this type of question relies solely on the rising intonation you use.

🔊 **CD1, TR 3, 1:27**

Itu menarik.	*It's interesting.*
Itu menarik?	*Is it interesting?*
Dia capék.	*She's tired.*
Dia capék?	*Is she tired?*
Ini anjing kamu.	*This is your dog.*
Ini anjing kamu?	*Is this your dog?*

anjing *dog*
menarik *interesting*
capék *tired*

QV

Using Indonesian

EXERCISE 7

Choose the correct response from the choice of three for each question or statement and write it in the space provided.

a Maaf, apa anda supir taksi?
    1 Terima kasih.
    2 Ya betul, mau ke mana Pak?
    3 Tidak apa-apa.

b Mari saya bantu.
    1 Terima kasih, kopor-kopor saya di luar.
    2 Saya sedang menonton TV.
    3 Saya berbicara bahasa Indonesia dengan baik.

c Mau ke mana Pak?
    1 Mau ke hotél Ciputra.
    2 Senang bertemu dengan kamu.
    3 Tidak, terima kasih.

d Apa anda sedang menunggu seseorang?

    1 Ya, saya sedang menunggu supir taksi.

    2 Tidak, dia turis.

    3 Senang berkenalan dengan anda juga.

EXERCISE 8

Over to you!

◀) **CD1, TR 3, 1:55**

While you are working at your desk, your Indonesian friend Mustafa (**A**) comes up to you to ask for help with something. Use the English in the prompts to answer Mustafa's questions in Indonesian. You are (**B**).

◀ CD1, TR 4, 0:24

A	Bisa anda membantu saya?
B	*I'm sorry. I'm busy.*
A	Apa anda sedang belajar bahasa Indonesia?
B	*Yes.*
A	Bisa saya kembali lagi nanti?
B	*OK.*
A	Selamat belajar!

QUICK VOCAB

sibuk *busy*
belajar *to study*
sedang belajar *studying*
kembali *to come back*
lagi *again*
nanti *later*
Selamat belajar! *Happy studying*

Insight

Extending from the meaning given above, you can probably see why **Kembali** also means *Don't mention it*, in reply to **terima kasih**.

When you have finished writing the answers, check that you know what Mustafa is asking you, then use the recording to practise the dialogue.

Taxi drivers

When Mark arrives at the airport in Jakarta, the setting for Part Two of this unit, he becomes the object of attention of the many private taxi drivers who vie for his custom. In fact, in the dialogue, the amount of attention attracted by someone who is ostensibly foreign, owing primarily to his or her ethnicity, is rather understated! Although not really menacing, the taxi drivers can be extremely persistent as they see an opportunity to solicit a high taxi fare from a foreigner not yet accustomed to prices and Indonesian ways. Bear in mind that what the taxi drivers may tell you about prices and availability of other services may not necessarily reflect the truth. If you are on a low budget and you arrive in the capital, you can take a bus from the airport to the city centre or a variety of other bus terminals. If you have a particular destination in mind, however, then taking a taxi is by far a more convenient alternative. You can always bargain with the taxi drivers and set a price beforehand or simply decline their offers politely (**Tidak, terima kasih**), go straight out of the airport building and take a Blue Bird or a Silver Bird, both of which use a meter. Moreover, it is generally safer for a foreigner to use this kind of taxi.

TEST YOURSELF

1 How would you say *Thank you very much*?

2 How would you say *Don't mention it*?

3 What is the difference in meaning between **saya guru** and **guru saya**?

4 What is the difference between **bahasa kami** and **bahasa kita**?

5 Which word would you use to make an invitation?

6 Why are tenses so easy to express in Indonesian?

7 Which word would you use to begin an apology?

8 What happens to **kamu** when it is added to a noun to mean *your*?

9 Give an alternative question marker to **apakah**.

10 How can you make a statement into a question without adding any words?

3

Getting to know you

In this unit you will learn how to
- **give information about yourself and ask about other people**
- **express nationalities and languages**
- **ask basic questions**

PART ONE

Dialogue

On the way to the hotel, Ken, Anton and Bambang pass the time by getting to know each other a little more.

Ken	Bagaimana kabar anda Bapak Bambang?
Bapak Bambang	Kabar baik dan anda Bapak Knight?
Ken	Saya juga, terima kasih.
Bapak Bambang	Bagaimana dengan penerbangan anda?
Ken	Sangat menyenangkan, walaupun sedikit melelahkan.
Bapak Bambang	Anda berbicara bahasa Indonesia dengan lancar sekali.
Ken	Terima kasih. Saya belajar dari isteri saya. Dia berasal dari Bandung. Apakah Bapak sudah berkeluarga?
Bapak Bambang	Belum. Saya masih bujangan.

(Contd)

Bapak Anton	Saya sudah berkeluarga.
Ken	Maaf. Bisa anda berbicara dengan lambat?
Bapak Anton	Baiklah. Maafkan saya.

QUICK VOCAB

bagaimana? *how?*
Bagaimana kabar anda? *How are you?*
kabar baik *I am fine*
dan anda *and you?*
Bagaimana dengan *How is...? How was...?*
penerbangan *flight*
sangat *very*
menyenangkan *pleasant*
walaupun *although*
melelahkan *tiring*
lancar *fluent*
dengan lancar sekali *very fluently*
isteri *wife*
masih *still*
bujangan *single*
berkeluarga *married*
lambat *slow*
dengan lambat *slowly*
baiklah *all right*
maafkan *to forgive*
maafkan saya *I'm sorry*

TRANSLATION

Ken	How are you, Mr Bambang?
Mr Bambang	Fine, and you, Mr Knight?
Ken	I'm (fine) too, thank you.
Mr Bambang	How was your flight?
Ken	(It was) very pleasant, although a little tiring.
Mr Bambang	You speak Indonesian very fluently.
Ken	Thank you. I learn (it) from my wife. She is from Bandung. Are you married, Mr Bambang?
Mr Bambang	Not yet, I am still single.

Mr Anton	I am married.
Ken	Sorry, could you speak (more) slowly?
Mr Anton	OK then. I am sorry.

How the language works 1

1 To ask *How are you?* in Indonesian you can use **Bagaimana kabar anda?** or **Apa kabar?** To answer you could use **Kabar baik, terima kasih,** *I am fine, thank you* or you could just use **baik** for short.

Insight

Kabar on its own means *news*.

Other common answers are **séhat,** *I'm healthy* or **alhamdulillah, baik,** *I'm well, thanks be to God.* The last response is partly Arabic and widely used by Muslims.

séhat *healthy*

Insight

You should only use **alhamdulillah, baik** if you, too, are Muslim.

2 Countries, nationalities and languages.

Inggeris	*England*	**Belanda**	*Holland*
Amérika	*America*	**Malaysia**	*Malaysia*
Kanada	*Canada*	**Singapura**	*Singapore*
Irlandia	*Ireland*	**Cina**	*China*
Skotlandia	*Scotland*	**Jepang**	*Japan*
Wales	*Wales*	**Spanyol**	*Spain*
Sélandia Baru	*New Zealand*	**Jérman**	*Germany*
Australia	*Australia*	**Perancis**	*French*

To talk about nationality simply take **orang** which means *person* and add the name of the country to it:

orang Amérika   *an American (person)*
Saya orang Irlandia *I am Irish. (I am an Irish person.)*

 orang *person*

Talking about languages is just as simple. Take **bahasa** which means *language* and add the name of the country that corresponds to the language you want to express:

bahasa Italia   *Italian (language)*
Dia bisa berbicara bahasa Perancis. *She can speak French.*

Insight

When Indonesians talk about their own language they often just refer to it as **bahasa**, taking it as read from the situation that it is **bahasa Indonesia** they are talking about.

EXERCISE 1

How would you say:

a	a Spaniard	**f**	an American
b	Chinese	**g**	a New Zealander
c	a Scot	**h**	Malay
d	a Malaysian	**i**	a Singaporean
e	Dutch	**j**	Japanese?

Insight

The Malay language, of which Indonesian is a form, may also be referred to as Bahasa Melayu.

3 Some question words. So far we have seen how to make yes/no-type questions in Indonesian. The other type of questions are those that require an answer and begin in English with question words such as *what?*, *who?*, *how?* and *when?*

▶ **apa** *what?*
Apa itu?   *What's that?*

Note that although this looks exactly like the short form for **apakah**, it also has a completely separate meaning, *what?*

▶ **siapa** *who?*
Siapa ini?   *Who's this?*

▶ **kapan** *when?*
Kapan rapat?   *When is the meeting?*

▶ **Bagaimana** what *kind of?/what's _____ like?/how's?/how are?/ how was/how were? etc.*

Bagaimana film itu?   *How was that film?*
Bagaimana isterimu?   *How's your wife?*

Insight

In the dialogue, Bambang asked **Bagaimana dengan penerbangan anda?** **Bagaimana dengan** is a more colloquial usage which can be used to ask how something is or was.

siapa *who*
kapan *when*
rapat *meeting*
film *film*

4 In English, nouns can be described by an adjective, for example, *a big car*, *a happy occasion*, or they can be described by another noun whereby the first noun gives more information about the second, for instance, *lifestyle*, *bookshop* and *fighter pilot*. In English, the describing word occurs *before* the main noun.

In Indonesian, nouns can be modified by adjectives, by nouns and even by verbs which also carry out the role of describing the noun. When any of these are used to describe a noun they are placed *after* the noun they refer to.

Study the following. The describing words are underlined:

- ► with adjectives
  mobil <u>baru</u>   *a <u>new</u> car*
  gambar <u>indah</u>   *a <u>beautiful</u> picture*

- ► with nouns
  pusat <u>kota</u>   *<u>town</u> centre*
  orang <u>Wales</u>   *a <u>Welsh</u> person*

With nouns that describe other nouns you may find it easier in many cases to think of it as *the centre of town* or *a person of Wales* as word order is similar in both languages this way.

- ► with verbs
  tempat <u>parkir</u>   *<u>parking</u> space*
  kamar <u>mandi</u>   *<u>bath</u>room*

- ► When more than one describing word, including possessive pronouns (*my, your, our* etc.) and personal names, occurs in a phrase, the word order is the *reverse* of the English:

  sekolah bahasa Indonesia   *Indonesian language school*
  paspor teman saya   *my friend's passport*

EXERCISE 2

How would you say:

a heavy luggage
b sports clothes
c bed (say: *a place to sleep*)
d My Indonesian language teacher's friend
e My friend's Indonesian language teacher?

berat *heavy*
olahraga *sports*
pakaian *clothes*
tidur *to sleep*

Here are some phrases that you will find very useful in helping you to communicate with Indonesians:

Maaf, saya tidak mengerti.	*I'm sorry, I don't understand.*
Bisa anda ulangi lagi?	*Could you repeat that please?*
Bisa anda tulis?	*Could you write it down please?*
Bisa anda éja?	*Could you spell it please?*
Bisa anda berbicara lebih lambat?	*Could you speak more slowly please?*
Bisa anda berbicara lebih keras?	*Could you speak more loudly please?*

Insight

Note that in many of these expressions, **bisa...?** corresponds to the English *could you...?* and can be used in a variety of situations.

mengerti *to understand*
ulangi *to repeat*
tulis *to write*
éja *to spell*
keras *loud*
lebih keras *more loudly*

Understanding Indonesian

EXERCISE 3

Say whether the following statements based on the dialogue are
true or false.

a Penerbangan Bapak Knight sangat melelahkan.
b Isteri Bapah Knight tidak berasal dari Bandung.
c Bapak Knight belajar bahasa Indonesia dari isterinya.
d Bapak Bambang sudah berkeluarga.

 isterinya *his wife*

....

Insight
As we shall see in a later unit, adding **-nya** to a noun can be
used to show possession.

....

EXERCISE 4

◄) **CD1, TR 4, 1:40**

First familiarize yourself with the vocabulary on the next page,
then listen to Ibu Rani interviewing a young man and circle the
correct answer to each question:

a What nationality is the speaker?
   Australian – Indonesian – Dutch – Malaysian

b How well can he speak Indonesian (according to the interviewer)?
   like a native – fluently – only a little

c What other language can he speak?
   Chinese – Portuguese – English – German

d What problem does he have with the interviewer's Indonesian?
   It's too fast – It's too unclear – It's heavily accented

seperti *like*
asli *authentic, native*
seperti orang asli *like a native*
Portugis *Portuguese*
jelas *clear*
tidak jelas *unclear*
aksén *accent*
kental *thick, strong*
aksén yang kental *a strong accent*

Insight

Yang means *that, which* or *who* in such phrases as *The book which I like*. So, while we translate phrases such as **aksén yang kental** as *a strong accent*, what it literally means is *(an) accent that (is) strong*.

PART TWO

Dialogue

◀》 **CD1, TR 4, 5:12**

Mark is staying at Reza's house on a housing estate. Reza's neighbour is an elderly gentleman who tends to be a bit nosey! Mark and Reza are just leaving the house when they meet Pak Tanto who is sitting on his verandah.

Pak Tanto	Mau ke mana, Néng? Siapa Mas itu?
Reza	Saya mau jalan-jalan, Pak. Dia teman saya dari Leeds.
Pak Tanto	Leeds? Di mana itu? Di Amérika?
Reza	Bukan, di Inggeris.
Pak Tanto	Jadi dia orang Inggeris. Saya dulu pernah belajar bahasa Inggeris, tapi sekarang saya sudah lupa.
	(Contd)

Mark	Jangan kuatir, saya bisa berbicara bahasa Indonesia.
Pak Tanto	Di mana kamu tinggal di Jakarta?
Reza	Dia tinggal di rumah saya.
Pak Tanto	Kapan tiba di Jakarta?
Mark	Kemarin soré dengan Garuda.
Pak Tanto	Berapa lama mau tinggal di sini?
Mark	Mungkin dua minggu saja.
Pak Tanto	Bagaimana orang Indonesia? Kamu suka?
Mark	Meréka sangat ramah, seperti Bapak. O, ya siapa nama Bapak?
Pak Tanto	Panggil saja saya, Pak Tanto. Selamat berlibur.
Mark	Terima kasih. Sampai bertemu lagi.

QUICK VOCAB

Néng *miss, young lady*
Mas *young man*
jalan-jalan *walk*
Saya mau jalan-jalan. *I am just off for (a) walk.*
dari mana *where from*
bukan *no*
jadi *so…*
dulu *long time ago*
pernah *once*
sekarang *now*
lupa *to forget*
sudah lupa *already forgotten*
jangan *don't*
kuatir *worry*
Jangan kuatir. *Don't worry.*
tinggal *to stay, to live*
rumah *house*
tiba *arrive*
kemarin *yesterday*
soré *afternoon*
kemarin soré *yesterday afternoon*
berapa lama *how long*
di sini *here*

mungkin *maybe*
dua *two*
minggu *week, weeks*
saja *just*
ramah *friendly*
O, ya *by the way*
panggil *to call*
Panggil saja saya... *Just call me...*
Selamat berlibur! *Enjoy your stay!*
Sampai bertemu lagi! *See you again!*
berlibur *to be on holiday*
bertemu *to meet*

TRANSLATION

Mr Tanto	Where are you going, young lady? Who is that young man?
Reza	I'm just off for a walk. He is my friend from Leeds.
Mr Tanto	Leeds? Where is that? In America?
Reza	No, in England.
Mr Tanto	So he's an Englishman. I studied English a long time ago, but I've already forgotten (it).
Mark	Don't worry, I can speak Indonesian.
Mr Tanto	Where are you staying in Jakarta?
Reza	He is staying at my house.
Mr Tanto	When (did you) arrive in Jakarta?
Mark	Yesterday afternoon with Garuda.
Mr Tanto	How long will (you) stay here?
Mark	Maybe just two weeks.
Mr Tanto	How are Indonesian people? Do you like (them)?
Mark	They are very friendly, like you. By the way, what's your name?
Mr Tanto	Just call me Pak Tanto. Have a nice stay!
Mark	Thank you. See you later.

How the language works 2

1 Negation. Indonesian makes sentences or phrases negative by using **tidak** or **bukan** depending on the situation. It is important that you understand the distinction between the usage of these two words.

▶ To make a *verb* negative in English, we use *don't* or *doesn't* before the verb. For example, we would say *He **doesn't** speak English* or *They **don't** eat pork*.

In Indonesian, insert **tidak** directly before a verb to make it negative:

dia minum *he drinks*   **dia tidak minum** *he doesn't drink*
saya tahu *I know*   **saya tidak tahu** *I don't know*

▶ In Indonesian *adjectives* are also made negative by using **tidak**:

dia séhat *he is healthy*   **dia tidak séhat** *He isn't healthy*
meréka mabuk *they*   **meréka tidak mabuk** *They aren't*
  are drunk   *drunk*

▶ When what you want to make negative is *a noun* (a thing) or a *pronoun*, **bukan** must be used. Again it is inserted directly before the noun (or pronoun) if refers to.

Saya orang Indonesia.   *I am an Indonesian.*
Saya bukan orang Indonesia. *I am not an Indonesian.*
Ini kucing.   *This is a cat.*
Ini bukan kucing.   *This is not a cat*
Dia présidén? Bukan dia.   *Is he the president? It's not him.*

tahu *to know*
mabuk *drunk*
présidén *president*

EXERCISE 5

Complete the sentence with either **tidak** or **bukan**.

a Dia _____ sopan.
b Meréka _____ buta.
c Kami _____ tinggal di Dénpasar.
d Itu _____ mobil saya.
e Dia _____ gembira.

sopan *polite*
buta *blind*
gembira *happy*

▶ Finally, both **tidak** and **bukan** mean *no* as a one-word response to a yes/no question. You need to recognize what the *focus* word is in the question. Is it a noun, verb or adjective?

Apa kakakmu penari? Bukan.	*Is your sister a <u>dancer</u>? No.*
Apa dia péndék? Tidak.	*Is she <u>short</u>? No.*
Apa dia bekerja **di Bali?** Tidak.	*Does she <u>work</u> in Bali? No.*

EXERCISE 6

Answer *no* to these questions:

a Apa itu pénsilmu?
b Apa pénsilmu patah?
c Apa ibumu ceréwét?
d Apakah meréka tahu?

kakak *elder sister/brother*
péndék *short*
pénsil *pencil*
patah *broken*
ceréwét *talkative*

2 In the dialogue did you notice that Pak Tanto asked Mark **Kapan tiba di Jakarta?** and **Berapa lama mau tinggal di sini?** without including a pronoun? This is perfectly acceptable and widely used in conversational style. Indonesians like to express themselves in the simplest and most economical way possible which leads to their omitting certain words from the sentence when the context is fully understood. In this case, it is obvious that Pak Tanto is addressing Mark and no-one else. It would be unthinkable to miss words out like this in correct English, even when the context is fully understood. The omission in this sentence is optional. It would be perfectly correct to say **Kapan kamu tiba di Jakarta?** and **Berapa lama kamu mau tinggal di sini?**. However, the forms in the dialogue come naturally to native Indonesian speakers so you should be aware of them.

Insight

As you work through this book and, especially if you have the opportunity to converse with Indonesian speakers, you will begin to get a natural feel for which words may be dropped when the context is understood.

3 To ask *where?*, *where to?* and *where from?* Indonesian uses:

di mana...?	*where...?*
Di mana kamu tinggal?	*Where do you live?*
ke mana...?	*where to...?*
Ke mana kamu pergi?	*Where are you going (to)?*
dari mana...?	*where from...?*
Dari mana kamu berasal?	*Where do you come from?*

These three questions are made up of a preposition (a word that indicates location) and **mana**. Note that the two components that make up these questions cannot be separated as in the corresponding English sentences. For instance, in the last example, notice how *where* can occur at the beginning of the phrase with the *from* at the end. This is *not* possible in Indonesian.

Insight

You will find these questions easier to understand and use if you think of how they would appear in older-style English: *To where are you going? From where do you come?*, as this is what you are effectively saying in Indonesian.

EXERCISE 7

Fill in the blanks with the appropriate question according to the meaning:

a _____ dia masuk?
b _____ dia belajar?
c _____ meréka membawa kopor itu?
d _____ kami datang?

masuk *to enter*
membawa *bring/take*
datang *to come*

4 Used on its own, **berapa?** means *how many?*

berapa mobil?	*how many cars?*
berapa kucing?	*how many cats?*

However, **berapa** is often combined with other words to create specific questions that ask about the quantity of something. In the dialogue you were introduced to:

Berapa lama?　　*How long?/For how long?*

This question is made up of **berapa** and **lama** which means *a long time*.

··

Insight

Note that **berapa lama?** can only be used to refer to time. If you want to ask *how long?* to refer to physical length the question **berapa panjang?** must be used.

··

Similarly, **berapa kali?**, *how many times?*

Berapa kali kamu datang ke Indonesia?	*How many times have you come to Indonesia?*

Many useful questions can be formed with **berapa**. It is worth bearing this in mind as you work through the units, as other questions using **berapa** will be presented in appropriate units.

> **Insight**
> The answer to a question with **berapa** will, more often than not, have a number in the answer.

kali *time*

EXERCISE 8

Complete these questions with **berapa lama** or **berapa kali** as appropriate.

a _____ penerbangan dari London ke Jakarta?
b _____ anda makan nasi goréng?
c _____ kita menunggu?
d _____ dia tinggal di Indonesia?
e _____ dia menélpon?

makan *to eat*
nasi goréng *Indonesian style fried rice*
menélpon *to telephone/to make a phone call*

5 In Part One of this unit you were introduced to the question word **siapa**. When you ask for someone's name in English, you use *what?* (*What's your name?*) Indonesian, by way of contrast, uses **siapa!**

Siapa **nama anda?**	*What's your name?*
Siapa **nama orang itu?**	*What's the name of that person?*

But, if you are inquiring about the name of something other than a living being, you must use **apa**:

Apa nama kota ini?　　　*What's this town called?*

kota *town/city*

If you mix these up, you can cause confusion. If you ask someone the name of her pet dog, for instance, the question would be **Siapa nama anjing ini?** If you were to ask, **Apa nama anjing ini?** you would be asking about the *breed* of dog.

6 **Pernah** and **tidak pernah** relate to the past in a specific way. From the English speaker's point of view, it is easier to grasp how to use **tidak pernah** first. **Tidak pernah** simply translates *never* as in such sentences as:

Saya *tidak pernah* **pergi ke Lombok.**　*I have **never** been to Lombok.*
Kami *tidak pernah* **melihat dia.**　　*We have **never** seen her.*

melihat *to see*

Pernah expresses *ever* as in the English *Have you **ever** been to Lombok?* However, whereas English only uses *ever* in the question form, Indonesian uses it in the positive statement too. In this sense it expresses something you have done in the distant past and can often be translated as *once* in English:

Saya *pernah* **pergi ke Bali.**　　*I **once** went to Bali.*
Dia *pernah* **belajar memasak.**　*She **once** learnt cookery.*
Apa kamu *pernah* **ke Lombok?**　*Have you **ever** (been) to Lombok?*

Insight
Note that in the last example **pergi** can be omitted as it is understood from the context which **ke** – *to* creates.

memasak *to cook*

EXERCISE 9

How would you say:

a I have never seen that film (movie).
b Have you ever been to Medan?
c We (use **kami**) once ate durian.
d He once lived in America?

QV

durian durian (see Unit 14)

7 Selamat, a word connected with the idea of prosperity, welfare, happiness and salvation is used in many an Indonesian greeting. In addition to several set greetings, some of which you will see in the following list, you can combine **selamat** with any verb to convey an idea of well wishing in that particular action etc. Here are some common ones you may find useful:

Selamat belajar!	*Enjoy your studies!*
Selamat makan!	*Enjoy your food!*
Selamat bekerja!	*Enjoy your work!*
Selamat terbang!	*Have a good flight!*
Selamat ulang tahun!	*Happy birthday!*
Selamat tidur!	*Good night!*
Selamat Lebaran!	*Happy Eid!*
Selamat Natal!	*Merry Christmas!*
Selamat jalan!	*Goodbye!*
Selamat tinggal!	*Goodbye!*
Selamat bersenang-senang!	*Have a good time!*

Insight

Why are there two words for *goodbye* in Indonesian?
If you are the one who is leaving you say **Selamat tinggal** to whomever you are taking leave of and, if you are the one staying, you wish the person leaving a happy journey, **Selamat jalan!**

Using Indonesian

EXERCISE 10

See if you can make these sentences in Indonesian:

a They didn't arrive yesterday.
b This isn't the flight to Jakarta.
c I don't speak Arabic.
d My wife isn't Indonesian.
e That isn't an orang outang.
f Endang is not stubborn.

bahasa Arab *Arabic*
orang utan *orang outang*
keras kepala *stubborn*

Insight

Orang-utan is, in fact, a Malay/Indonesian word. **Orang** means *person* and **hutan** means *forest*. So **orang-utan** means *forest person*. This is not the only word we've adopted into English from Malay. For instance, *amok*, as in *to run amok* is borrowed from the Malay/Indonesian **amuk**.

EXERCISE 11

Look at the following sentences. Use the rules given earlier to determine whether the sentence uses **bukan** or **tidak** in the right way. If there is a mistake, correct it. Check your answer in the key.

a Dia tidak orang Brazil.
b Dia bukan pemain sépak bola.
c Kami tidak bahagia.
d Saya bukan bodoh.
e Kemarin meréka bukan datang.

orang Brazil *Brazilian*
pemain *player*
sépak bola *football (i.e. soccer)*
pemain sépak bola *football player*
bahagia *happy*
bodoh *stupid*

EXERCISE 12

Look at the answers. What were the questions?

a Séhat.
b Penerbangan sangat melelahkan.
c Tidak, saya masih bujangan.

d Nama saya Angela.
e Ya, saya pernah ke Miami.
f Meréka mau tinggal di Solo cuma dua minggu.
g Bukan, saya bukan orang Thailand.

cuma *just, only*
Thailand *(pronounced **Tailan**) Thailand*

EXERCISE 13

Over to you!

Imagine you are an Australian called Stuart from Canberra (**A**).
One day you are out and about in your home town and you notice
a foreign tourist having difficulty making herself understood (**B**).
You notice that her guidebook is in Indonesian so you take the
opportunity to practise the Indonesian you learnt at school
(**di sekolah**).

A	*Are you Indonesian? How are you?*
B	Ya, kabar baik, terima kasih.
A	*Excuse me? What's your name?*
B	Nama saya Triwulandari. Panggil saja Tri.
A	*My name's Stuart. Just call me Stu.*
B	Maaf, bahasa Inggeris saya tidak lancar.
A	*Don't worry. I once learnt Indonesian at school.*
B	Bagus kalau begitu.
A	*Where are you staying?*
B	Saya tinggal di hotél Hilton.
A	*How is Australia?*
B	Bagus sekali.
A	*How long will you stay in Canberra?*
B	Cuma dua minggu.
A	*Have a nice holiday!*
B	Terima kasih. Sampai berjumpa lagi.

CD1, TR 4, 6:48

bagus sekali *great*
Sampai berjumpa lagi! *See you!*

Some conversation pointers

Some pointers about Indonesian culture are indispensable when it comes to successful communication. A westerner's lack of understanding of the Indonesian standpoint can sometimes lead to misunderstanding and embarrassment.

Did you notice that, in the first dialogue in this unit, in the conversation about marriage, Bambang does not say directly that he is not married, but says that he is *still single*, **masih bujangan** i.e. not married *yet*. This reflects the traditional family values of Indonesia. Whereas it is perfectly acceptable in many western countries to say one is single, for the Indonesians one is either already married – **sudah berkeluarga** – or one is not married yet – **belum berkeluarga**. It is always assumed that you will get married one day.

As a westerner, you may find it better to stick to this formula rather than saying that you are not married, as you might arouse unexpected concern for your future in the Indonesians you meet!

In addition to these expressions, you may also hear and use **menikah** (or **nikah**, in informal conversation) and **kawin** both meaning *married*. Be warned, however that the use of **kawin** is becoming increasingly associated with animals rather than human beings and in a few years its usage will probably become restricted to beasts alone!

First-time western visitors to Indonesia are often indignant about the apparent noseyness of Indonesians as they seem forever to be inquiring about where you are going! **Mau ke mana?**, *Where are you off to?* In reality, this is just a very common greeting which is not really meant to be taken literally and, most of the time, the person who asks does not really expect anything other than the standard reply, **Jalan-jalan**, *Oh, I'm just off for a walk.*

Forms of address

Generally, men are addressed as **Bapak** which means *Sir* and *Mr*, when used with the person's name. Women are addressed as **Ibu** meaning *Madam* or *Mrs* when used with a name. Unlike English, the first name can be used after **Bapak** or **Ibu** or, as in English, the family name can be used. Therefore, *Ken Knight* could be either **Bapak Ken** or **Bapak Knight**. **Bapak** is often shortened to **Pak** and **Ibu** to just **Bu** when the person is being addressed directly.

Mas meaning *brother* and **mbak** which means *sister* are Javanese words that are used by the speaker to address people who are older. They can also be used with the person's name as with **Bapak** and **Ibu**.

In West Java, the Sundanese use **A'ak** for **Mas** and **Tétéh** for **Mbak**.

To address someone younger, especially in West Java, **ujang** is used for a male and **neng** is used for a female. Although these words mean *little boy* and *little girl* respectively, the person does not have to be a child to be addressed in this way.

Two more forms of address you may come across are **adik** (which is often shortened to just **dik**) which can be used when speaking to someone younger, male or female, and **abang** which is only used to address males who are older than the speaker.

You can attract someone's attention by using these forms, for example **maaf mas**, *excuse me, young man.* Although this may sound patronizing in English, these forms are polite and are widely used in Indonesian.

Remember also that all these forms can be used to mean *you* as Indonesian often uses a title or someone's name where we would use *you* in English, even though you are addressing that person directly.

PAKAIAN TRADISIONAL (TRADITIONAL DRESS)

| Java | Sumatera | Kalimantan | Irian Jaya |

Learning tip

Make pocket-sized flashcards with Indonesian vocabulary or expressions on one side and the English on the other or make a small vocabulary and expression book that you can carry around with you so that you can revise the material from the unit you are studying and keep previously covered material alive during all those spare moments when you are waiting in queues, taking the bus etc.

TEST YOURSELF

1 How do you say *How are you?* in Indonesian?

2 How would you answer the question above?

3 What does **orang Perancis** mean?

4 How would you refer to the *English language* in Indonesian?

5 How would you say *I don't understand* in Indonesian?

6 What is unusual about the way you ask someone's name in Indonesian?

7 How should you use **bukan** and **tidak**?

8 Are adjectives placed after or before the noun in Indonesian?

9 How would you say *never* in Indonesian?

10 What is the difference between **Selamat tinggal** and **Selamat jalan**?

4

Working and studying

In this unit you will learn how to
- *talk about your job and ask about what other people do*
- *express your capabilities*
- *talk about education and study*

PART ONE

Dialogue

During his short stay in Indonesia, Ken needs a competent personal assistant to help him. One of the short-listed applicants for the job is a Rita Sutanto, whom Ken is interviewing.

Rita	Selamat pagi, Pak!
Ken	Selamat pagi, silahkan duduk! Saya memerlukan seorang sektretaris untuk membantu saya. Bisakah saudara ceritakan tentang pendidikan saudara?
Rita	Saya telah menyelesaikan pendidikan saya di Akademi Sekretaris 'Tarakanita' di Jakarta.
Ken	Kapan saudara tamat?
Rita	Lima tahun yang lalu.
Ken	Apa keahlian saudara?
Rita	Saya bisa berbicara tiga bahasa, Inggeris, Perancis dan Jepang dengan baik. Saya juga mampu mengetik dengan cepat.

Ken	Apa saudara terbiasa menggunakan komputer?
Rita	Tentu, Pak. Saya juga terbiasa dengan mesin fax dan e-mail.
Ken	Apakah saudara bisa surat-menyurat?
Rita	Saya ahli dalam bidang itu.
Ken	Apakah saudara masih bekerja di perusahaan lain?
Rita	Ya, saya masih bekerja di perusahaan Unilever sebagai sekretaris.
Ken	Berapa gaji yang saudara harapkan?
Rita	Dua juta per bulan, jika memungkinkan.
Ken	Kapan saudara bisa mulai bekerja?
Rita	Bulan depan.
Ken	Apakah saudara bisa bekerja penuh waktu?
Rita	Maaf Pak, saya hanya bisa bekerja paruh waktu, tiga hari dalam seminggu.
Ken	Baiklah kalau begitu, saya akan pertimbangkan lagi dan memberi kabar secepatnya.

duduk *sit down*
silahkan duduk *please sit down.*
memerlukan *to need*
sekretaris *secretary*
untuk *for*
ceritakan *to tell*
tentang *about*
pendidikan *education*
telah *already*
menyelesaikan *to finish*
telah menyelesaikan *finished*
akademi *academy*
tamat *to graduate*
lima *five*
tahun *year*
lima tahun yang lalu *five years ago*
keahlian *skill*
mampu *capable*
mengetik *to type*
terbiasa *to be used to*

QUICK VOCAB

cepat *fast*
dengan cepat *quickly*
menggunakan *to use*
komputer *computer*
tentu *of course*
mesin fax *fax machine*
e-mail *email (pronounced as in English)*
surat-menyurat *to handle correspondence*
ahli *expert*
dalam *inside*
ahli dalam *an expert in*
bidang *field*
lain *other, another*
perusahaan lain *another company*
sebagai *as*
gaji *salary*
harapkan *to expect*
dua juta *two million*
per bulan *per month*
jika *if*
jika memungkinkan *if possible*
mulai *to start*
bulan depan *next month*
penuh *full*
waktu *time*
penuh waktu *full time*
paruh *half, part*
paruh waktu *part time*
tiga *three*
hari *day*
tiga hari *three days*
Baiklah kalau begitu. *That's fine/that's all right then.*
akan *will/shall*
pertimbangkan *to consider*
memberi *to give*
memberi kabar *let you know/to inform*
secepatnya *as soon as possible*

TRANSLATION

Rita	Good morning, Sir!
Ken	Good morning, please take a seat. I need a secretary to help me. Could you tell me about your education?
Rita	I finished my education at the Tarakanita Secretarial Academy in Jakarta.
Ken	When did you graduate?
Rita	Five years ago.
Ken	What are your skills?
Rita	I can speak three languages well – English, French and Japanese. I am also able to type fast.
Ken	Are you used to using a computer?
Rita	Of course, Sir. I'm also used to (using) fax and email.
Ken	Can you handle correspondence?
Rita	Yes, I am an expert in that field.
Ken	Are you still working for another company?
Rita	Yes, Sir, I'm still working for Unilever as a secretary.
Ken	What salary do you expect?
Rita	Two million per month, if possible.
Ken	When are you able to start work?
Rita	Next month.
Ken	Can you work full time?
Rita	I'm sorry, Sir, (but) I'm only able to work part time. Three days a week.
Ken	That's fine. I'll think about it more and let you know as soon as possible.

How the language works 1

1 Silahkan is a useful and polite word to use when urging someone to do something. It is one of the ways to say *Please (do something)* in Indonesian. Just combine it with a verb.

Silahkan duduk!	*Please sit down!*
Silahkan berdiri!	*Please stand up!*

| **Silahkan cuci!** | *Please wash!* |
| **Silahkan ikut saya!** | *Please follow me!* |

berdiri *to stand up*
cuci *to wash*
ikut *to follow*

EXERCISE 1

Try forming **Silahkan...** phrases with the following words and then write the meanings:

a menyanyi
b berbicara
c minum
d menari
e masuk

menyanyi *to sing*
menari *to dance*
masuk *to enter*

2 Expressing ability. There are three ways to talk about what you can do in Indonesian. You can use **bisa**, **dapat** or **mampu**, all of which mean *can* or *to be able to*. Place them before the verb they refer to:

Saya *dapat* **berhitung.**	*I **can** count.*
Meréka *dapat* **mengajar bahasa Spanyol.**	*They **can** teach Spanish.*
Dia *bisa* **berkomunikasi dengan baik.**	*He **can** communicate well.*
Saya *mampu* **menjual produk itu.**	*I **can** sell this product.*

berhitung *to count*
berkomunikasi *to communicate*
menjual *to sell*
produk *product*

> ## Insight
> **Mampu** is a good word to use when talking about your capabilities. Indonesians will be impressed to hear you using this!

3 **Bisa** and **dapat** can both be used to form phrases that make a request which corresponds to *Could you...?* in English, as in *Could you help me?* As in the dialogue they can both occur with **-kah** attached. **Bisakah anda ceritakan tentang pendidikan saudara?** As with **apakah**, the **-kah** makes the question even more polite, which is appropriate for a formal situation such as the job interview in the dialogue.

4 You have already come across a way of indicating *how* an action is performed. Such a word is known as an *adverb*. It tells you more about the action expressed in the verb. These are usually formed by adding *-ly* to an adjective in English, for example: *quick → quickly*.

Look at these examples:

Saya berbicara Inggeris *dengan baik.*   *I speak English* **well.**
Dia mampu mengetik *dengan cepat.*   *He can type* **quickly.**

You will see that in Indonesian they are formed by **dengan** plus adjective. Adding any adjective to **dengan** has the same effect as adding *-ly* to a noun in English, turning it into an adverb:

otomatis   *automatic*
dengan **otomatis**   *automatica***lly**

otomatis *automatic*

EXERCISE 2

How would you say:

a Please drive carefully!
b Please write accurately!
c Please read quietly!

mengemudi *to drive*
teliti *accurate*
hati-hati *careful*
tenang *quiet*

5 Job talk

arsiték *architect*
dokter *doctor*
dokter gigi *dentist*
perawat *nurse*
ibu rumah tangga *housewife*
ilmuwan *scientist*
montir *mechanic*
dosén *lecturer*
wartawan, wartawati *journalist*
pegawai negeri *public servant*
ahli hukum *lawyer*
nelayan *fisherman*
pelukis *artist*
penulis *writer*
penyanyi *singer*
pemusik *musician*
petani *farmer*
perawat *nurse*
juru foto *photographer*
juru masak *chef*
pelayan *waiter*
Apa pekerjaan anda? *What's your job?*

Insight

As with **mahasiswa/mahasiswi,** that we met in Unit 1, some occupations have different forms depending on whether it is a man or a woman being referred to. Ones ending in **-wan**, end in **-wati** for females. For example, **pustakawan/pustakawati** *librarian*.

When stating what job someone does, the word **seorang** is often inserted just before the job title:

Dia seorang wartawati.   *She's a journalist.*

Insight

Used in this way **seorang** corresponds to *a* or *an* in English. Although it is entirely optional, native speakers tend to express jobs in this way.

Understanding Indonesian

EXERCISE 3

Using the dialogue say whether the following statements are true or false.

a Rita menyelesaikan pendidikan di Jakarta.
b Rita hanya mampu menggunakan komputer dan email.
c Dia tidak dapat mengerjakan surat-menyurat.
d Dia mampu mengetik dengan cepat.
e Dia tidak bisa mulai kerja minggu depan.

mengerjakan *to do*
kerja *work*

EXERCISE 4

Imagine you work for an international employment agency. A company has asked you to find a salesperson who is between 30–55 years of age, has a university diploma, has at least five years' experience in sales and is computer literate. An Indonesian speaker is preferred but fluent English is a must. There are four people on your books who may be suitable. Read the information about each person and choose which one best fulfils the requirements the company is looking for.

Nama	Yenny Hayes
Umur	30 tahun
Warga negara	Indonesia/Australia
Pendidikan	Universitas (Sarjana)
Pengalaman kerja	Pemasaran 4 tahun
Ketrampilan	Komputer, bahasa Inggeris

Nama	Guntur Supratna
Umur	40 tahun
Warga negara	Indonesia
Pendidikan	Sarjana (Universitas)
Pengalaman kerja	Pemasaran/penjualan 10 tahun
Ketrampilan	Komputer, bahasa Inggeris (lancar)

Nama	Douglas Cross
Umur	36 tahun
Warga negara	Kanada
Pendidikan	Diploma (akademi)
Pengalaman kerja	Pemasaran 7 tahun
Ketrampilan	Komputer, bahasa Inggeris, bahasa Perancis

Nama	David Teng
Umur	31 tahun
Warga negara	Singapura
Pendidikan	Universitas
Pengalaman kerja	Pemasaran 6 tahun
Ketrampilan	Komputer, bahasa Inggeris dan bahasa Mandarin

PART TWO

Dialogue

Reza is taking Mark around her university, where she studies computer science.

◄» CD1, TR 5, 1:59

Reza	Mark, ini kampus saya. Kami punya dua kampus, A dan B. Sekarang kita berada di kampus A.
Mark	Di mana kampus B?
Reza	Kampus B di Dépok, jauh dari sini, kira-kira satu jam. Saya akan mengajak kamu ke sana, kalau kamu tertarik. Hari ini kamu kelihatan capék.
Mark	Tentu saya tertarik, hari ini saya tidak keberatan pergi ke sana.
Reza	Baiklah kalau begitu.
(Di kampus B.)	
Mark	Di mana kelas kamu?
Reza	Di lantai dua. Mari ikut saya.
Mark	Kamu belajar apa?
Reza	Komputer. Karena saya ingin menjadi seorang pembuat program komputer.
(Meréka naik ke atas.)	
Reza	Ini ruang belajar saya.
Mark	Di perusahaan apa kamu mau bekerja nanti?
Reza	Di perusahaan swasta.
Mark	Di mana kamu bisa mencari pekerjaan?
Reza	Dari iklan di koran. Saya sudah kirim riwayat hidup ke satu perusahaan swasta. Saya ingin bekerja paruh waktu.
Mark	Saya harap kamu berhasil.

kampus *campus*
punya *to have*
sekarang *now*
berada *to be (at a place)*
jauh *far*

jauh dari sini *far from here*
kira-kira *around, approximately*
satu *one*
jam *hour*
akan *will*
mengajak *to invite*
kalau *if*
tentu *of course*
tertarik *interested*
Tentu saya tertarik. *Of course I'm interested.*
hari ini *today*
kelihatan *to look like/to seem*
tidak keberatan *I don't mind*
ke sana *(to) there*
kelas *class*
lantai *floor*
mari ikut saya *follow me*
karena *because*
ingin *want*
menjadi *to become*
pembuat *maker*
pembuat program komputer *computer programmer*
naik ke atas *to go upstairs*
ruang *room/space*
ruang belajar *classroom*
bekerja *to work*
swasta *private*
perusahaan swasta *private company*
mencari *to look for*
pekerjaan *job*
iklan *advertisement*
kirim *to send*
riwayat *story, biography*
hidup *life*
riwayat hidup *curriculum vitae*
harap *to hope*
berhasil *succeed*
Saya harap kamu berhasil. *I wish you luck. (I hope you succeed.)*

TRANSLATION

Reza	Mark, this is my campus. We have two campuses, A and B. Now we are at campus A.
Mark	Where is campus B?
Reza	Campus B is in Depok, far away from here, about one hour. I will take you there if you are interested. Today you look so tired.
Mark	Of course I'm interested. I don't mind going there today.
Reza	All right.
Mark	Where is your class?
Reza	On floor two. Please follow me.
Mark	What do you study?
Reza	Computer science. Because I want to be a programmer.
Reza	This is my classroom.
Mark	What company do you want to work for later on?
Reza	For a private company.
Mark	Where can you find a job?
Reza	From an advert in the newspaper. I've already sent my CV to one private company. I want to work part time.
Mark	I wish you luck.

How the language works 2

1 Tenses. In English, when you talk about what you are doing now, what you did yesterday and what you will do tomorrow, you convey the meaning through a change in the form of the verb you use, for example: *I am eating, I ate, I will eat*. The form of the verb is usually enough to indicate tense, i.e. when the action takes place. If you hear *I went* then you know immediately that the speaker is referring to the past. In fact, English has a very complex tense system. If you have bad memories of learning a foreign language before and are struggling with the complications of learning tenses, then you will be happy to hear that you are about to make a quantum leap in your study of Indonesian!

Indonesian verbs do not indicate person; they do not indicate tense either. This means that, for instance, **pergi** can translate as *go*, *went*, *has been* etc. depending on the context in which it occurs.

Insight

This does not pose a translation problem for English speakers as your knowledge of English will automatically compensate and place the action in the correct time frame.

Indonesian has two ways of indicating tense: The first way is by using a *time expression* which will give you a time frame and a tense for the verb.

Some basic units of time are:

hari	*day*
minggu	*week*
bulan	*month*
tahun	*year*

Adding either **depan** or **yang akan datang** to any of these or a day of the week or month puts the time unit into the future and automatically creates a future tense for anything you put with it and translates as *next…*:

tahun depan	*next year*
minggu yang akan datang	*next week*

Similarly, adding **yang lalu** to any of the time units just mentioned above creates a past tense and translates as *last…* or *… ago*:

bulan yang lalu	*last month*

Note also:

hari ini	*today*
bésok	*tomorrow*
kemarin	*yesterday*

dua hari yang lalu *the day before yesterday (two days ago)*
dua hari yang akan *the day after tomorrow*
  datang

When you are talking about events that happened in the very near past or future, usually the same day or in the same 24-hour period, you need to be aware of the usage of particular time expressions. These only occur with **pagi**, *morning*, **soré**, *late morning*, **siang**, *afternoon*, and **malam**, *evening*.

With one or two exceptions **tadi** is used to refer to the past in this extremely limited time frame and **nanti** is used to refer to the future.

Thus:

tadi malam	*yesterday evening*
tadi pagi	*this morning*
nanti malam	*tonight*
nanti soré	*this afternoon*

You need to note the form **bésok pagi** (rather than **nanti pagi**) for *tomorrow morning* as this is the only exception.

Note, finally, that if you are talking about something that will happen later on in the same time frame you are currently experiencing, for instance, it is evening and you want to talk about something that will happen on that same evening, the preferred form is **malam ini**. Note also **pagi ini** etc.

EXERCISE 5

How would you say:

a last year
b next month
c the year before last
d last week
e this afternoon?

The second way to indicate tense is by use of a *tense marker*. These are generally adverbs that, by the very nature of their meaning, carry with them the idea of tense when used with a verb. For example, you have already met **sedang** which means *now*. When you combine **sedang** with a verb, it forms the equivalent of a continuous tense which is expressed by *to be … -ing* in English:

Saya mengajar biologi.   *I teach biology.*
Saya *sedang* **mengajar biologi.**   *I **am teaching** biology.*

You have also come across **sudah** which you know means *already* but when used as a tense marker indicates a past tense:

Meréka *sudah* **datang.**   *They **have arrived**/they **arrived**.*

A tense marker with a similar meaning is **telah** which you met in the dialogue in Part One:

Saya *telah* **menyelesaikan pendidikan.**   *I **finished** my education.*

In spoken Indonesian you will almost always use **sudah** because **telah** is considered highly formal. It is fitting for the job interview situation in the dialogue but it would seem out of place in everyday conversation. In writing, however, it would be appropriate to substitute **telah** for **sudah**.

Insight

In the conversation in Part One, Rita uses **telah**, even though the Indonesian being used is spoken, because she is being interviewed for a job and wants to make a good impression.

EXERCISE 6

How would you say:

a he wrote
b they are typing
c I am speaking

d she read
e Are you studying? (use kamu)

Some subjects you might study at school are as follows:

bisnis manajemén *business management*
keuangan *finance*
perbankan *banking*
pertanian *agriculture*
ilmu lingkungan *environment*
sumber daya manusia *human resources*
hubungan masyarakat *human relations*
keahlian téknik *engineering*
akutansi *accounting*
ilmu wisata *tourism*
pengajaran *teaching*
ilmu kedokteran *medicine*
hukum *law*
ilmu sastra *humanities*
arsitéktur *architecture*
kimia *chemistry*
biologi *biology*
matématika *mathematics*
géografi *geography*
kesenian *art*

Using Indonesian

EXERCISE 7

Match the pictures opposite with the professions.

a Dia seorang dokter gigi.
b Dia seorang petani.
c Toni seorang nelayan.
d Yanto seorang pelukis.

i

ii

iii

iv

Read the sentences and fill in the appropriate words from the list that follows.

a _____ dan _____ bekerja di rumah sakit.
b _____ mengurus anak dan suami di rumah.
c Hotél itu mempunyai _____ terkenal.
d Kami memerlukan seorang _____untuk merancang rumah baru kami.
e Perusahaan surat kabar itu memerlukan seorang _____.

ibu rumah tangga	arsiték
dokter	juru masak
perawat	wartawan

rumah sakit *hospital*
mengurus *to look after*
suami *husband*
terkenal *famous*
merancang *to design*

EXERCISE 8

Over to you!

An Indonesian (**A**) who runs a language school is looking for someone to help her teach English at her school. You (**B**) are being interviewed about the position.

A	Apa pekerjaan anda pada saat ini?
B	*I am a language teacher.*
A	Apa keahlian anda?
B	*I have experience teaching English and I can speak three languages.*
A	Di mana anda belajar mengajar?
B	*At Babel Language School.*
A	Berapa gaji yang anda harapkan?
B	*Five million, if possible.*
A	Kapan anda bisa mulai bekerja?
B	*Next month.*
A	Mudah–mudahan anda berhasil.

pada saat ini *at present*
sekolah bahasa *language school*
mudah-mudahan *hopefully*

Agriculture

Indonesia is traditionally an agricultural country with most of the population living in villages and working on farms. Most Indonesian farmers work the land for their own survival. Rice is the staple diet so rice fields abound! Known centuries ago as the *Spice Islands* owing to the export in spices, Indonesia still farms spices, as well as rice, coffee, tea, coconuts, corn and rubber for export.

The role of women

In the cities and in the workplace the role of women has changed radically in the last few years and it is now possible for women to hold the same positions as men. This became most apparent in the government where, for the first time in Indonesian history, a woman, Megawati Soekarno Putri, served as president between 2001 and 2004.

Education

Education for Indonesian children begins at kindergarten, **taman kanak-kanak** (shortened to **TK**), when they are five years old.

After **TK** they go to elementary school, **sekolah dasar** (**SD**) for six years from the age of seven.

Following elementary school, pupils go to junior high school **sekolah lanjutan tingkat pertama** (**SLTP**) for three years. Junior high schools used to be called **sekolah menengah pertama** which was shortened to **SMP**. Even though the name of the school has been changed, Indonesians still refer to junior high school as **SMP**.

After **SMP** comes senior high school, **sekolah lanjutan tingkat atas** (**SLTA**). As with junior high, Indonesians still use the old acronym **SMA**, which refers to the former name, **sekolah menengah atas**. In the second of three years at senior high school, students can choose to major in natural sciences (**ilmu pengetahuan alam**), social science (**ilmu pengetahuan sosial**) or languages. Following **SMA** students can continue their studies at a university or an academy.

TEST YOURSELF

1 Which word would you use when making a polite request?

2 What do **bisa** and **dapat** mean?

3 Which word can you use to express your abilities in a more impressive way?

4 How do you form an adverb in Indonesian?

5 Which word is often inserted before a job title in Indonesian?

6 How would you say *next month* in Indonesian? (three ways)

7 How would you say *tomorrow morning* in Indonesian? (Be careful!)

8 How would you create a continuous tense in Indonesian?

9 Which two words can be used to form a past tense in Indonesian?

10 Which would you use at a job interview, where you are the interviewee?

Family and home

In this unit you will learn how to
- *talk about members of your family*
- *express where things are in your house*
- *say the numbers 1 to 10*

PART ONE

Dialogue

Ken and Anton take the opportunity to get to know each other a little better during a coffee break in the company canteen.

CD1, TR 6, 0:03

Ken	Bapak sudah berkeluarga, bukan?
Anton	Ya, Isteri saya dari Padang. Kami punya tiga orang anak. Yang pertama laki-laki, masih sekolah dasar. Yang kedua kembar perempuan. Meréka sangat lucu sekali.
Ken	Berapa umur meréka?
Anton	Sepuluh tahun dan tujuh tahun. Dan Bapak punya berapa orang anak?
Ken	Saya punya dua anak. Yang sulung perempuan, dan yang bungsu laki-laki.
Anton	Apa isteri Bapak bekerja?

Ken	Tidak. Dulu dia sekretaris, tapi sekarang cuma ibu rumah tangga. Menjaga anak-anak dan suami. Dia isteri yang baik. Apa isteri Bapak bekerja?
Anton	Dia seorang guru bahasa Inggeris. Tapi kami punya pembantu untuk menjaga anak-anak.
Ken	Bagus kalau begitu. Isteri dan anak-anak saya akan datang minggu depan dari Sélandia Baru. Meréka ingin bertemu kakék, nénék dan sepupu-sepupunya.
Anton	Apa kakéknya masih bekerja?
Ken	Dia dulu seorang guru besar di Universitas Pajajaran, tapi sekarang sudah pensiun. Isteri saya punya keluarga besar. Dia punya dua saudara laki-laki dan dua saudara perempuan. Meréka semua sudah menikah.
Anton	Jangan lupa kenalkan meréka, kalau meréka datang ke Jakarta. Saya akan mengundang meréka untuk makan malam.
Ken	Pasti, terima kasih.

pertama *first*
kedua *second*
laki-laki *male, man*
perempuan *girl*
kembar *twin*
kembar perempuan *twin girls*
lucu *cute*
berapa *how many*
orang anak *children*
umur *age*
yang *the one*
sulung *first born*
bungsu *youngest (child)*
berapa umur *how old*
sepuluh *ten*
tujuh *seven*
anak-anak *children*
delapan *eight*

enam *six*
cuma *just/only*
ibu rumah tangga *housewife*
menjaga *to look after*
pembantu *maid*
bagus *good*
begitu *so*
bagus kalau begitu *that's fine/that's all right then*
minggu depan *next week*
kakék *grandfather*
nénék *grandmother*
sepupu *cousin*
sepupu-sepupunya *their cousins*
dulu *formerly*
guru besar *senior lecturer*
besar *big*
pensiun *retired*
saudara laki-laki *brother*
saudara perempuan *sister*
menikah *married*
jangan *don't*
lupa *to forget*
jangan lupa *don't forget*
kenalkan *to introduce*
mengundang *to invite*
makan malam *dinner*
pasti *sure, of course*

Insight

We will look at this later in the course, but the use of **orang**, as in **tiga orang anak**, is a distinct feature of Indonesian, and most other East- or South-Asian languages. It is related to the **seorang** we met in the last unit. People are often counted in 'orang's, so three children are often counted as **tiga orang anak**. It is similar to the way we count cattle in 'heads' and hair in 'tufts'. There are other counting words for various categories of objects that we shall discuss fully in Unit 14.

TRANSLATION

Ken	You're already married, aren't you?
Anton	Yes, my wife is from Padang. We have three children. The first one is a boy (who is) still (at) elementary school. The second ones are twin girls. They are very, very cute.
Ken	How old are they?
Anton	Ten years and seven years old. And you, how many children do you have?
Ken	I have two children. The first born is a girl and the youngest is a boy.
Anton	Does your wife work?
Ken	No. She used to be a secretary but now she's just a housewife. (She) looks after (her) children and husband. She is a good wife. Does your wife work?
Anton	She is an English teacher but we have a housemaid to look after the children.
Ken	That's good. My wife and children will arrive next week from New Zealand. They want to see their grandfather, grandmother and cousins.
Anton	Does their grandfather still work?
Ken	He was a senior lecturer at Pajajaran University, but now he is retired. My wife has a big family. She has two brothers and two sisters. They are all married.
Anton	Please don't forget to introduce them [to me] if they come to Jakarta. I will invite them for dinner.
Ken	Sure. Thank you

How the language works 1

1 In spoken English, we add phrases like … *don't you?*, … *isn't she?* to the end of statements to form what are known as *question tags*. In English, the tag changes depending on the content of the statement it refers to, for instance, ***She speaks Malay, doesn't she?***, ***They were at the airport, weren't they?***

In Indonesian, you only need to use one tag, **bukan?**, which is often shortened just to **kan?** in more casual speech:

Meréka sudah berangkat ke Jakarta, *bukan*?	*They've already left for Jakarta,* **haven't they?**
Kamu mau membeli mobil, *bukan*?	*You want to buy a car,* **don't you?**

berangkat (ke) *to leave for*
membeli *to buy*

It is very important, however, to note that you must *always* use **bukan** (or **kan**) when you are adding a question tag to a negative statement, even when you have used **tidak** in the statement already, according to the rules given in Unit 3. **Tidak** can <u>never</u> be used as a question tag:

Meréka *tidak* **datang,** *bukan*?	*They didn't come,* **did they?**
Dia *tidak* **marah,** *kan*?	*She isn't angry,* **is she?**

marah *angry*

EXERCISE 1

Turn these statements into questions using question tags, then translate them, noting the simplicity of the Indonesian question tags compared to the English ones.

a Dia sedang tidur.
b Itu salah.
c Meréka bukan tentara.

salah *wrong*
tentara *soldier(s)*

2 **Sangat** and **sekali** can both be used to translate *very*; however each is used in a different position in relation to the word you want to refer to. When you use **sangat** you need to place it *before* the word it refers to but when you use **sekali** you need to place it *after* the word. You can use these with adjectives or adverbs in the following way:

sangat **ganteng**	**very** *handsome*
ganteng *sekali*	**very** *handsome*
dengan cepat *sekali*	**very** *fast*

ganteng *handsome*

05

Insight

In colloquial language, Indonesians tend to prefer to use **sekali** rather than **sangat**.

As in the dialogue, you can use both **sangat** and **sekali** together to mean *very, very* or *extremely*:

sangat **lucu** *sekali*   **very, very** *cute*

EXERCISE 2

Give the Indonesian for the following. Give both forms where possible:

a very dark
b very wide
c very good
d extremely strong
e extremely tired

gelap *dark*
luas *wide*
kuat *strong (physically)*
lelah *tired*

05

3 Numbers.

◀) **CD1, TR 6, 2:03**

Numbers 1 to 10 form the basis for all the numbers that come after, so learning them thoroughly now will really pay off later.

satu	*one*
dua	*two*
tiga	*three*
empat	*four*
lima	*five*
enam	*six*
tujuh	*seven*
delapan	*eight*
sembilan	*nine*
sepuluh	*ten*

Note also:

pertama	*first*
kedua	*second*
ketiga	*third*

Insight

After **pertama**, adding **ke-** to any number will form the ordinal.

4 In this unit, we have come across the word **yang** which has several important uses in Indonesian, some of which will be examined here and some in later units.

▶ **Yang** corresponds to *the one which (is)*, *the one who (is)*, *the ones who (are)* and *the ones which (are)* in English. It can refer to things as well as people:

Yang sulung perempuan.   *The (one who is) first born is a girl.*
Yang laki-laki berumur   *The one who is male is 7 years old.*
  7 tahun.

Mau yang kecil? Tidak, yang besar.	*Do you want the small one (i.e. the one that is small)? No, the big one (the one that is big).*
Kamu perlu yang ini? Tidak, yang lain.	*Do you need this one (the one that is this)? No, the other one (the one that is other).*
Saya mau yang itu.	*I want that one.*
Yang menolong saya sepupu Eva.	*The one who helped me is Eva's cousin.*

kecil *small*
menolong *to help*

▶ By extension, **yang** can be used, as in the dialogue, with ordinal numbers meaning *the first one*, *the second one* etc.:

Yang pertama laki-laki.	*The first one (i.e. the one who is first) is male.*
Yang ketiga sudah siap.	*The third one is ready.*

siap *ready*

▶ **Dia isteri *yang* baik.** It is very common for Indonesian speakers to insert **yang** between the noun and the adjective, even though it may not seem necessary given the rules for noun + adjective you learnt in Unit 3. It is sometimes used by the speaker to stress the quality expressed by the adjective in relation to the noun it refers to. It could be used by the speaker to add emotional emphasis creating a meaning such as *She is a good wife*, stressing the quality *good*, although you will hear it used naturally and regularly by Indonesians simply as a speech habit and not always to add emphasis.

5 Talking about your family.

ayah	*father*
ibu	*mother*
putera	*son*

putri	*daughter*
kakék	*grandfather*
nénék	*grandmother*
paman or **om**	*uncle*
bibi or **tante**	*aunt*
suami	*husband*
isteri	*wife*

Many family words in Indonesian are not gender specific:

saudara	*brother/sister*
adik	*younger brother/sister*
kakak	*older brother/sister*
ipar	*brother/sister-in-law*
anak	*child/son/daughter*
cucu	*grandchild/grandson/granddaughter*
sepupu	*cousin*
keponakan	*niece/nephew*
mertua	*father/mother-in-law*
kembar	*twin(s)*

This is not usually a problem as either context will tell you or you may already be aware of the gender of the person the speaker is referring to. When clarification is needed **laki-laki** is applied to all these words to indicate a male and **perempuan** is applied to indicate a female.

Laki-laki and **perempuan** can also be used with **anak**, *child*, to mean *boy* or *girl* or with **orang**, *person*, to indicate *man* or *woman*, although **perempuan** or **laki-laki** alone can also mean *woman* or *man* respectively.

> ### Insight
> **Orang tua** means *old person* or *old people* but it can also mean *parent* or *parents*. *Grandparents* is rendered by **kakék nénék** in Indonesian.

EXERCISE 3

Write the gender-specific forms of the following:

a granddaughter
b father-in-law
c nephew
d older sister

To talk about what you have you can use **punya** or **mempunyai** interchangeably.

Saya *punya* **anak kembar.**	*I have twins.*
Saya *mempunyai* **anak kembar.**	*I have twins.*
Kami *mempunyai* **rumah bagus.**	*We have a nice house.*

6 **Punya** can combine with **siapa** to form the question *whose?*
It can occur at the beginning or end of a sentence but the two parts cannot be separated. Look at the following examples:

Gelas ini *punya siapa?*	**Whose** *is this glass?*
Punya siapa **gelas ini?**	**Whose** *is this glass?*

gelas *glass*

EXERCISE 4

Write out both versions of these questions:

a Whose book is that?
b Whose job is it? (use **ini**)
c Whose child is this?
d Whose car is that?

▶ **Siapa** on its own can also mean *whose?* but with this meaning the word order is important. In this case **siapa** must immediately *follow* the noun it is referring to, as an adjective does:

Gelas *siapa* **ini?**	**Whose** *glass is this?*

EXERCISE 5

Go back to Exercise 4 and write out the sentences again using just **siapa**.

7 -nya. Another Indonesian word with many uses is **-nya**. It is very commonly used as an alternative to **dia** or **meréka** when they occur as possessive pronouns (*his/her/their*). **-nya** cannot occur as a separate word in a sentence. Instead, it is attached to the end of the word or words it refers to to create one word (like **-mu** in Unit 3):

permainan dia	*his toy*
permainan + nya = permainannya	*his toy*
rumah besar meréka	*their big house*
rumah besar + nya = rumah besarnya	*their big house*

 permainan *toy*

(Note in the last example, the **-nya** is attached to the adjective as the noun and the adjective in this case form a single unit. If you attached the **-nya** to the **rumah**, as in **rumahnya besar**, it would change the meaning to *Their house is big*.)

EXERCISE 6

Give the alternative forms of the following:

a jam tangan dia (*her watch*)
b sekolah dasar meréka (*their elementary school*)
c kebun meréka (*their garden*)
d CD player dia (*her CD player*)
e Keponakan perempuan dia lucu sekali. (*His niece is very cute.*)

 kebun *garden*
CD player *CD player*

The important point to remember when using **-nya** is that it has to refer back to something already mentioned or a context that has already been established.

Kakak saya akan tiba bésok.
Isterinya **bekerja di kantor periklanan.**

My brother is arriving tomorrow.
His wife *works in an advertising bureau.*

kantor periklanan *advertising bureau*

Insight

The context you establish does not have to be verbal. You could just as easily point to someone and say, *His wife works in advertising* and use **-nya** as just seen.

---

8 **Saya akan mengundang** *meréka* **untuk makan malam,** *I will invite* **them** *to dinner*. **Meréka** means *they*, but it also means *them*. In English, some of the personal prounouns change to *me*, *him*, *her*, *us* and *them* when they occur as objects (when they are on the receiving end of the action) or when they occur after words like *for*, *to* etc. In Indonesian they remain the same, (with *one* exception we'll look at below):

Kami mengenal meréka.
Ken menolong kami.

We know **them**.
Ken helps **us**.

There is the potential for confusion with some object pronouns because **dia** is used to refer to both males and females. Look at the following: **Kami melihat dia,** *We saw him*. But it can also mean *We saw her*. The context of the situation will usually tell you which is intended.

The exception occurs in sentences such as *He knows her* or *She knows him* because you cannot have **dia** for both the subject (the person who is doing the action, in this case *knowing*) and the object (here the one who is being known). In such a situation you must use **-nya** for the object pronoun and attach it to the verb:

Dia mengenal + nya = Dia mengenalnya.   *He knows her* etc.

mengenal *to know*

EXERCISE 7

How would you say:

a We are waiting for them.
b She phoned me.
c They disturbed him.
d He loves her.
e We went with them?

menélpon *to telephone*
mengganggu *to disturb*
mencintai *to love*

9 Berapa umur anda? *How old are you?* There are two ways of expressing age in Indonesian.

▶ The first uses **umur** which is a noun, therefore you need to use a pronoun or a name after **umur**, which means *age*:

Umur Tuti 10 tahun.	*Tuti is 10.*
Umurnya 10 tahun.	*She is 10.*

▶ The second uses the verb **berumur**, *to be X years old*. As it is a verb the pronoun or name occurs in front:

Tuti berumur 10 tahun.	*Tuti is 10 years old.*
Dia berumur 10 tahun.	*She is 10 years old.*

EXERCISE 8

Give the alternative forms of the following:

a Kembar saya berumur empat tahun.
b Umur Agus sembilan tahun.
c Yang sulung berumur tiga tahun.
d Umur cucunya lima tahun.

▶ The use of **umur** is similar in construction to the use of **nama** in **Nama saya…**, *My name is…* As with **umur** there is an alternative way to give someone's name in Indonesian which uses a verb **bernama** – *to be called*.

Nama saya Ratna.	*My name's Ratna.*
Saya bernama Ratna.	*I am called Ratna.*

Insight

It is easy to see that both verbs, **berumur** and **bernama**, are formed from **umur** and **nama** respectively. This is a common feature of Indonesian which we will look at in more depth in a later unit.

10 Dulu means *formerly* but it can also function as a tense marker to indicate *used to* as in *She **used to** be a teacher*. **Dulu dia seorang guru. Dulu** can occur first in the sentence or after the subject of the sentence:

Dulu kami tinggal di Surabaya.	*We used to live in Surabaya.*
Dulu dia miskin.	*She used to be poor.*
Kami dulu sering kencan di tempat ini.	*We often used to go dating in this place.*

miskin *poor*
sering *often*
kencan *to go dating*

11 The other tense marker you have met in this unit is **akan** which always indicates a future action or event. Unlike **dulu** it is used purely as a tense marker and translates *will*, *shall* and *to be going to…* in English:

Meréka akan pergi ke suatu tempat.	*They will go somewhere.*
Tuti akan menjemput nénék.	*Tuti will pick grandma up.*

suatu tempat *somewhere*
menjemput *to pick up*

Understanding Indonesian

EXERCISE 9

True or false? Answer the following questions based on the dialogue.

a Isteri Anton ibu rumah tangga berasal dari Padang.
b Ken mempunyai dua anak laki-laki.
c Anak-anak Anton berumur sepuluh tahun dan tujuh tahun.
d Isteri Ken masih bekerja sebagai sekretaris.
e Isteri Anton seorang guru bahasa Perancis.
f Keluarga Ken akan datang minggu depan.
g Semua kakak dan adik isteri Ken sudah berkeluarga.

EXERCISE 10

◀) **CD1, TR 6, 2:32**

First familiarize yourself with the vocabulary. Look at the five
pictures of families (a–e), and choose which picture fits with what
each person (1–5) says about his or her family. If you are not using
the recording, turn to the Listening Transcripts section and treat
this as a reading exercise.

QUICK VOCAB

pelajar *student*
duda *widower*
cerai *divorced*
murid *pupil/elementary school student*
keduanya *both of them*
manager *manager* (pronounced as in English, but with **r** clearly
   annunciated)
perancang mode *fashion designer*
pakaian anak-anak *children's wear*
bujangan *bachelor*
kuliah *university lecturer*
butik *boutique*

anak tunggal *only child*
dosén *lecturer*
mertua *parent-in-law*
montir *mechanic/repair person*
béngkél *workshop/garage*
sebuah *a*
sebuah béngkél *a workshop*
penjahit pakaian *tailor*

PART TWO

Dialogue

Reza wants to introduce Mark to some real Indonesian hospitality so she invites him to stay with her grandmother who lives in a village.

Reza	Nék, ini teman saya Mark. Dia akan tinggal dengan kita di sini beberapa hari.
Nénék	Selamat datang, Nak Mark. Saya sudah siapkan kamar.
Mark	Terima kasih. Jangan répot-répot.
Nénék	Tidak apa-apa. Saya punya banyak kamar karena saya punya tujuh anak. Tapi sekarang anak-anak saya sudah kawin semua. Saya tinggal sendiri dengan pembantu. Kamar-kamar tidur di sini banyak yang kosong.
Mark	Berapa kamar tidur nénék punya?
Nénék	Lima kamar tidur. Kamar tidur saya paling besar. Dulu saya dan suami tidur di sini, tapi dia sudah meninggal dua tahun yang lalu.
Mark	Ini kamar siapa?
Nénék	Ini kamar anak saya yang pertama. O, ya, Reza akan menunjukkan kamar-kamar yang lain. Anggap saja rumah sendiri. Jangan malu-malu.
Reza	Jangan kuatir Nék. Ayo Mark ikut saya. Kita mulai dari belakang. Ini dapur, di sebelahnya ruang makan. Setelah itu di depannya ruang keluarga.
Mark	Buku-buku itu punya siapa?
Reza	Oh, itu buku-buku sejarah punya kakék. Dia suka sekali membaca. Kalau kamu suka, kamu bisa pinjam dengan nénék.
Mark	Terima kasih.
Reza	Itu kamar tidur saya dan di sampingnya kamar tidur kamu.
Mark	O, ya, di mana kamar mandi?
Reza	Maaf saya lupa. Ada dua kamar mandi, satu di lantai atas dan satu lagi di lantai bawah. Tapi berbéda dengan kamar mandi di luar negeri. Kami mandi pakai gayung.
Mark	Menarik sekali.
Reza	Saya harap kamu betah tinggal di sini.

QUICK VOCAB

beberapa *a few, some*
beberapa hari *a couple of days*
siapkan *to prepare*
kamar *room*
répot *busy, occupied*

Jangan répot-répot. *Don't trouble yourself too much.*

kawin *married*

sendiri *alone*

kamar tidur *bedroom*

paling besar *biggest*

meninggal *die*

menunjukkan *to show (someone something)*

sendiri *one's own*

rumah sendiri *own house*

anggap *to consider*

Anggap saja rumah sendiri. *Make yourself at home.*

malu *shy*

kuatir *to worry*

jangan kuatir *don't worry*

sejarah *history*

suka *like*

pinjam *to borrow*

di samping *next to*

mandi *take a shower/take a bath*

kamar mandi *bathroom*

lantai *floor, storey*

atas *over, on top*

lantai atas *upstairs*

bawah *under, below*

lantai bawah *downstairs*

berbéda *different*

berbéda dengan *different from*

luar *outside, exterior*

negeri *country*

luar negeri *abroad, foreign country*

pakai *to use*

gayung *scoop*

menarik *interesting*

betah *to feel at home*

Saya harap kamu betah *I hope you feel at home here.*
 tinggal di sini. *(Make yourself at home.)*

TRANSLATION

Reza	Grandma, this is my friend, Mark. He's going to be staying with us here for a couple of days.
Grandmother	Welcome, young Mark. I already prepared a room (for you).
Mark	Thank you. Don't trouble yourself too much.
Grandmother	It's no problem. I have a lot of rooms because I have seven children but now they are all married. I live alone with a maid. There are a lot of unused bedrooms here.
Mark	How many bedrooms do you have?
Grandmother	Seven. My bedroom is the biggest. My husband and I used to sleep there but he died two years ago.
Mark	Whose room is this?
Grandmother	This is my eldest son's room. By the way, Reza will show you round the other rooms. Make yourself at home. Don't be shy.
Reza	Don't worry, Grandma. Come on, Mark, follow me. We'll start from the back (of the house). This is the kitchen and next to the kitchen is the dining room. And then, after the dining room is the living room.
Mark	Whose books are those?
Reza	Oh, those are Grandad's history books. He loved reading. If you like, you can borrow (them) from Grandma.
Mark	Thank you.
Reza	That is my bedroom and next to it is your bedroom.
Mark	By the way, where is the bathroom?
Reza	Sorry, I forgot. There are two bathrooms, one upstairs and one downstairs. But it's different from western bathrooms. We take a shower with a scoop.
Mark	(That's) very interesting.
Reza	I hope you (will) feel at home here.

How the language works 2

1 **anak-anak,** *children,* **buku-buku,** *books.*

▶ When we talk about something being *plural* we mean that we are talking about more than one thing. In English we usually indicate a plural by adding *-s* or *-es* to the singular form, *bus, buses* etc. In Indonesian, the noun is simply doubled to create a plural.

orang	*person*
orang-orang	*people*

▶ If you need to make a plural of a noun that is modified by another noun (see Unit 2) note that only the main noun is doubled:

rak buku	*book shelf*
rak-rak buku	*book shelves*

rak *shelf*

▶ Having said that, plural forms are nowhere near as common in Indonesian as they are in English. In fact, plurals are only really used in Indonesian when it is not obvious from the context that more than one thing is intended. Thus, if you use a number or a word that indicates a quantity, you do not need to double the noun:

empat orang	*four people*
banyak anak	*a lot of children*

This also applies to **berapa.** Where we always use a plural in English when we ask *How many?* you only need to use the singular form in Indonesian:

Berapa orang?	*How many people?*

EXERCISE 11

Rewrite these sentences making the plural form of the word indicated in brackets. When doing this exercise, pay attention to the meaning of the sentence. Do you need to double the noun or can you leave it as it is? Could the sentence be ambiguous if you do not use a double plural? Where you decide to use double plurals, indicate what the sentence would mean had you not doubled the noun.

a (Anak) meréka pergi ke sekolah di désa itu.
b Saya mempunyai empat (saudara perempuan).
c Berapa (buku) yang anda pinjam?
d Apa kamu suka (film) Stephen Spielberg?
e Di mana (tas) saya?

QV

désa *village*
tas *bag*

2 As with *who?* in English, **siapa** combines with other words to form questions such as:

Who from?	**dari siapa?**
Who for?	**untuk siapa?**
Who to?	**kepada siapa?**
Who with?	**dengan siapa?**

However, as with **ke mana?** and **dari mana?** (Unit 3), the main difference in usage is that the components of the Indonesian questions cannot be separated. For example, in modern English it is usual to say **Who did he do it for?** or **Who did you go with?**, splitting the two parts of the question. The Indonesian questions, however, follow the pattern of older hyper-perfect English forms (**For whom** did he do it?, **With whom** did you go?). Thinking of these questions in this way will help you greatly in formulating this type of question in Indonesian. Compare the following.

Dari siapa **surat ini?**	*Who is this letter from?*
Dengan siapa **meréka berolahraga?**	*Who do they do sports with?*
Untuk siapa **kita masak?**	*Who do we cook for?*
Kepada siapa **kamu menulis surat?**	*Who did you write the letter to?*

berolahraga *to do sports*
masak *to cook*

Insight

You know that **ke** means *to* or *towards*! When a person is involved **ke** becomes **kepada**.

EXERCISE 12

Add **untuk siapa, dari siapa, kepada siapa** and **dengan siapa** to complete the following questions (use each question only once):

a ____ meréka pergi ke pésta?
b ____ bingkisan ini?
c ____ kita menyanyi?
d ____ kami mengirim surat?

bingkisan *present, parcel*
mengirim *to send*

In the same way, certain other questions can be formed with **apa**:

what with?   **dengan apa?**
what for?   **untuk apa?**

Again, the two components cannot be separated, and they correspond to the English forms *with what?* and *for what?*:

Kamu sedang menulis *dengan apa?*	**What** *are you writing* **with**?
Kamu memanaskan makanan *dengan apa?*	**What** *do you heat the meal* **with**?
Dengan apa **kita membayarnya?**	**What** *do we pay for it* **with**?
Untuk apa **kita datang ke sini?**	**What** *did we come here* **for**?
Uang ini *untuk apa?*	**What** *is this money* **for**?

memanaskan *to heat*
makanan *food*
membayar *to pay*
uang *money*

3 Indonesian uses the following words to express static location:
depan *front*, **belakand** *back*, **atas** *on*, **bawah** *under*, **antara**
between, **dalam** *inside*, **luar** *outside*, **samping** *side* and **sebelah**,
which also means *side*.

All these words can be combined with **di** to form the following
expressions:

> **di depan** *in front of*
> **di belakang** *behind*
> **di bawah** *below*
> **di antara** *in between*
> **di dalam** *inside*
> **di luar** *outside*
> **di samping** *beside, next to*
> **di sebelah** *beside, next to*

Jakét keselamatam di bawah tempat dudak *Life-jacket is under
the seat*
Meréka tinggal di sebelah rumah kami *They live next door to us*
Di sebelah combines with **kiri**, *left* and **kanan**, *right*, to form:
di sebelah kiri *on the left-hand side*
di sebelah kanan *on the right-hand side*
Di Inggeris kami mengemudi di sebelah kiri *In England we drive
on the left*

jakét keselamatan *life jacket*
tempat duduk *seat*
mengemudi *to drive*

Using Indonesian

EXERCISE 13

Look at the picture below and answer the questions that follow.

a Siapa anak laki-laki di depan Siti?
b Siapa anak perempuan di depan Salim?
c Siapa anak perempuan di sebelah kanan Salim?
d Siapa anak laki-laki di antara Rudi dan Ana?
e Siapa anak laki-laki di belakang Tono?
f Siapa anak perempuan di samping Tati?

EXERCISE 14

Look at the picture of the house opposite and answer the following questions.

a Ruang apa di samping kiri kamar tidur?
b Kamar apa di antara dua kamar tidur?
c Ruang apa di depan ruang makan?
d Ruang apa di antara dapur dan ruang tamu?

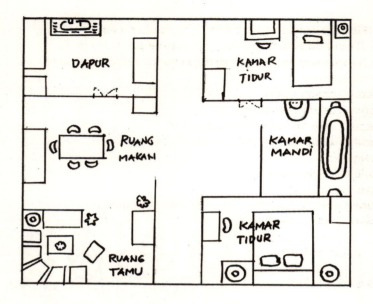

EXERCISE 15

Look at the picture of the buildings. Complete the following
sentences with **di antara, di sebelah kanan, di sebelah kiri, di depan**
or **di belakang** according to the location of the buildings mentioned
in relation to each other.

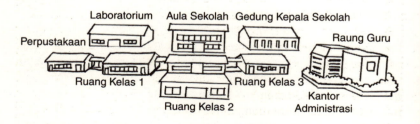

a Perpustakaan ada _____ ruang kelas 1.
b Laboratorium ada _____ perpustakaan.

c Gedung kepala sekolah ada _____ aula sekolah.

d Kantor administrasi ada _____ ruang guru.

e Ruang guru ada _____ ruang kelas 3.

perpustakaan *library*
laboratorium *laboratory*
kepala sekolah *head teacher/principal*
kantor administrasi *administration office*
aula *hall*
aula sekolah *school hall*
gedung *building*
ruang guru *staff room*
ruang kelas *classroom*

EXERCISE 16

Over to you!

◀) **CD1, TR 6, 6:37**

You (**B**) are on vacation in Indonesia and your friend has invited you to stay with her family. When you arrive at your friend's house, you find that dinner has been prepared and you waste no time in getting to know your friend's mother (**A**) who is eager to find out more about you!

A Saya sudah siapkan makanan untuk kamu. Jangan malu malu!
B *Thank you. Don't trouble yourself too much.*
A Apa kamu sudah berkeluarga?
B *Yes, I am. I have two children.*
A Berapa umur meréka?
B *The first is seven and the second is four.*
A Ini kamar kamu, di dalamnya ada kamar mandi.
B *Where is the kitchen?*
A Di belakang dekat ruang makan. Anggap saja rumah sendiri.
B *Thank you. Whose room is that?*
A Ini kamar saya. Mudah-mudahan kamu betah tinggal di sini.

Bathing facilities

Most Indonesian houses and very small hotels are not equipped with western style bathing and toilet facilities.

In the **kamar mandi** which means *bathroom* (**kamar**, *room*, **mandi**, *to bathe*) you will find a **bak,** a large vessel filled with cold water which you pour over yourself with the help of a pail that is usually on hand. Although the western image may be somewhat different, this is what Indonesians mean when they say they are going to take a shower! You should not get into the **bak** even though some may be big enough to climb into, neither should you contaminate the water with soap, as others have to use water from the same receptacle.

Some houses may have a traditional toilet that is nothing like a western toilet. It is more like a hole in the ground that you must squat over in order to use! Hygienic it may be, but it is surely one of the cultural differences that western visitors to Indonesia will find least comfortable to adapt to. The shape of the toilet will indicate where your feet should be placed for accurate aim.

Indonesians are very thorough when it comes to cleaning themselves after using the toilet. Paper alone will not do! You are expected to wash yourself thoroughly with water from a **bak** which will most likely be next to the toilet, by means of a hand pail or even a separate hand shower. If you have ever used an Indonesian toilet and you were wondering what the shower attachment on the wall next to the toilet was for... now you know!

One final (but vital) note on the subject of toilets in Indonesia. If you use a public toilet, it is wise to take your own paper with you as it is often not provided.

Arabic greetings

As Indonesia is essentially a Muslim country, the traditional Arabic greeting **Assalamualaikum** which means *Peace be upon you*, and to which the reply is **Waalaikum salam**, which means *Peace be upon you too*, is often used. You may find it useful when visiting a Muslim Indonesian family at their home, or even as a greeting on the telephone.

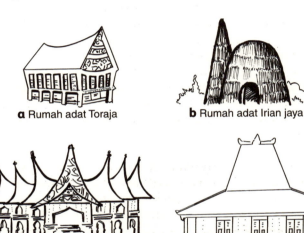

a Rumah adat Toraja

b Rumah adat Irian jaya

c Rumah adat Minangkabau

d Rumah adat Jawa Tengah

Insight
Rumah adat means *traditional house*.

TEST YOURSELF

1 Which one word is used as a question tag in Indonesian?

2 Which comes before the adjective: **sangat** or **sekali**?

3 How do you form an ordinal number from two onwards?

4 How would you translate *the one who*?

5 Which two ways do you know to say *have* in Indonesian?

6 What does **-nya** mean, and how does it function?

7 What are the two different ways to express your name and age?

8 How do you express *used to* in Indonesian?

9 Which tense marker means *will*?

10 How does Indonesian form plurals?

11 Why is it often unnecessary to express plurals in Indonesian?

6

Tourist information

In this unit you will learn how to
- *ask about what there is to see and do*
- *express existence*
- *use numbers 1 to 99*
- *tell the time*
- *say the days of the week*

PART ONE

Dialogue

Ken's wife Jamilah, their son Calvin and their daughter Silvia have arrived in Jakarta. They are planning to go for a week's holiday in Bali so they go to the Anta Travel Agency to see what is on offer.

CD1, TR 7, 0:03

Pegawai	Selamat pagi, Bu! Bisa saya bantu?
Ibu Jamilah	Ya. Kami perlu beberapa informasi tentang Bali dan Lombok. Kira-kira apa yang dapat kami lihat dan lakukan di sana?
Pegawai	Banyak yang dapat ibu kunjungi di sana. Ada pantai, gunung, candi, danau.
Ibu Jamilah	Apa ada pertunjukan kecak dan tari-tarian?
Pegawai	Ya, setiap hari Selasa jam 20.30 malam di hotél Santika.

(Contd)

Ibu Jamilah	Apa ada pakét wisata yang bisa kami beli?
Pegawai	Ya. Ada yang tiga hari, lima hari dan ada yang tujuh hari.
Ibu Jamilah	Apa nama hotelnya?
Pegawai	Ada beberapa pilihan, ada yang di tepi pantai, di kota dan yang suka gunung, kami pilihkan di daérah Kintamani.
Ibu Jamilah	O, ya apa ada rumah makan yang bagus dan nyaman?
Calvin	Orang tua saya mau bernostalgia.
Pegawai	Ada rumah makan yang besar dan romantis di daérah Kuta. Berapa lama mau tinggal di sana?
Ibu Jamilah	Sekitar satu minggu. Apa ada juga pakét wisata yang murah dan bagus?
Pegawai	Ada, tapi tidak termasuk makan. Ini ada beberapa brosur tentang pakét wisata.
Ibu Jamilah	Dengan penerbangan apa ke sana? Saya suka penerbangan yang langsung dan tepat waktu.
Pegawai	Ada dua pilihan – Garuda dan Mandala Airlines.
Ibu Jamilah	Terima kasih atas informasinya. Kami akan diskusikan lagi di rumah. Jam berapa kantor ini tutup?
Pegawai	Jam lima soré. O, ya ini kartu nama saya. Silahkan menghubungi saya, kalau ada sesuatu yang belum jelas.

QUICK VOCAB

informasi *information*
lihat *to see*
lakukan *to do*
di sana *there*
kunjungi *to visit*
tepi *edge, border*
di tepi pantai *on the beach front*
pantai *beach*
gunung *mountain*
candi *temple*
danau *lake*

pertunjukan *performance*
Kecak *a Balinese dance*
tari-tarian *dancing*
setiap *every*
setiap hari *every day*
Selasa *Tuesday*
pilihan *option/choice*
daérah *area*
rumah makan *restaurant*
orang tua *parents*
bernostalgia *nostalgic*

romantis *romantic*
sekitar *around*
pakét *parcel, package*
wisata *tour*
pakét wisata *package tour*
murah *cheap*
termasuk *included, including*
brosur *brochure*
langsung *direct*

tepat waktu *on time/punctual*
diskusikan *discuss*
kantor *office*
tutup *closed*
kartu nama *name card*
menghubungi *to contact*
sesuatu *something*
jelas *clear*
belum jelas *not yet clear*

TRANSLATION

Employee	Good morning, Madam. Can I help you?
Jamilah	Yes, we need some information about Bali and Lombok. What sort of things can we see and do there?
Employee	There are a lot (of places) you can visit there. There are beaches, mountains, temples, lakes.
Jamilah	Are there any performances of *kecak* and dancing?
Employee	Yes, every Tuesday at 8.30 in the evening at the Santika Hotel.
Jamilah	Is there a package tour that we can buy?
Employee	Yes, there are ones for three days, five days and seven days.
Jamilah	What's the name of the hotel?
Employee	There are several options: there are some (those that are) on the beach front, some in the city and for those who like mountains we select (ones) in the Kintamani area.
Jamilah	By the way, is there a good and comfortable restaurant (there)?
Calvin	My parents want to be nostalgic!
Employee	There are big and romantic restaurants in the Kuta district. How long will (you) stay there?
Jamilah	Around one week. Is there also a good, budget package tour?
Employee	There is, but meals are not included. Here are several brochures about package tours.

(Contd)

Jamilah	Which airline goes there? I like flights that are direct and on time.
Employee	There are two options – Garuda and Mandala Airlines.
Jamilah	Thank you for the information. We'll discuss (it) further at home. What time does the office close?
Employee	At five in the afternoon. This is my name card. Please contact me if there is anything that it not clear.

How the language works 1

1 To express the existence of something in Indonesian you only need to use one word, **ada**. This translates both *there is* and *there are* in English:

Ada **air mancur di pusat kota.** *There is a fountain in the city centre.*
Ada **bunga-bunga di taman itu.** *There are flowers in that garden.*

> **Insight**
> Remember that **ada** also means *to have*, and can also translate *is* with location words. Context will tell you which.

air *water*
air mancur *fountain*
bunga *flower*
bunga-bunga *flowers*

To ask about the existence of something you can simply use **apa ada...?**:

Apa ada **kantor polisi di sini?** *Is there a police station here?*
Apa ada **penerbangan yang murah?** *Are there (any) cheap flights?*

polisi *police*
kantor *office*
kantor polisi *police station*

Finally, as **ada** is a verb, it is negated with **tidak**. It translates *there is no* and *there are no/there aren't any*:

Tidak *ada* **margarin di lemari és.**   *There is no margarine in the fridge.*
Tidak *ada* **ikan di sungai ini.**   *There aren't any fish in this river.*

Insight

As with **berapa** and other quantity words, you do not need to indicate plurals when using **tidak ada** as we do with the English equivalent.

Tidak ada bunga.   *There aren't any flowers.*

QUICK VOCAB

taman *garden*
margarin *margarine*
lemari *cupboard*
és *ice*
lemari és *fridge*
ikan *fish*
sungai *river*

EXERCISE 1

Form the following sentences in Indonesian.

a There is a souvenir shop.
b There are some traditional restaurants.
c There aren't any hotels.
d Is there any information?
e Is there a sports centre?
f There isn't an art gallery.

QV

toko cinderamata *souvenir shop*
tradisional *traditional*
pusat kegiatan olahraga *sports centre*
balai kesenian *art gallery*

2 More on using **yang**. When a noun is described by two or more adjectives in English we simply list them in order before the noun, as in a ***beautiful, friendly** flight attendant* and ***large, romantic** restaurants*. Notice how these phrases are represented in Indonesian: **pramugari yang ramah dan cantik** and **rumah makan yang besar dan romantis**. You will notice that the two adjectives, which still follow the noun, are separated by **yang** and **dan** so you end up with phrases that more literally translate as *a flight attendant who is beautiful and friendly* and *restaurants which are large and romantic*.

Insight
    Pramugari is a *female flight attendant, an air-hostess; an air steward* is **pramugara**.

From this you can see that the pattern is:

noun	**yang**	first adjective	**dan**	second adjective
kota	**yang**	**damai**	**dan**	**indah**

a peaceful, beautiful city

pésta	**yang**	**meriah**	**dan**	**ramai**

a lively, crowded party

If you need to have three adjectives to describe the same noun as in *a **friendly, beautiful, slim** flight attendant* or ***large, romantic, cheap** restaurants* you simply place two of the adjectives together after the **yang** and the third after the **dan**.

pramugari *yang* **ramah, cantik** *dan* **langsing**
rumah makan *yang* **besar, romantis** *dan* **murah**

In theory, if you want to add even more adjectives to describe one noun you can amass all but one in between the **yang** and **dan** being sure to leave one to place after the **dan**.

You might find it useful to think of it in the same way we list adjectives in English:

*She was beautiful, charming, lovable, honest **and** cute.*

A final, but important point to note is that this rule applies to true adjectives only and <u>not</u> to nouns or verbs acting as adjectives (refer back to Unit 2):

rumah makan Indonesia yang romantis, unik dan murah

romantic, excellent, cheap Indonesian restaurants

QUICK VOCAB

damai *peaceful*
indah *beautiful (of places)*
meriah *lively*
ramai *crowded*
langsing *slim*
unik *unique/excellent*

Insight

Although **unik** has the same meaning as in English, it has also come to refer to something excellent which is not necessarily unique.

EXERCISE 2

How would you say:

a a long, boring film
b keen, clever children
c a long, tiring journey
d a lively, crowded, expensive holiday resort
e a big, comfortable, stylish room?

QUICK VOCAB

panjang *long*
membosankan *boring*
antusias *enthusiastic, keen*
pandai *clever*
perjalanan *journey*
tempat/beristirahat *holiday resort*
mahal *expensive*
modern *stylish*

3 Telling the time. First, you will need numbers up to 60, although if you have learnt numbers 1 to 10 from the last unit, it is very easy to form numbers up to 99.

Sepuluh, as you know, means *ten*, but it also means *one ten*. The **se-** only indicates something in the singular or to do with the number one.

As the *-teens* were formed with **-belas**, the *-ties*, that is *twenty*, *thirty*, *forty* etc. are formed with **puluh**. Thus:

dua puluh	*twenty*
tiga puluh	*thirty*
empat puluh	*forty*

Note that to make compound numbers you use the same pattern as in English, i.e. take *forty*, **empat puluh**, and add *one*, **satu**, making **empat puluh satu**, *forty-one*.

EXERCISE 3

Can you form these numbers?

a 54
b 78
c 81
d 99

There are two ways of telling the time in Indonesian, as in English. To answer the question **Jam berapa?**, *What time is it?*, you always start with **jam** in the reply.

To express the *o'clock* start with **jam** and add the number for the hour to it:

Jam satu.	*It's one o'clock.*
Jam lima.	*It's five o'clock.*

It is important to know that **jam** + number for the hour forms the basis for telling the time in Indonesian. Minutes past and to the hour come after this base.

To express minutes past the hour use **léwat** or **lebih**. Look at the following examples. Remember that time phrases always start with **jam** and the minutes past or to come after.

Jam dua léwat sepuluh.	*It's ten past two.*
Jam empat léwat lima belas.	*It's 15 minutes past four.*

Minutes *to* the hour is expressed by **kurang**:

Jam sembilan kurang sepuluh.	*It's ten to nine.*
Jam delapan kurang lima.	*It's five to eight*

Quarter past and *quarter to* can also be expressed using **seperempat** which means *quarter*. *Quarter past* is **léwat seperempat** (or **lebih seperempat**) and *quarter to* is **kurang seperempat**:

Jam tiga léwat seperempat.	*It's quarter past three.*
Jam tiga kurang seperempat.	*It's quarter to three.*

Half past is expressed using **setengah** meaning *half* but care needs to be taken when using this, as it is thought of as *half **to** the next hour. Therefore, what we think of as *half past six* in English must be rendered as *half **to** seven* in Indonesian! Moreover, with **setengah** only, the pattern changes with **setengah** occurring *before* the hour:

Jam *setengah* **tujuh.**	*It's half past six.*
Jam *setengah* **sembilan.**	*It's half past eight.*

EXERCISE 4

Write the following times in Indonesian.

a It's seven o'clock.
b It's half past four.

c It's 9.45.
d It's quarter past ten.
e It's quarter to two.

As in English, you can also tell the time simply by using a number from 1 to 59 after the hour.

Jam enam tiga puluh lima = 6.35

Note also that *oh* as in *ten oh five* is expressed using **kosong**.

Jam sepuluh kosong lima = 10.05

a.m. can be expressed by adding **pagi** and **siang** and p.m. can be expressed by adding **soré** or **malam** after the time. Which one you use will depend on the way the day is divided according to Indonesian ways. (Refer to Unit 1 for specific details of each time frame.)

Résépsi pernikahan mulai jam 10 pagi.	*The wedding reception starts at 10 a.m.*
Pesawat dari Sydney mendarat jam 6 soré.	*The aircraft from Sydney lands at 6 p.m.*
Pertunjukan berakhir jam 11 malam.	*The show finishes at 11 p.m.*
Dia selalu pergi ke kantor jam 6.30 pagi.	*He always goes to work at 6.30 a.m.*

résépsi *reception*   **berakhir** *to finish*
pernikahan *wedding*   **selalu** *always*
pesawat *aircraft*

The 24-hour clock is used in Indonesian with more frequency than you might expect to find in your home country. You will see it used on invitations and in TV programme listings etc. It is formed exactly as in English, with 18.20, for example, being expressed as *eighteen twenty*:

Pesawat Garuda ke London akan lepas landas pada jam delapan belas dua puluh.	*The Garuda flight to London will take off at 18.20.*

Berita terakhir di TV adalah jam dua puluh satu tiga puluh. *The last news on TV is at 21.30.*

lepas landas *to take off*
berita *news*
terakhir *the last*
adalah *is, to be*

Insight

Adalah can be used to convey the verb *to be* (*am, is , are*) in Indonesian. Its usage is entirely optional, and is restricted to highly formal speech and educated written Indonesian.

The days of the week in Indonesian are as follows:

◀)) **CD1, TR 7, 2:19**

Senin	*Monday*
Selasa	*Tuesday*
Rabu	*Wednesday*
Kamis	*Thursday*
Jumat	*Friday*
Sabtu	*Saturday*
Minggu	*Sunday*

Insight

Capital letters are used for days of the week in Indonesian, as they are in English.

You can use the days of the week as they stand, but colloquially, Indonesians prefer to express them by adding each to **hari** which means *day*. So they say:

hari Senin	*Monday*
hari Selasa	*Tuesday*
hari Rabu	*Wednesday* etc.
Hari ini hari apa?	*What day is it today?*

Hari ini hari Senin.	*Today is Monday.*
Kemarin hari apa?	*What day was it yesterday?*
Kemarin hari Minggu.	*Yesterday was Sunday.*
Bésok hari apa?	*What day is it tomorrow?*
Bésok hari Selasa.	*Tomorrow is Tuesday.*
Lusa hari apa?	*What day is it the day after tomorrow?*
Lusa hari Rabu.	*The day after tomorrow is Wednesday.*

bésok *tomorrow*
lusa *the day after tomorrow*
dua hari yang lalu *the day before yesterday*

EXERCISE 5

Answer the questions using short sentences as in the examples just given.

a Kemarin hari Kamis. Hari ini hari apa?
b Hari ini hari Rabu. Bésok hari apa?
c Dua hari yang lalu Senin. Lusa hari apa?
d Lusa hari Jumat. Bésok hari apa?

To say *on* a certain day of the week Indonesian uses **pada**. Note that you must include **hari** if you use **pada**. Thus: **pada hari Selasa**, *on Tuesday*.

Insight

In spoken Indonesian **pada** is almost always omitted, so **hari Selasa** can also mean *on Tuesday*.

When you ask the question *On what day?* you can say either **pada hari apa?** or just **hari apa?**

Hari apa dia datang?   *On what day is he coming?*

5 Apa yang dapat kami lihat. Under certain circumstances, when you want to ask *what?*, it is necessary to insert **yang** after the question word **apa**, creating the question form **apa yang?** When you are going to make a sentence in Indonesian using **apa,** where we use *what?*, ask yourself whether you can replace *what* with the phrase *What is it that...?*, for example, **What (is it that) we can do there?** and this will show you whether **yang** needs to be inserted.

Look at the following examples:

Apa yang boléh saya lakukan di tempat itu?   *What may I do in that place?*

Apa yang bisa meréka buat untuk kita?   *What can they do for us?*

Apa yang sedang dia tulis sekarang?   *What is she writing now?*

....

Insight

You have already encountered different forms of the same verb in this course, such as **menonton,** meaning *to watch* and **tonton,** also meaning *to watch*. If the verb you want to use begins with **me-** and has another form, such as **mengerjakan/ kerjakan,** it is the form without the **me-** (which is subject to spelling changes we'll cover fully in unit 17) that must be used with **apa yang.** Thus, **Apa yang kamu tonton?** *What are you watching?* **Apa yang dia kerjakan?** *What is he doing?* (not **apa yang dia mengerjakan?**)

....

buat *to do*

You may also notice that an inversion occurs with **kami dapat** becoming **dapat kami.** This is because a verb should directly follow **yang.** Although some speakers do not adhere to this rule, it is bad form not to do so.

In the same way, **siapa** may also be followed by **yang.** The question form **siapa yang** is used when *Who?* is followed by a verb, for instance, when you want to ask, *Who lives here?* You cannot use **siapa** alone in this type of question.

As with **apa yang** it may also help if you consider whether *Who?* can be replaced by *Who is it that…? Who (is it that) speaks French?*

Look at these examples:

Siapa yang punya peta Dénpasar?	*Who has a map of Denpasar?*
Siapa yang mengarang buku itu?	*Who wrote that book?*
Siapa yang mau mendaki gunung bésok?	*Who wants to go mountain climbing tomorrow?*

Insight

You'll notice, in the examples above, that **mengarang** and **mendaki** are **me-** verbs, both of which also have the shorter forms of **karang** and **daki** with the same meaning. In all of these examples, it is the person doing the action (i.e the subject of the verb) being referred to. However, when **siapa yang** refers to the receiver of the action (i.e. the object of the verb) only the shorter (base) form can be used. **Siapa yang dia tolong?** *Who does she help?* In correct English this should be *Whom does she help?* That gives you the clue – if it is *whom* in English then you should not use the **me-** verb.

peta *map*
mengarang *to write, compose*
mendaki *climb*

6 When you make part-sentences such as *The man **who** sells fruit* and *The building **which** is behind the museum* the parts of the sentences in bold are both rendered by **yang** in Indonesian:

Orang yang menjual buah-buahan ayah saya.	*The man who sells fruit is my father.*
Gedung yang terletak di belakang musium, kedutaan besar.	*The building which is located behind the museum is the embassy.*

Insight

*Notice the comma in the Indonesian sentence. It indicates a slight pause that you need to take when saying this sentence. Can you spot the reason? **musium kedutaan besar** without the pause means *the embassy museum*! This leaves what appears to be an unfinished sentence – *The building which is located behind the embassy museum…* Remember that is not usually translated in Indonesian. Remember also that we commonly drop words such as *which* and *who* in spoken English, so you may need to bear this in mind when creating Indonesian sentences, as the **yang** will *always* be needed in such sentences. *The cake you bought* should really be *The cake which you bought*. Thinking of it in this way will indicate that you need **yang** in Indonesian: **Kué yang kamu membeli**.

buah-buahan *fruit*
gedung *building*
terletak *to be located*
musium *museum*
kedutaan besar *embassy*

EXERCISE 6

Try writing these part-sentences in Indonesian.

a the house he built
b the town we visited
c the girl who used to work here

Understanding Indonesian

EXERCISE 7

Read or listen to the dialogue again and say whether these statements are true or false.

a Jamilah mau informasi tentang Yogyakarta.
b Ada pertunjukan Kecak dan tari-tarian setiap hari Selasa jam setengah sembilan malam.
c Orang tua Calvin ingin bernostalgia di rumah makan.
d Ada pakét wisata yang murah, bagus dan termasuk makan.
e Biro perjalanan tutup jam enam soré.

EXERCISE 8

Look at the times on the clocks and match them to the correct times:

a jam setengah lima
b jam empat kurang seperempat
c jam tujuh lima puluh lima
d jam satu dua puluh
e jam enam belas kosong lima
f jam setengah satu
g jam sembilan léwat empat puluh lima
h jam tiga lebih seperempat

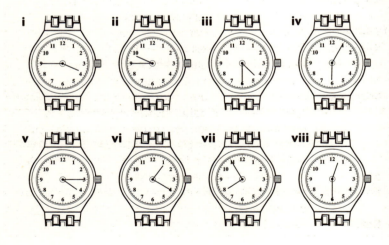

PART TWO

Dialogue

Reza and Mark are in a tourist information centre in Jakarta asking about things to do.

CD1, TR 7, 2:55

Reza	Permisi, Bu, apa kami bisa minta informasi mengenai kota Jakarta?
Karyawan	Tentu saja. Ada banyak tempat yang layak dikunjungi bagi turis.
Reza	Bagaimana kalau kita mulai dari Jakarta pusat?
Karyawan	Ide yang bagus. Ada musium Gajah, pelabuhan Sunda Kelapa dan Monas.
Mark	Apa itu Monas?
Karyawan	Oh, itu singkatan dari monumén Nasional. Anda bisa naik ke atas monumén itu dan melihat kota Jakarta.
Reza	Kalau tidak salah, ada musium di lantai bawah tanah.
Karyawan	Betul sekali. Setiap hari Minggu pagi tempat itu ramai dengan orang yang berolahraga.
Reza	Selain itu apa lagi yang menarik untuk dikunjungi?
Karyawan	Taman Mini Indonesia Indah. Anda dapat melihat kebudayaan dari seluruh propinsi di Indonesia.
Mark	Menarik sekali, apa saja yang bisa kami lihat?
Karyawan	Rumah adat, musium Islam, taman anggrek, taman burung, pakaian tradisional, kadang-kadang ada pertunjukan kesenian atau acara pernikahan. O, ya anda bisa berkunjung ke Kebun Raya Bogor. Kira-kira 30 menit dari Taman Mini.
Mark	Saya sudah tidak sabar lagi.
Karyawan	Untuk lebih jelasnya ini ada brosur-brosur yang bisa anda bawa pulang.
Reza	Terima kasih atas bantuannya.

karyawan *employee, member of staff*
permisi *excuse me*
minta *to ask for, to request*
mengenai *about*
tentu saja *of course*
layak *worth*
dikunjungi *to be visited*
layak dikunjungi *worth seeing/worth a visit*
bagi *for*
turis *tourist*
ide *idea*
gajah *elephant*
pelabuhan *port*
singkatan *abbreviation*
monumén *monument*
naik ke atas *climb up to the top*
kalau tidak salah *if I'm not mistaken*
bawah tanah *underground*
betul sekali *that's right, so there is*
selain *apart (from)*
selain itu *apart from that*
apa lagi *what else?*
kebudayaan (budaya n) *culture*
seluruh *all of the*
propinsi *province*
adat *tradition*
rumah adat *traditional house*
musium Islam *museum of Islam*
anggrek *orchid*
burung *bird*
kebun raya *botanical garden*
kadang-kadang *sometimes*
pertunjukan kesenian *performing art show*
acara *programme*
acara pernikahan *wedding ceremony*
berkunjung *to visit*

kebun *garden*
menit *minute*
sabar *patient*
Saya tidak sabar lagi. *I can hardly wait.*
bawa *to take, to carry*
pulang *to come back home*
bawa pulang *to take home*
bantuan *help*

Insight

Karyawan refers to *a male employee*; **karyawati** refers to *a female employee*.

TRANSLATION

Reza	Excuse me, Madam, can we get (ask for) information about Jakarta?
Employee	Of course. There are a lot of places that are worth visiting for tourists.
Reza	What if we start from central Jakarta?
Employee	Good idea. There is the Gajah (elephant) Museum, Sunda Kelapa Port and Monas.
Mark	What's 'Monas'?
Employee	It's an abbreviation for 'Monumen Nasional' (National Monument). You can climb up to the top and see the city of Jakarta.
Reza	If I'm not mistaken, there is a museum too, underground.
Employee	That's right. Every Sunday morning that place is crowded with people doing sport.
Reza	Apart from that, what else is there of interest to visit?
Employee	The Beautiful Miniature of Indonesia. You can see the culture from all of the provinces of Indonesia.
Mark	Very interesting. Just what can we see (there)?
	(Contd)

Employee	Traditional houses, Museum of Islam, orchid garden, a bird park, traditional dress, sometimes there is a performing arts show or a wedding ceremony. You can go to Bogor Botanical Garden. It's about 30 minutes from Taman Mini (Miniature of Indonesia).
Mark	I can hardly wait
Employee	For more details, there are brochures you can take home.
Reza	Thank you for your help.

Insight

Taman Mini Indonesia Indah (**Taman Mini** for short), *Beautiful Indonesia In Miniature*, is a cultural theme park outside Jakarta, encompassing the diverse cultures and colours of Indonesia. You can take a virtual tour of this online at www.tamanmini.com. Why not also visit the website of Bogor's botanical gardens at www.bogorbotanicgardens.org?

How the language works 2

1 To say *what* + noun, as in *what day?* or *what flight?* Indonesian uses **apa**, but with this meaning, **apa** follows the noun it refers to. For example:

hari *apa*	**what** *day?*
penerbangan *apa?*	**what** *flight?*
Rumah *apa* **ini? Ini rumah makan.**	**What** *room is this? It's the dining room.*

EXERCISE 9

How would you say:

a What flower is this?
b What programme is that?
c What language is this?

2 Lagi is a useful word with various uses in Indonesian, two of which we will look at here.

▶ With a positive statement or question, **lagi** means *further*, *more* or *again*.

Apa *lagi*?   *What* **else**?
Silahkan ulangi itu *lagi*.   *Please repeat that* **again**.
Berapa jam *lagi* **kita**   *How many* **more** *hours shall*
   menunggu?   *we wait?*

EXERCISE 10

How would you say:

a Do you want some more?
b I must take a bath again.

▶ With a negative statement or question, it means *not... any more* or *not... any longer*.

Dia bukan guru *lagi*.   *She's not a teacher* **any more**.
Dia bukan pacar saya *lagi*.   *He is not my boyfriend* **any more**.
Saya bukan pemilik   *I am not the owner of that*
   perusahaan itu *lagi*.   *company* **any more**.

pacar *boyfriend/girlfriend*
pemilik *owner*

06

....
Insight

You'll also come across the related verb pacaran, common in conversational usage. It means 'to date'.

The word pacar has given rise to a related verb, pacaran, very common in conversation, especially amongst young people. It means 'to date' and can sometimes have slightly negative connotations...

(Contd)

Mothers may be heard admonishing their young offspring, Kamu maish kecil, jangan pacaran dulu! with the meaning of, You're still young, you shouldn't be dating yet!

Similarly, Dia selalu pacaran sampai lupa pekerjaan rumah – She's always dating so she forgets her homework.

The form berpacaran also exists: Mereka sudah berpacaran selama tujuh tahun. They have been dating for seven years.

EXERCISE 11

What about these sentences:

a She is not a dancer any more.
b He is not rich any more.

kaya *rich*

3 You will hear **saja** used a lot in everyday Indonesian speech. While it really means *only* or *just*, as in **Saya mau satu saja**, *I want just one*, it is very frequently used for emphasis. We often do the same in English using *just* for instance in the question *Just what do you want?* In the dialogue, Mark says **Apa saja yang bisa kami lihat?** The meaning is *Just what can we see there?*

However, **saja** used for emphasis does not always correspond to *just* in English. It is used in a variety of expressions, such as **Kalau saja...!** *If only...!*

Kalau saja kita tiba tepat pada waktunya!	*If only we had arrived on time!*

Other examples:

Ke mana saja kamu selama ini?	*Just where have you been all this time?*
Siapa saja yang datang ke pésta?	*Just who came to that party?*

tepat pada waktunya *on time*
selama ini *all this time*

Baru saja is a tense marker that is used to express *have just done something*:

Dia baru saja bangun.	*She has just woken up.*
Saya baru saja menyelesaikan PR.	*I have just finished my homework.*

bangun *to wake up*
menyelesaikan *to finish*
PR *homework*

Insight

PR (pronounced as the letters are in Indonesian – refer to the pronunciation guide to this course if you need to refresh your mind) is short for **pekerjaan rumah**. Remember, Indonesian likes brevity.

EXERCISE 12

How would you write these sentences in Indonesian?

a He has just arrived.
b We have just had dinner.

makan malam *dinner, to have dinner*

Insight

The words for meals are easy to form in Indonesian. Just add the corresponding time of day to **makan**, i.e. **makan pagi**, *breakfast*; **makan siang**, *lunch* etc. These also mean *to have breakfast, to lunch*, etc.

---

4 Terima kasih atas..., *Thank you for...* Notice that when you express thanks for something in Indonesian, *for* is rendered by **atas** and not by **untuk**, as you might expect:

Terima kasih atas bantuannya.   *Thanks for the help.*

Using Indonesian

EXERCISE 13

Reconstruct these sentences so that they make sense starting with the word in **bold** in each case.

a hari Minggu – **kami** – Ciater – ke – akan – pergi – pada
b ada – air panas – kolam renang – dan lain lain – rumah makan – di **Ciater**
c pusat kota – **dari** – memakan waktu – jam – dua – ke sana

kolam renang *swimming pool*
dan lain lain *and so on*
memakan waktu *take time*

EXERCISE 14

Read the schedule Mr Knight's secretary made for him, then answer the questions below in Indonesian.

Senin	10.15	janji dengan Bapak Habibie
	11.00	mengambil tikét
	14.40	janji dengan Bapak Rustam
Selasa	15.45	ke bandara/berangkat ke Surabaya dengan Garuda
Rabu	12.10	makan siang dengan Ibu Fraulina
Kamis	09.25	menjemput Bapak Knight dari Surabaya
Friday	08.30	rapat karyawan

janji *appointment*
mengambil *to get, to take*
bandara *airport*
makan siang *lunch*

Insight

Bandara is short for **bandar udara**. **Bandar** means *harbour* and **udara** means *air*. You might also hear the English word *airport* in normal Indonesian conversation, especially among businessmen in areas where foreigners are a common sight, such as in Jakarta.

a Jam berapa kamu harus mengambil tikét?
b Jam berapa ada janji dengan Bapak Rustam?
c Jam berapa Bapak Knight makan siang dengan Ibu Fraulina?
d Hari apa Bapak Knight pulang dari Surabaya?
e Jam berapa ada rapat karyawan?

EXERCISE 15

Over to you!

You (**B**) are in a travel agent's asking the person who works there (**A**) for information about Medan.

A	Selamat pagi. Bisa saya bantu?
B	*Yes, I need some information about Medan.*
A	Kami punya pakét wisata untuk lima hari.
B	*What can I see there?*
A	Ada Danau Toba, gunung, perkebunan téh, musium dan masih banyak lagi.
B	*Is there a good beach for surfing?*
A	Ya.
B	*With which airline can I get there?*
A	Dengan Garuda atau Mandala.
B	*Are meals included?*
A	Ya. Sudah termasuk tikét pesawat, hotél, makanan dan tour.
B	*How much does it cost?*

CD1, TR 7, 4:57

(Contd)

perkebunan téh *tea plantation*
masih banyak lagi *and more besides*
pantai yang bagus *a good beach*
berselancar *to surf*
untuk berselancar *for surfing*
pesawat *aeroplane*
tikét pesawat *air ticket*
daftar *list*
daftar harga *price list*
makanan *meal*
tour *tour*

Something for everyone!

There is something for every type of tourist in Indonesia. Bali is
the place to go for sun, sea, surf and nightlife but if you are more
adventurous, Indonesia can offer you a wealth of unforgettable
experiences. Each of the main islands is distinctly different from the
others, both in culture and religion. The main religion of Indonesia
is Islam, with about 90% of Java, the most populated island and
home to the capital Jakarta, being Muslim. In fact, Indonesia is the
largest Muslim country in the world outside the Arabian peninsula.
Whatever the religion, be it Muslim, Hindu, Buddhist or Christian,
the Indonesians co-exist peacefully often with places of worship for
the various religions existing side by side.

For the nature lover, Indonesia can offer a wealth of exotic flora and
fauna. Indonesia boasts the second largest rainforest in the world,
which is home to thousands of species of birds, mammals, trees and
orchids, many of which are unique to Indonesia. If Indonesia can
boast only the second largest rainforest in the world, it can boast the
biggest and the best of much else! The islands of Indonesia make up

the largest archipelago in the world; Indonesia is the most volcanic country on the planet with 70 of its 400 or so volcanos still active, including **Anak Krakatau**, *Child Of Krakatoa*, the infamous volcano **Krakatau** (*Krakatoa*) that erupted in 1883 killing tens of thousands and leaving destruction in its wake; it is home to more species of mammal than any other country in the world; Yogyakarta is the site of the biggest Buddhist temple in the world, **Borobudhur**. Sumatra is home to the biggest flower in the world, known in Indonesian as **bunga bangkai**, *carcass flower*, owing to the highly unpleasant smell the flower emits when in bloom. You can see (and smell) the flower at the **Kebun Raya** (*Botanical Gardens*) in Bogor. Another world's biggest also hails from Indonesia, this time from the island of Komodo. The largest lizards in the world, known as the Komodo, can grow up to three metres in length. This has earned them the apt name of *Komodo Dragon* in English!

Insight

Kebun raya, as you know, means *botanical gardens*, but although **kebun** means *garden*, **raya** does not, itself, mean *botanical*. It has nothing to do with it! In fact, **raya** means *great* or *large*, and features in various significant expressions: **jalan raya** means *main road*, **Jakarta Raya** means *Greater Jakarta* and the main religious event of the Muslim year is referred to in Indonesian as **Hari Raya**, (which is also referred to as **Hari Idul Filtri**).

Learning tip

Indonesian does not have the same enormous base to draw vocabulary from that English does. This often means that concepts are expressed more literally than in English, for example, **tempat** means *place* and **tidur** means *to sleep*. Combined, **tempat tidur** means *place to sleep* i.e. *bed*. Similarly **rumah** means *house* and **makan** means *to eat* so **rumah makan** means *eating house*, i.e. *restaurant*. This does not mean that Indonesian is not a poetic language. It can be that too, for example, **matahari** meaning *sun* literally means *the eye of the day*.

Look at the meanings of the following words, some of which you have already met in this course, and see if you can give the English equivalents of the vocabulary created from the combined words.

sakit	*ill*	**kebun**	*garden*
air	*water*	**binatang**	*animal*
panas	*hot*	**minyak**	*oil*
mancur	*to spurt*	**wangi**	*fragrant*

a rumah sakit
b air panas
c air mata
d air mancur
e kebun binatang
f minyak wangi

TEST YOURSELF

1 How do you say *there is* or *there are* in Indonesian?

2 What do you need to do to form the *-teens* in Indonesian?

3 How do you form the *-ties* as in 30, 40 etc?

4 Which word do you always need to include when telling the time?

5 How would you say *quarter past five* in Indonesian?

6 How would you say *on Wednesday* in Indonesian?

7 How do you use **apa yang** and **siapa yang**?

8 How would you say *what day?* in Indonesian?

9 What does **lagi** mean in positive and negative sentences?

10 In the Indonesian expression meaning *thank you for*, what word translates *for*?

7

Invitations

In this unit you will learn how to
- **make, accept and decline an invitation**
- **give reasons**
- **say the months**

PART ONE

Dialogue

Anton invites Ken and his family over to his house for dinner, but unfortunately Ken's family already has other plans.

Anton	Saya dan isteri saya ingin mengundang bapak sekeluarga untuk makan malam hari Sabtu.
Ken	Terima kasih, tapi sayang sekali kami tidak bisa. Kebetulan kami sudah ada rencana ke Bandung hari Sabtu ini.
Anton	Bagaimana kalau sesudah pulang dari Bandung? Kapan kembali ke Jakarta?
Ken	Boléh, kami pulang hari Senin pagi.
Anton	Baik kalau begitu. Datanglah ke rumah saya hari Jumat malam.
Ken	Hm… Maaf mungkin saya tidak bisa, karena harus mengantar anak saya ke rumah sakit, tapi hari Sabtu saya tidak ada kerja apa-apa.

Anton	Tidak apa-apa. Saya pikir hari Sabtu lebih baik. Apa bapak suka makanan yang pedas?
Ken	Saya makan apa saja, tidak ada masalah. Isteri dan anak-anak saya suka sekali.
Anton	Bagus. Isteri saya akan membuat sambal khusus. O, ya apa anak-anak bapak betah tinggal di sini?
Ken	Tentu. Meréka suka bergaul, jadi temannya banyak.
Anton	Sampaikan salam saya untuk meréka.
Ken	Terima kasih, kami akan datang sekitar jam 12 siang.

sekeluarga *one family, (here) together with your family, as a whole family*
sayang *it's a pity*
sayang sekali *unfortunately*
kebetulan *by chance/by accident*
rencana *plan*
sesudah *after*
boléh *may, OK then, sure*
datanglah (datang) *please come*
mungkin *maybe*
mengantar (antar) *to take*
rumah sakit *hospital*
Saya tidak ada kerja apa-apa. *I don't have anything to do.*
masalah *problem*
tidak ada masalah *no problem*
pikir *think*
lebih baik *better*
pedas *spicy*
Saya makan apa saja. *I eat anything.*
membuat *to make*
sambal *chilli sauce*
khusus *special*
bergaul *to socialize*
sampaikan (sampai) *to pass on*
salam *regards*
Sampaikan salam saya untuk meréka. *Give them my regards.*

QUICK VOCAB

TRANSLATION

Anton	My wife and I would like to invite you and your family for dinner this Saturday.
Ken	Thank you, but unfortunately we can't. We already have plans to go to Bandung this Saturday.
Anton	What if (you come) after coming back from Bandung? When (are you) coming back to Jakarta?
Ken	OK then, we're coming back on Monday morning.
Anton	All right. Come to (our) house on Friday night.
Ken	Sorry, maybe I can't because I should take my son to the hospital but Saturday I don't have anything to do.
Anton	It's no problem. I think Saturday is better. Do you like spicy food?
Ken	I eat anything, it's no problem. My wife and children like (it) a lot.
Anton	Good, my wife will make a special sambal. By the way, do your children feel at home here?
Ken	Of course. They like socializing so they have a lot of friends.
Anton	Give them my regards.
Ken	Thank you. We will come around 12 in the afternoon.

How the language works 1

1 When dealing with numbers we came across **se-** prefixed to numbers that indicated *one* such as **seratus**, *one hundred* and **seribu**, *one thousand*.

A further but very common usage of the **se-** prefix with nouns is to indicate *the same*, for example, **sekantor**, *the same office*:

Kami bekerja sekantor.   *We work in the same office.*

> **Insight**
> Note that with this type of usage **di**, *in*, is not required.

EXERCISE 1

Use another two important similar expressions: **sekelas,** *in the same class,* and **seumur,** *to be the same age* to make these two sentences:

a Kami ada ujian _____. *We have a test in the same class.*
b Dia _____ dengan saya. *She is the same age as me.*

ujian *test/exam*   av

Se- can also mean *all* or *the whole (of)*:

Saya ingin mengundang bapak   *I would like to invite you* **and all**
 sekeluarga ke pésta.   **your family** *to a party.*

··
Insight
It is best to learn the words from this section as set
expressions.
··

2. a **Boléh** can be used when accepting an offer or an invitation:

Bagaimana kalau kita ke bioskop *Shall we go to the cinema*
 nanti malam?   *tonight?*
Boléh!   *Sure!*

bioskop *cinema*   av

Note that **Bagaimana kalau,** literally *What if …?,* is often used to
make a suggestion, where it means something like *How about …?*
So the question above, put more literally, would be *How about we
go to the cinema tonight?*

b It is also used in making polite requests where we use *may* or
can in English. For example, we might say *May I use this?* or *Can
I use this?* This usage of *can* should be distinguished from **bisa** in
Indonesian. While **bisa** can be used in making simple requests, it is
more polite to use **boléh,** especially if you are asking for permission.
Therefore **boléh** carries the meaning of *to have permission to.*

Boléh **saya menggunakan itu?**   **May** *I use that?*
Boléh **kami parkir di sini?**   **May** *we park here?*

QV **parkir** *to park*

EXERCISE 2

How would you say the following?

a May I open the window?
b May we smoke?
c May I turn on the radio?

buka *to open*
jendéla *window*
merokok *to smoke*
hidupkan *to turn on*
radio *radio*

c Question words such as **boléh** and **bisa** can be made more formal by the addition of **-kah: boléhkah, bisakah.** Nowadays, this form is almost entirely confined to written Indonesian, but it may also be used in speech on especially formal occasions.

Bisakah anda menjelaskan   *Could you explain that problem?*
masalah itu?

QV **menjelaskan** *to explain*

d **Boléh** followed by **jadi** means *maybe* or *likely*, as in:

Boléh jadi **dia akan datang pada**   *It's* **likely** *he'll come on Tuesday.*
hari Selasa.

3 To ask *why?* in Indonesian use **kenapa?** or **mengapa?** They both mean *why?* but **kenapa?** is the form widely used in conversation. **Mengapa?** is preferred in writing.

Unlike other question words, which may appear in various positions, these question words can only occur at the beginning of the sentence.

Kenapa dia marah?	*Why is he angry?*
Kenapa mobil itu berhenti?	*Why did that car stop?*
Kenapa kamu tidak minum?	*Why don't you drink?*
Kenapa meréka tertawa?	*Why are they laughing?*
Kenapa kamu tidak menélpon?	*Why don't you call?*

berhenti *to stop*
tertawa *laugh*
menélpon *to phone*

Of course, to answer this question you will need the word **karena** which means *because*.

It can be used just like *because* in English as the answer to **kenapa?** (**mengapa?**):

Kenapa kamu tidak mampir ke tempat tinggal saya kemarin? Karena saya sibuk.	*Why didn't you come over to my place yesterday? Because I was busy.*
Mengapa dia sedih? Karena dia baru saja putus dengan pacarnya.	*Why is she sad? Because she has just broken up with her boyfriend.*

mampir *to come over (to a place)*
tempat tinggal *place (where someone lives)*
sedih *sad*
putus *to break up*

Karena can also be used independently as in:

Karena sibuk dia lupa menélpon isterinya.	*Because he was busy, he forgot to phone his wife.*

4 **Sampaikan salam saya untuk meréka,** *Give them my regards.* Look at the way this useful phrase is structured in Indonesian. **Sampaikan salam,** *pass greetings,* **saya,** *of me,* **untuk meréka,** *to them.*

EXERCISE 3

How would you say...

a Give her my regards.
b Give Sue our regards.
c Give them our regards.
d Give them regards from me and my family.

5 An introduction to word bases. English has a vast vocabulary. This is due, in part, to the fact that the vocabulary of English makes use of root words from several different languages. This often means that parts of speech (i.e. nouns, verbs, adjectives etc.) referring to related concepts bear no relation to one another. Indonesian vocabulary, by way of contrast, tends to build related words, or words that relate to a single topic area, around the same root.

Compare the Indonesian with the English in the following words, all related to the topic of teaching and learning. Note the ever-present base **ajar** in the Indonesian and no similar roots in the English translations we have used to illustrate this vital difference between the two languages.

belajar	*to learn*
mengajar	*to teach*
pelajar	*student*
pelajaran	*lesson*
pengajar	*instructor*
terpelajar	*educated*

To describe how words are built up in Indonesian we will regularly be referring to three basic concepts:

- ▶ **prefix** – this is a bit added to the *beginning* of a word, such as the *im-* in *impossible* in English.
- ▶ **suffix** – this is a bit added on to the *end* of a word. You have already come across the Indonesian possessive **-mu** (Unit 2) and **-nya** (Unit 5).
- ▶ **base word** – this is the word in its simplest form to which prefixes or suffixes may be added. A base word may be a noun, a verb or an adjective.

Insight

These may be called root words in some textbooks or dictionaries.

A prefix or a suffix, or a combination of both, added to a base word can create related vocabulary. There is often a pattern whereby a specific prefix or suffix creates a new and particular part of speech. This happens in English too. For example, some verbs, with the suffix *-ion* added, create a related noun, the meaning of which is derived from the verb. For example, *to suggest* is the verb, but when we add *-ion* we end up with the noun *suggestion*. In Indonesian, the addition of prefixes and suffixes to base words is an integral part of how the vocabulary is built up, and there is often a definite pattern to the resulting words created.

An ability to see how words are built up from their bases will not only help you learn related vocabulary more easily, but it will also give you a better chance of deducing the meaning of new words you may come across. At this stage it is better just to notice how the prefixes and suffixes affect the base word. You will soon begin to get a feel for the patterns in which prefixes and suffixes modify the base and create a word with a separate meaning.

From now on, base words are included next to modified words in the vocabulary sections. They appear in brackets followed by *n*, *v* and *a* to indicate whether the base word is a noun, verb or adjective. Base words from all units appear in the vocabulary list in a similar fashion.

Understanding Indonesian

EXERCISE 4

True or false? Read the following questions based on the dialogue and decide which are true and which are false.

a Anton mau mengundang Ken sekeluarga untuk makan malam.
b Ken pulang dari Bandung hari Jumat.
c Ken tidak suka makanan pedas.
d Anak-anak Ken mempunyai banyak teman.
e Ken sekeluarga akan datang hari Sabtu jam 11 siang.
f Ken mengantar anaknya ke rumah sakit hari Jumat.
g Pada hari Sabtu Ken sangat sibuk.

EXERCISE 5

Match up the questions with the answers.

1 Kenapa kamu sakit perut?
2 Mengapa dia terlambat?
3 Mengapa bajunya basah?
4 Kenapa polisi menangkapnya?
5 Kenapa kamu tidak membalas surat saya?
6 Mengapa dia gagal dalam tés itu?

a Karena saya sibuk.
b Karena tidak belajar.
c Karena makan cabe terlalu banyak.
d Karena mobilnya mogok.
e Karena tidak punya SIM.
f Karena hujan.

perut *stomach*
sakit perut *stomach ache*
basah *wet*
menangkap (tangkap, v) *to catch*
membalas (balas, v) surat *to answer a letter*

baju *clothes*
gagal *fail*
tés *test*
gagal dalam tés *to fail a test*
cubé chilli terlalu bauyak *too many*
mogok *broken down*
SIM (Surat Izin Mengemudi) *driving licence*
hujan *rain, it's raining*

PART TWO

Dialogue

Reza has received a telephone call from a friend inviting her to go to a discotheque. She is wondering whether Mark would like to go too.

Reza	Mark, teman saya mengajak saya ke diskotik nanti malam. Kamu mau ikut?
Mark	Tentu. Saya mau minum anggur, sama cari pacar.
Reza	Ya sambil menyelam, minum air.
Mark	Ada gula ada semut.
Reza	Dasar laki-laki!
Mark	Saya cuma bercanda. Apa minuman di sana mahal?
Reza	Saya tidak tahu. Tapi saya rasa tidak terlalu mahal. Jangan kuatir. Dia akan mentraktir kita.
Mark	Hm. Terima kasih. Naik apa kita ke sana?
Reza	Dengan mobil. Dia akan menjemput kita jam 10 malam.
Mark	Siapa saja yang pergi?
Reza	Kita bertiga, saya, kamu dan Roni.
Mark	Apakah harus bayar tikét masuk?
Reza	Tidak, kita cuma bayar minuman.
Mark	Apa itu klub malam yang terbaik di sini?
Reza	Ya, tempat kumpul anak-anak muda.
Mark	Musik apa yang ada di sana?

(Contd)

● CD1, TR 8, 1:47

Reza	Bermacam-macam. Meréka punya 'live music' dengan penyanyi dari luar negeri.
Mark	Masak?
Reza	Benar. Kamu harus berpakaian yang rapi.

QUICK VOCAB

diskotik *discotheque*
ikut *(here) to come along*
nanti malam *tonight*
anggur *wine*
sambil *while*
menyelam (selam, v) *to dive*
Sambil menyelam minum air. *To drink water while you are diving (proverb similar in meaning to to kill two birds with one stone).*
gula *sugar*
semut *ant*
Ada gula ada semut. *Where there's sugar there are ants (proverb).*
dasar *nature*
Dasar laki-laki! *Typical man!*
bercanda (canda, v) *to kid*
cuma bercanda *just kidding*
rasa *to think, to believe*
minuman (minum, v) *drinks*
mahal *expensive*
terlalu *too*
terlalu mahal *too expensive*
mentraktir *to treat*
Naik apa ke sana? *How do we get there?*
dengan mobil *by car*
bertiga *three of us*
bayar *to pay (for)*
tikét masuk *entry (ticket)*
klub malam *nightclub*
terbaik *the best*
kumpul *hang around, 'hang out'*

tempat kumpul *a place to 'hang out'*
anak muda *young person*
anak-anak muda *young people*
musik *music*
bermacam-macam *many different kinds*
berpakaian (pakai, v) *to dress, to get dressed*
rapi *neatly*
berpakaian rapi *dress well*

TRANSLATION

Reza	Mark, my friend has invited me to go to the disco tonight. Do you want to come?
Mark	Of course. I want to drink wine and look for a girlfriend.
Reza	Yes, kill two birds with one stone
Mark	Where there's sugar there are ants.
Reza	Typical man!
Mark	I am just teasing. Are the drinks there expensive?
Reza	I don't know. But I guess they're not. Don't worry. He will treat us.
Mark	Thank you. How do we get there?
Reza	By car. He will pick us up at 10 this evening.
Mark	Who else is going?
Reza	Three of us – me, you and Roni.
Mark	Is there an entrance fee?
Reza	No. We just pay for drinks.
Mark	Is that the best nightclub here?
Reza	Yes, it's *the* place for young people to hang out.
Mark	What kind of music do they have there?
Reza	Many different kinds. They have live music with singers from abroad.
Mark	Really?
Reza	That's right. You must dress well.

How the language works 2

1 bertiga, three of us. From two onwards, you can specify a group by prefixing the number with **ber-**:

dua	*two*	**berdua**	*as a pair*
empat	*four*	**berempat**	*in a group of four*

In English, when we say *in a group of three* or *the four of them* etc., we usually only include the number for a specific purpose, such as to stress the number of people in the group. Otherwise we normally just say *together*. Indonesian, however, tends always to be specific in this situation, as long as the group is small and, of course, as long as you know how many people are in the group. These **ber-** + number words are usually used with a pronoun, as in the following examples:

Meréka selalu bertiga.	*They are always together (the three of them).*
Kami berdua pergi berlibur ke danau Toba di Sumatra Utara.	*The two of us went on holiday to Lake Toba in North Sumatra.*
Meréka berlima keluar untuk makan malam di rumah makan yang baru di pusat kota.	*The five of them went out for dinner to that new restaurant in the town centre.*

utara *north*
keluar *to go out*

EXERCISE 6

See if you can form these sentences:

a They came together (in a pair).
b The three of us are good friends.
c The ten of us climbed Mount Salak.

bersahabat (sahabat, *n*) *to be friends*
bersahabat dengan baik *to be good friends*
mendaki (daki, *v*) *to climb*
Gunung Salak *Mount Salak*

If you know the number in the group you should try and be specific by using language such as that just discussed. If you do not know the number, you can use **bersama-sama** to mean *together*:

Meréka selalu bersama-sama.	*They are always together.*
Meréka makan malam bersama-sama.	*They have dinner together.*

If you want to express *together with* use **bersama dengan**:

Saya bersama dengan dia berenang di pantai.	*I swim together with him at the beach.*
Ibu itu bersama dengan anak-anaknya bekerja keras.	*That woman, together with her children, works hard.*

berenang *to swim*

2 Months of the year

🔊 **CD1, TR 8, 3:13**

Januari	*January*
Fébruari	*February*
Maret	*March*
April	*April*
Méi	*May*
Juni	*June*
Juli	*July*
Agustus	*August*
Séptémber	*September*
Oktober	*October*
Novémber	*November*
Désémber	*December*

In the same way **hari** is used with days of the week, **bulan** which means *month* (and also means *moon*) occurs before the name of the month when you wish to express *in* + month, which also uses **pada**:

pada bulan Méi *in May*

> ### Insight
> In speech it is common to drop the **pada** when the meaning is understood, so **bulan Méi** can also mean *in May*.

3 Verb + **-an**. Many nouns ending in **-an** are created from verb base words. Their meaning is closely related to the verb they come from.

pakai	*to wear*
pakaian	*clothes*
makan	*to eat*
makanan	*food*

EXERCISE 7

Note the meanings of the verb bases in the left-hand column. Look at the nouns created from the respective verbs in the right-hand column and see if you can deduce the meanings:

a minum *to drink*   minuman
b jawab *to reply*   jawaban
c main *to play*   mainan
d pilih *to choose*   pilihan
e beli *to buy*   belian
f hibur *to entertain* hiburan
g kerja *to work*   kerjaan
h pikir *to think*   pikiran

A few noun bases and verb bases also have the suffix **-an** attached to them, which makes other nouns, although the meaning created by the suffix is not always as easy to see as with verb base **-an** nouns.

With noun bases the meaning of the suffixed noun tends to be an extension of the noun base:

laut	*sea*	**lautan**	*ocean/seas*
gambar	*picture*	**gambaran**	*description*
jalan	*street*	**jalanan**	*road*
rambut	*hair*	**rambutan**	*a type of hairy fruit*
duri	*thorn*	**durian**	*a kind of spikey fruit*

With adjective bases the noun created reflects the quality expressed by the adjective:

kotor	*dirty*	**kotoran**	*rubbish/trash*
manis	*sweet*	**manisan**	*sweets*
asam	*sour*	**asaman**	*pickles*

Using Indonesian

EXERCISE 8

Look at the texts and fill in the invitations accordingly.

a Ani akan mengundang Yenny dan Rizal minggu depan tanggal 24 Juni di rumahnya Jalan Mawar no 1. Jakarta untuk merayakan pésta Ulang tahun. Jam 4 soré.

PÉSTA ULANG TAHUN
Tempat...........................
Jam..............................
Siapa yang diundang..............
....

b Reza ingin mengundang Mark ke pésta perkawinan Tati malam Sabtu, tanggal 7 Juni 2012 jam 7 malam di Gedung Kartika.

PÉSTA PERNIKAHAN
Tempat.........................
Tanggal.........................
Jam.............................

c Saya akan mengajak orang tua saya untuk menghadiri acara wisuda di kampus Universitas Pajajaran, tanggal 9 Juni 2012, hari Senin, jam 10 pagi.

WISUDA
Tempat.........................
Tanggal.........................
Jam.............................

d Kami akan mengundang teman-teman sekelas untuk acara pésta Tahun Baru di Puncak tanggal 31 Désémber, hari Kamis jam 8 malam.

TAHUN BARU
Tempat.........................
Tanggal.........................
Hari.............................
Jam.............................

QUICK VOCAB

merayakan (raya, *a*) *to celebrate*
pésta *parts*
ulang tahun *birthday*
jam *hour, (here) time*
siapa yang diundang *who is invited*
pésta perkawinan *wedding party*
tanggal *date*
menghadiri (hadir, *v*) *to attend*
wisuda *graduation*
tahun baru *new year*

EXERCISE 9

Over to you!

Your new Indonesian acquaintance (A) has decided to invite you (B) out for dinner at the Hotel Mulia. Respond in Indonesian as indicated.

A Saya ingin mengundang bapak beserta isteri untuk makan malam.
B Thank you. When?
A Bésok sekitar jam tujuh malam di hotél Mulia. Apa bapak dan ibu ada waktu?
B That's OK. I don't have work tomorrow.
A Apakah bapak dan ibu minum-minuman beralkohol?
B I'm sorry, we are not used to it.
A Jangan kuatir, saya akan pesan sari buah atau minuman tanpa alkohol.
B Thank you! See you then.
A Salam untuk ibu.

beserta *together with*
sekitar *around, about*
minuman beralkohol *alcoholic drinks*
biasa *to be used to (something)*
pesan *to order*
tanpa *without*
sari *extract*
sari buah *fruit juice*
minuman tanpa alkohol *alcohol-free drinks*
salam untuk *say 'hi' to... (a more informal way of saying it)*
salam untuk ibu *say 'hi' to your wife.* (Note that in this context **ibu** is automatically taken to mean your wife.)

QUICK VOCAB

Invitations – Indonesian style

If you invite Indonesians out for a meal or other form of entertainment, they will assume that you intend to pay the bill. Similarly, if you are invited out by an Indonesian, he or she will expect to treat you.

An interesting quirk! In western countries we invite each other *round for a coffee*, when the goal is to socialize and chat. In Indonesia people are invited to each other's houses for a chat, **Datanglah ke rumah saya, kita ngobrol-ngobrol** even though you can count on coffee or tea or some other beverage being served!

Some Indonesians might invite you for **rujakan** which can also imply a chat. **Rujak** is a mixture of various kinds of raw fruit such as paw-paw, mango and pineapple that is accompanied by a **sambal** (a relish) made, in this case, from chilli and brown sugar. Of course, while you are eating your **rujak** you are engaging in conversation too.

Note also that if you are invited to an Indonesian home it is a customary courtesy to take your shoes off before entering.

Insight

Ngobrol is a highly colloquial form, characteristic of the informal speech of Jakarta. The standard form of the verbs *to chat* is mengobrol. We'll take a closer look at Jakarta style speech in Unit 17.

TEST YOURSELF

1 What does **se-** mean when added to a noun?

2 What phrase is often used to make a suggestion?

3 What is a polite way to ask *May I...?*

4 Which two words can mean *Why?* and which is the more conversational one?

5 How would you say *in a group of five* in Indonesian?

6 How would you say *together with* in Indonesian?

7 How would you say *in August* in Indonesian?

8 From what are nouns with the suffix **-an** derived?

9 What effect does **-an** have on noun bases?

10 What does a noun resulting from **-an** mean when applied to adjective bases?

8

Asking the way

In this unit you will learn how to
- *ask for directions*
- *understand the directions*

PART ONE

Dialogue

Ken and his family finally decided to book a package tour offered by the travel agency. On the way to pick up the voucher, Ken gets lost and has to ask a passer-by for help.

CD1, TR 9, 0:03

Ken	Maaf Pak, numpang tanya? Di mana biro perjalanan Anta Tour?
Pejalan kaki	Boléh saya tahu alamatnya? Di jalan apa?
Ken	Di Jalan Thamrin. Apa nama jalan ini?
Pejalan kaki	Oh ini namanya Jalan Sudirman.
Ken	Bagaimana menuju ke sana?
Pejalan kaki	Dekat sekali. Ambil jalan ini lurus saja, sampai ketemu lampu mérah, kemudian bélok kanan. Kira-kira 50 méter, ada hotél Mandarin. Biro perjalanan itu ada di sebelahnya.
Ken	Apa itu dekat bioskop?

| Pejalan kaki | Tepat sekali, kantor itu ada di antara bioskop dan hotél Mandarin. |
| Ken | Terima kasih. |

tanya to ask
numpang tanya do you mind if I ask you...?
biro bureau, office
biro perjalanan travel agency
pejalan walker
kaki foot
pejalan kaki pedestrian
boléh saya tahu may I know, could you tell me
alamat address
jalan street
di jalan apa? on what street?
Bagaimana menuju ke sana? How to get there?
dekat near
ambil to take
lurus straight on
sampai until, as far as
ketemu to meet, to get to
lampu light
mérah red
lampu mérah traffic light
kemudian then
bélok to turn
kanan right
bélok kanan turn right
tepat exact
tepat sekali that's exactly right

TRANSLATION

Ken	Excuse me, Can I ask you? Where is the Anta travel agency?
Passer-by	Could you tell me the address? On what street?
	(Contd)

Ken	On Thamrin Street. What's the name of this street?
Passer-by	It is called Sudirman Street.
Ken	How can I get there?
Passer-by	It is very near. Take this street, straight on until you find the traffic light, then turn right. About 50 metres, there is a hotel Mandarin. That agency is next to it.
Ken	Is it close to the theatre?
Passer-by	That's exactly right. That office is between the cinema and the hotel Mandarin.
Ken	Thank you.

How the language works 1

1 When you need to ask for directions to a place in Indonesian, you can use **di mana?**, *where is?* or you could use the phrase **Bagaimana menuju ke?**

Di mana Monas?   *Where's Monas?*
Bagaimana menuju ke Monas?   *How do I get to Monas?*

Insight

If you need to stop a passer-by, after you have said **Maaf**, *Excuse me*, it is nice to start with the useful phrase **Numpang tanya**, *May I ask you…*

EXERCISE 1

Ask how to get to…

a the Aryaduta Hotel
b the airport
c Cihampelas.

Understanding Indonesian

EXERCISE 2

Answer the following true/false questions based on the dialogue.

a Ken mau pergi ke Biro Perjalanan Wita Tour.
b Ken tersesat di jalan Thamrin.
c Biro perjalanan ada di jalan Sudirman.
d Kantor itu ada di antara hotél dan bioskop.
e Setelah lampu mérah Ken harus bélok kiri, kira-kira 50 méter.
f Kantor Anta Tour tidak jauh.

bélok kiri *to turn left*

QV

EXERCISE 3

🔊 **CD1, TR 8, 1:14**

First familiarize yourself with the vocabulary. Listen to each short dialogue featuring someone asking the way to a place. For each dialogue, circle the place the person is trying to get to. If you are not using the recording, turn to the transcript in the Listening transcripts section and treat this as a reading exercise.

a Istana Bogor – Kebun Raya Bogor – Pasar Bogor
b Musium Nasional – Bank BCA – Monumén Nasional
c SMU 3 – SMU 2 – SMU 5
d SMU Ragunan – Kebun Binatang Cisarua – Kebun Binatang Ragunan
e Sahid Jaya – Hotél Mulia – Plaza Senayan

istana *palace*
binatang *animal*
bank *bank*
kebun binatang *zoo*
perempatan *intersection/crossroads*
tugu *monument*

QUICK VOCAB

maksud *to mean*
menyebut (sebut, v) *to name/to call*
lapangan *field/pitch*
saya mau tanya *I'd like to ask*
coba *to try*
coba tanya *try asking*
ujung *end*
cara *way, method*
salah *wrong*
bundaran *roundabout*
setelah *after*

Insight

Another word for *crossroads* that you might hear is **perapatan**.

PART TWO

Dialogue

Reza cannot accompany Mark to the BIP Mall so she gives him directions telling him how to get there. Somehow he still manages to get lost...

◉ CD1, TR 8, 3:04

Pejalan kaki	Mas kelihatan bingung. Apa bisa saya bantu?
Mark	Ya saya tersesat.
Pejalan kaki	Mau pergi ke mana?
Mark	Saya mau pergi ke BIP di Jalan Dago. Bagaimana ke sana?
Pejalan kaki	Jauh sekali kalau berjalan kaki.
Mark	Tidak apa-apa saya suka jalan kaki.
Pejalan kaki	Ikuti jalan ini, lurus saja sampai ketemu bundaran, lalu ambil bélokan pertama. Jalan terus sampai ke perempatan. BIP terletak setelah tiga bangunan dari perempatan.

Mark	Sulit saya untuk mengingatnya. Bisa kamu tunjukkan di peta ini?
Pejalan kaki	Mari saya lihat. Sekarang kamu berada di sini dan ini gedung yang kamu cari.
Mark	Terima kasih sudah merepotkan Mas.
Pejalan kaki	Tidak – apa-apa. Malu bertanya sesat di jalan.

QUICK VOCAB

bingung *confused*
tersesat (sesat, v) *lost*
saya tersesat *I am lost*
berjalan (jalan, n) *to walk*
berjalan kaki *go on foot*
ikuti (ikut, v) *follow*
bélokan (bélok, v) *turning*
bélokan pertama *first turning*
jalan terus *go straight on*
sulit *difficult*
mengingat (ingat, v) *to remember*
tunjukkan (tunjuk, v) *to show*
cari *to look for*
merepotkan (repot, a) *to bother, to put (someone) to some
  trouble*
malu *shy*
bertanya (tanya, n) *to ask*
malu bertanya sesat di jalan *if you're too shy to ask you will get
  lost in the street* (proverb – can be used in other contexts too)

TRANSLATION

Passer-by	You look confused. Can I help you?
Mark	Yes. I'm lost.
Passer-by	Where do you want to go?
Mark	I want to go to BIP on Dago Street. How do I get there?
Passer-by	It's too far to walk.
Mark	No problem. I like going on foot.
	(Contd)

Passer-by	Follow this road, straight on until you come to a roundabout, then take the first turning. Keep walking until you come to a crossroads. BIP is (located) three buildings from the crossroads.
Mark	It's difficult to remember. Could you point to it on the map?
Passer-by	Let me see. You are here and this is the building you are looking for.
Mark	Thank you. Sorry to bother you.
Passer-by	No problem. If you don't ask, you don't get.

How the language works 2

1 Most Indonesian words beginning with **ber-** and **me-** are verbs. These prefixes can be attached to noun, adjective and verb bases.

When **ber-** and **me-** occur as prefixes to a verb base, they often have no particular function and express the same meaning as the verb base.

Some verbs of this type are:

▶ with **ber-**

berhenti	*to stop*	(*from* **henti**, *to stop*)
berbelanja	*to go shopping*	(*from* **belanja**, *to go shopping*)
bertanya	*to ask a question*	(*from* **tanya**, *to ask a question*)
bermain	*to play*	(*from* **main**, *to play*)
berenang	*to swim*	(*from* **renang**, *to swim*)

Insight
It is best to learn these verbs with the **ber-** prefix as a single unit as this is the form you will almost always use.

Note that there are some cases where, due to sound changes, **ber-** changes slightly.

Learn these two exceptions as they are common:

| **bekerja** | to work | (from **kerja,** to work) |
| **belajar** | to learn | (from **ajar,** to learn) |

▶ with **me-**

membeli	to buy	(from **beli,** to buy)
melihat	to see	(from **lihat,** to see)
mendengar	to hear	(from **dengar,** to hear)
mencari	to look for	(from **cari,** to look for)
menjual	to sell	(from **jual,** to sell)

(The **me-** prefix creates certain sound changes which will be dealt with in a later unit.)

Some verb bases that are verbs in their own right occur with **me-** which creates a verb with a different meaning, usually related. Some common ones are:

menunggu	to expect	(from **tunggu,** to wait)
meninggal	to die	(from **tinggal,** to stay or to live)
mendatang	to approach	(from **datang,** to come)
mendapat	to get	(from **dapat,** to be able)
membangun	to build	(from **bangun,** to wake up or to get up)

Using Indonesian

EXERCISE 4

Look at the map, then fill in the passages with the words specified in each section.

a Use **lurus, antara, menyeberang, bélok** to complete this text.

Bagaimana saya ke réstoran dari perpustakaan?

Jalan _____ ke Jalan Senopati, sampai ketemu lampu mérah yang kedua. _____ kanan terus ke jalan Majapahit, kemudian _____ jalan. Réstoran ada di _____ toko buku dan toko CD.

b Use **terus, menyeberang, keluar, bélok, belakang,** to complete this text.

Bagaimana saya ke kolam renang dari réstoran?

Ketika _____ dari réstoran, _____ kanan, jalan _____ sampai ketemu perempatan kemudian bélok kiri ke jalan Darmawangsa dan _____ jalan. Kolam renang ada di _____ sekolah dan universitas.

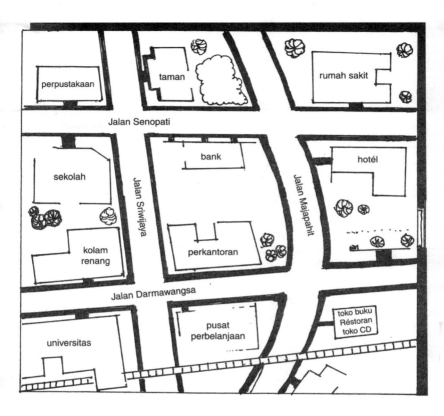

c Use **sudut**, **bélok**, **keluar** to complete this text.

Bagaimana saya ke rumah sakit dari taman?

Pertama _____ taman ke jalan Sriwijaya, kemudian _____ kiri, ke Senopati, jalan lurus. Rumah sakit di ____.

perkantoran *office complex*
pusat perbelanjaan *shopping centre*
ketika keluar *when you have come out of*
keluar *to go out, to come out*
sudut *corner*
toko *shop*
CD *CD*

EXERCISE 5

Over to you!

You (**B**) are wandering the streets looking for a post office. A passer-by (**A**) can see that you are lost so she offers to help you...

CD2, TR 1, 0:02

A	Kamu kelihatan bingung. Bisa saya bantu?
B	I'm lost. I want to go to a post office.
A	Gampang sekali. Ikuti jalan utama ini sampai ketemu perempatan. Bélok kiri dan lurus saja. Kantor pos terletak di samping kiri jalan.
B	Is it (that) near the Hard Rock Café?
A	Tepat sekali. Juga ada McDonald's di sebelahnya.
B	Could you point it out on this map? Where are we now?
A	Tentu. Kita sekarang ada di Jalan Sudirman. Ini kantor pos di sebelah McDonald's.
B	Thank you.

QV

gampang *simple, easy*
utama *main*
jalan utama *main road*

Body language

When you enter a foreign country you cannot escape entering that country's culture. No matter how good your intentions are, you may, without the proper advice, inadvertently end up creating embarassing and even potentially volatile situations. If you are from the UK, you may have had the experience of talking to a foreigner who unwittingly uses a two-finger salute, probably just to buy two of something in a shop, and witnessed the problems that this can cause. Ignorance of certain aspects of Indonesian culture can create a problem of similar magnitude!

If you should need to point at anything, refrain from using your finger. Instead, you should use your thumb and, specifically, the thumb of your *right* hand. The left hand is traditionally associated with using a toilet so it is considered highly impolite to use it for anything concerning your interactions with other people. For example, you should not hail a taxi with your left hand, neither should you use it to pass something to someone. If you *do* use your left hand for something by mistake, it is best to acknowledge your mistake immediately by saying **Maaf**. This will show Indonesians that you respect their culture, which will be highly appreciated, even if you do happen to err.

It is also considered insulting to point at anything with your foot. This is because the feet are regarded as the lowest part of the body and as such should not be used for pointing. Note also, that if you are sitting on the floor, you should ensure that the soles of your feet are not outstretched towards someone as this also conveys a silent, but poignant, insult. As the feet are the lowest part of the body, the head is regarded as the highest part, which acts as a vessel for the soul. You should refrain from touching people on the head for this reason.

For westerners, the act of putting our hands on our hips or crossing our arms in front of our chest is an innocent one. Be warned, however, that in Indonesia this is interpreted as a sign of arrogance or anger. Either way it is regarded as highly impolite and will not serve you well.

If you have to cross someone's path, interrupting, say, a conversation between two people, the correct and polite way to do this is to say **permisi**, bow a little and make a slow upward cutting motion with your hand held vertically, thumb uppermost.

Point with the thumb of your right hand!

TEST YOURSELF

1 What are two ways to ask for directions in Indonesian?

2 What useful phrase should you use when stopping someone and asking for information?

3 True or false: when **ber-** is attached to a verb it always alters the meaning.

4 How should you aim to remember **ber-** verbs?

5 What is unusual about the **ber-** prefix when used with *to work* and *to swim*?

6 What other common verb prefix did you learn in this unit?

7 Do verbs with the **me-** prefix always have the same meaning as the verb base?

8 What is the difference between **mengajar** and **belajar**?

9 What is the difference between **berbuat** and **membuat**?

10 How would you say *in between* in Indonesian?

9

Changing money

In this unit you will learn how to
- *change money*
- *understand and express higher numbers*
- *express distance, weight, height etc.*

PART ONE

Dialogue

Jamilah has been so busy shopping that she did not realize she was running out of rupiah until she was getting ready to pay.

📶 CD2, TR 2, 0:03

Ibu Jamilah	Maaf mbak, uang saya tidak cukup. Bisa saya bayar dengan dolar?
Penjaga toko	Maaf Bu, kami hanya menerima rupiah. Tapi di seberang jalan ada tempat tukar uang. Atau Ibu bisa tukar di bank di samping kanan toko itu.
Ibu Jamilah	Baiklah, tolong simpan barang ini. Saya akan kembali lagi.
(In the bureau de change.)	
Ibu Jamilah	Selamat pagi, bisa saya tukar dolar ke rupiah?
Pegawai	Ya, Dolar apa Bu, Amérika?

Ibu Jamilah	Bukan, Dolar Sélandia Baru. Berapa nilai tukar untuk hari ini?
Pegawai	Satu dolar Sélandia Baru sama dengan 4.552 rupiah. Berapa Ibu mau tukar?
Ibu Jamilah	500 Dolar. Berapa dalam rupiah?
Pegawai	500 kali 4.552 rupiah sama dengan 2.276.000 rupiah.
Ibu Jamilah	Tolong kasih saya beberapa lembar uang seratus ribuan dan beberapa lembar uang lima puluh ribuan.
Pegawai	Silahkan hitung kembali.
Ibu Jamilah	Ya, betul. Terima kasih.

cukup *enough*
dolar *dollar*
menerima *to accept*
tukar *to change*
tempat tukar uang *money changer, bureau de change*
simpan *to keep*
nilai *value*
nilai tukar *rate of exchange*
sama dengan *equal to, the same as*
kasih *to give*
kasih saya *give me*
lembar *(here) bank note*
hitung *to count*
hitung kembali *to count again*

TRANSLATION

Jamilah	I'm sorry, I don't have enough money. Can I pay in dollars?
Shop assistant	Sorry, Madam, but we only accept rupiah. But across the road there is a bureau de change. Or you can change it at the bank next to that shop on the right.
Jamilah	Good, please keep my stuff (to one side). I'll come back later.
Jamilah	Good morning, can I change dollars into rupiah?
	(Contd)

Clerk	Yes, what kind of dollars, Madam, US dollars?
Jamilah	No, New Zealand dollars. What's today's rate?
Clerk	It's one dollar to 4,552 rupiahs. How much do you want to change?
Jamilah	500 dollars. How much (is that) in rupiah?
Clerk	500 times 4,552. That's 2,276,000.
Jamilah	Please give it to me in 100,000 and then some 50,000 bills.
Clerk	Please count your money again.
Jamilah	Yes, it's correct. Thank you.

How the language works 1

1 When you are shopping in Indonesia you will need to know how to express and understand very high numbers. You already know that to form the -*teens* you follow the number by **belas** and to make the -*ties* you need to use **puluh**.

It is just as simple to form hundreds, thousands and millions.

For *hundreds* use **ratus**:

| **dua ratus** | *two hundred* |
| **lima ratus empat** | *five hundred and four* |

For *thousands* use **ribu**:

| **delapan ribu** | *eight thousand* |
| **enam ribu empat ratus dua belas** | *six thousand four hundred and twelve* |

For *millions* use **juta**:

| **empat juta** | *four million* |
| **tujuh juta empat ratus ribu** | *seven million four hundred thousand* |

Note that numbers that refer to *one* or *a* (as in ***one** million* or *a million*) are different and are formed with the prefix **se-** which means *one*.

seratus	*one hundred*
seribu	*one thousand*
sejuta	*one million*

EXERCISE 1

Write the following numbers in words (note that where we separate parts of a big number with commas in English, Indonesian does the same thing using full stops):

a 19.432
b 2.865.714
c 3.197
d 8.600.111
e 25.155.613

2 Years are formed in the same way as the numbers we have just looked at. They follow the word **tahun** which means *year*.

2003	**tahun dua ribu tiga**
1492	**tahun empat belas sembilan puluh dua**

In informal spoken language, years can be expressed in a slightly different way. The first two numbers are said as a normal number, but the last two are said separately. For example, if you want to express 1945, you would form this in Indonesian as *nineteen, four, five*:

1945	**tahun sembilan belas empat lima**
1492	**tahun empat belas sembilan dua**

Insight
As with days and weeks, **pada** can be used to express *in* with years, although it is not obligatory, furthermore, it is rarely used in spoken Indonesian.

3 In addition to meaning *You're welcome* and *to come back* **kembali** can also be used to mean *to (do something) again*. In this case it is placed directly after the verb it refers to.

Hitung kembali uangmu!	*Count your money again!*
Baca kembali perintahnya!	*Read the instruction again!*
Dia memeriksa kembali dompétnya.	*He checked his wallet again.*
Guru mengingatkan kembali pekerjaan rumah.	*The teacher gave a further reminder about the homework.*

perintah *instruction, command*
dompét *wallet*
mengingatkan (ingat, *v) to remind*

EXERCISE 2

How would you say:

a to enrol again
b to repeat again
c to research again
d to hit again?

mendaftar (daftar, *n) to enrol*
mengulangi (ulang, *v) to repeat*
meneliti (teliti, *a) to research, to examine carefully*
memukul (pukul, *n) to hit*

Adding the suffix **-an** to **puluh, ratus, ribu** and **juta** gives you *tens, hundreds, thousands* and *millions*:

Ratusan anak muda akan ambil bagian dalam perlombaan maraton amal.	*Hundreds of young people will take part in the charity marathon.*
Ribuan tikus besar menyerang sawah.	*Thousands of rats attacked the rice field.*

ambil bagian (dalam) *to take part (in)*
perlombaan (lomba, *n) race*
perlombaan maraton *marathon*
amal *charity*
tikus *mouse*
tikus besar *rat*
menyerang (serang, *n) to attack*
sawah *rice field*

Understanding Indonesian

EXERCISE 3

Answer the following true/false questions based on the dialogue.

a Jamilah tidak mempunyai cukup uang rupiah untuk berbelanja.
b Penjaga toko hanya menerima uang tunai.
c Jamilah akan kembali ke toko setelah menukar uang.
d Bank ada di seberang jalan.
e Tempat tukar uang ada di samping kanan toko.
f Jamilah ingin menukar uang sebanyak 500 dolar Amérika.

penjaga toko *shop assistant*
tunai *cash*
uang tunai *cash, ready money*
menukar (tukar, *v.) to change*
sebanyak *as much as, to the tune of (figuratively)*

EXERCISE 4

🔊 **CD2, TR 2, 1:28**

You are going to hear numbers being called out in a lottery game.
Check off the numbers for each of the players as you hear them
and note down who wins first, second and third by getting all four
numbers. The empty card is for you to play. Choose four numbers
between 1 and 100. **Semoga suksés!** (*Good luck!*)

Tuti	
30	38
25	69

Muhamad	
12	52
79	13

Sutrisno	
61	70
9	45

Noncik	
36	24
91	83

Budi	
99	17
22	50

PART TWO

DIALOGUE

Mark is looking for somewhere to change his money so that he can go shopping for souvenirs.

CD2, TR 2, 3:02

Mark	Reza, apa saya bisa menarik uang dengan kartu krédit di sini?
Reza	Ya. Ada mesin ATM di luar.
(Mark puts his card in the slot but the machine swallows it.)	
Mark	Reza, kartu krédit saya ditelan mesin ATM. Bisa kamu bantu saya? Saya cuma punya beberapa poundsterling.
Reza	Jangan kuatir. Saya akan mengurus kartu krédit kamu di bank dan kamu bisa tukar uang di sana. Kalau tidak cukup, saya akan pinjamkan kamu uang.
Pegawai	Bisa saya bantu, Pak?
Mark	Ya… saya mau tukar uang poundsterling ke rupiah. Berapa nilai tukar untuk hari ini?
Pegawai	1 poundsterling sama dengan 14.620 rupiah. Hari ini lebih bagus dari kemarin.
Mark	Beruntung sekali. Saya mau tukar 30 pound saja.
Pegawai	Baik, jumlah uang nya 438.600 rupiah.
Mark	Wow… banyak sekali. Saya bisa jadi orang kaya.
Pegawai	Bapak mau uang kecil atau uang besar?

| **Mark** | Tolong beri saya beberapa lembar uang 100.000-an dan sisanya saya minta beberapa uang kecil. |
| **Pegawai** | Tentu. Ini semua uangnya. Jangan lupa hitung kembali. |

menarik uang *to withdraw money*
mesin ATM *ATM*
ditelan (telan, *v***)** *to be swallowed*
kartu krédit *credit card*
pinjamkan (pinjam, *n***)** *to lend*
Uang poundsterling *British pound*
lebih bagus *better*
beruntung (untung, *n***)** *lucky*
uang kecil *small money*
uang besar *big money*
jumlah *amount, total*
sisanya (sisa, *n***)** *the rest (of it)*
beri *to give*

QUICK VOCAB

TRANSLATION

Mark	Reza, can I withdraw my money with a credit card here?
Reza	Yes. There is an ATM machine outside
Mark	Reza, my credit card has been swallowed by the ATM machine. Can you help me? I only have a little pound sterling (a few pounds).
Reza	Don't worry, I will see about the credit card in that bank and you can change your money there. If you need more I will lend you (some) money.
Clerk	Can I help you, Sir?
Mark	Yes, I would like to change pound sterling into rupiah. What's today's rate?
Clerk	14,620. Today (the rate) is better than yesterday.
Mark	(I'm) so lucky. I want to change 30 pounds only.
Clerk	Well, the total is 438,600.
Mark	Wow! It's a lot of money. I can be a rich man.
Clerk	Do you want (it in) small or big money?
Mark	Please give (it to) me in 100,000 bills and the rest in small money.
Clerk	OK. This is all your money. Don't forget to count (it) again.

How the language works 2

1 So far we have seen how **-nya** is used to mean *his* or *her*. It is frequently used where we would use *the* or *your* in English in sentences such as:

Bagaimana penerbangan*nya*?	*How was* **the** *flight? How was* **your** *flight?*
Bagaimana kelas*nya*?	*How was* **the** *class? How was* **your** *class?*
Ini kamus*nya*.	*This is* **the** *dictionary. This is* **your** *dictionary.*

It is especially used in this way to refer back to something that has been previously mentioned or a situation that is understood by both speakers. In the first example, it could be that you are being met by someone at the airport who asks you how your flight was, knowing that you have just arrived on a plane. The second could be asked by someone who knows that you have just had a class. As you can see from the third example, the usage of **-nya** in this way is not restricted to questions. This person may have borrowed your dictionary and is returning it, he or she might be handing you a book that was the subject of a previous conversation meaning *This is the dictionary I told you about*. There could be many situations that would warrant the use of **-nya** by an Indonesian speaker, but what all these situations have in common is that they refer to a situation or something previously *known* or *understood* by both speakers.

Similarly, in the dialogue, the clerk says **Ini semua uangnya** as a situation has been set up whereby, due to a previous interaction, Mark is waiting for money so the clerk says *Here is* **the** *money (that you have been waiting for)*.

Insight

This use of **-nya** is very common and, even though it may take a little time to get used to, you will start to get a feel for how it is used as you hear it used by Indonesians or see it used in the dialogues. In our previous examples it is not wrong to say **Bagaimana penerbangan kamu?** or **Ini kamus** in the same situations. It just so happens that native Indonesian speakers tend to use **-nya** in such cases.

By extension, you will notice that questions that ask about prices and fares use -nya:

Berapa harganya?	*How much does it cost?*
Berapa ongkosnya?	*What's the fare?*

ongkos *cost, fare*

In the same way, -**nya** is also used with weight and measure words. It refers to these words in such a way as to mean, for example, *Its length is 45 centimetres* where we would say *It is 45 centimetres long* in English. Such measure words are mostly formed from an adjective to which -**nya** is attached:

panjang	*long*
Panjangnya **45 séntiméter.**	*It is 45 centimetres long.*
tebal	*thick*
Buku itu tebalnya **300 halaman.**	*That book is 300 pages thick.*

An exception is **kecepatannya** which is formed from the noun kecepatan, *speed*:

Kecepatannya 70 km per jam.	*Its speed is 70 km per hour.*

tebal *thick*
halaman *page*
kecepatan *speed*
per jam *per hour*

EXERCISE 5

Use the adjectives in the vocabulary section beneath the exercise to express the following:

a It weighs 56 kilos.
b It is 45 centimetres high.
c It is 100 metres wide.
d It is 2 metres deep.
e It takes 7 hours.

berat	*heavy/weight*	**lama**	*long*
tinggi	*high/tall*	**séntiméter**	*centimetre*
lébar	*wide*	**méter**	*metre*
dalam	*deep*		

These adjectives combine with **berapa** to form questions related to measure:

berapa tinggi   *how tall?*

Insight

Make sure you do not confuse **lama** and **panjang** as they both translate as *long* in English. **Lama** refers to a length of time only, whereas **panjang** refers to physical distance only:

Berapa lama penerbangan dari Jakarta ke Manila?	*How long is the flight from Jakarta to Manila?*
Berapa panjang méja itu?	*How long is that table?*

---

méja *table*
panjang *long*

2 The **ber-** and **me-** prefixes with noun bases.

With **ber-**. Many verbs in Indonesian are nouns that have been modified by means of a prefix. You have already come across this in Unit 5 when you met **berumur** and **bernama**. For example, when **olahraga** which means *sport* occurs with **ber-** the result is the verb **berolahraga** which means to *play sport*. In the same way, **istirahat**, *(a) rest*, becomes **beristirahat**, *to rest*, and **bahasa** which means *language* becomes **berbahasa**, *to speak (such and such a language)*.

Insight

In the final example notice how the noun and the meaning of the noun become *absorbed* into the verb. You already know that **bahasa Inggeris** means *(the) English (language)*, **berbahasa Inggeris** means *to speak English*. It is an alternative to **berbicara bahasa Inggeris**.

Many **ber-** + noun verbs can be translated into English as *to be...* or to *have...*:

akal	intelligence	berakal	**to be** intelligent
libur	holiday	berlibur	**to be** on holiday
pendapat	opinion	berpendapat	**to be** of the opinion
untung	luck	beruntung	**to be** lucky (i.e. to have luck)
isteri	wife	beristeri	**to have** a wife (i.e. to be married)
anak	children	beranak	**to have** children

Ber- used in this way can create expressions such as:

Dia berkaki panjang. *He has long legs. (**kaki panjang** long legs)*
gedung berlantai empat *a four-storey building (a building that has four storeys)*

kaki *leg*

EXERCISE 6

Look at the nouns in the left-hand column noting the meaning. See if you can find suitable English meanings for the verbs in the right-hand column that use the nouns as a base.

a puasa	*fast (as in a religious fast)*	**berpuasa**	
b gerak	*movement*	**bergerak**	
c keluarga	*family*	**berkeluarga**	

With **me-**.

tari	*dance*	**menari**	*to dance*
rokok	*cigarette*	**merokok**	*to smoke*
bungkus	*parcel*	**membungkus**	*to wrap up*
gunting	*scissors*	**menggunting**	*to cut with scissors*

Insight

You will notice that, in some cases, when the **me-** prefix is added to create a verb, the noun (which has now become the base) undergoes a change in spelling and, therefore, pronunciation. Such sound changes are for ease of pronunciation (from an Indonesian point of view) and will be dealt with in more detail in Unit 17. For now, just concentrate on the meaning of the prefixed verbs.

EXERCISE 7

See if you can deduce the meanings of the **me-** verbs in the right-hand column created from the nouns in the left-hand column. You may find that with **me-** + noun verbs, the meanings are a little less easy to deduce than with the **ber-** + noun verbs.

a potong *slice*   **memotong**
b potrét *photograph*   **memotrét**
c rampok *robber*   **merampok**

Using Indonesian

EXERCISE 8

Read the English for the following facts about Indonesia. Rewrite the Indonesian sentences inserting the Indonesian form of the number in words.

a *The population of Indonesia is 192 million.*
Penduduk Indonesia ___ orang.
b *Mount Bromo is 2,750 metres high.*
Gunung Bromo tingginya ___ méter.
c *Indonesia gained independence in 1945.*
Indonesia memperoleh kemerdékaan pada tahun___.
d *Sulawesi has a population of 13 million people.*
Sulawési penduduknya ___ orang.
e *Indonesia is made up of 13,667 islands.*
Indonesia terdiri dari ___ pulau.
f *The Portuguese arrived in Indonesia in 1512.*
Bangsa Portugis tiba di Indonesia pada tahun ___.
g *There are 128 active volcanoes in Indonesia.*
Ada ___ gunung berapi yang masih aktif di Indonesia.
h *Mount Rinjani is 3,700 metres high.*
Gunung Rinjani tingginya ___ méter.
i *Waingapu has a population of 25,000 people.*
Penduduk Waingapu ___ orang.
j *The North Sulawesi Peninsula is 777 km long.*
Semenanjung Sulawési panjangnya ___ kilométer.
k *Lake Toba is 732 metres above sea level.*
Danau Toba terletak ___ méter di atas permukaan laut.
l *Palu City has a population of 150,000 people.*
Kota Palu penduduknya ___ orang.
m *Maumere was destroyed by an earthquake in 1992.*
Maumere dihancurkan oléh gempa bumi pada tahun ___.

---

penduduk (duduk, v) *population*
memperoléh (oléh, n) *to gain*
kemerdékaan (merdéka, n) *independence*
terdiri dari *to be made up of, to be composed of*
bangsa *nation*
api *fire*
gunung berapi *volcano*
masif aktif *active*
semenanjung *peninsula*
permukaan (muka, n) *surface*
laut *sea*

QUICK VOCAB

permukaan laut *sea level*
dihancurkan oléh (hancur, v) *to be destroyed by*
gempa *shaking*
bumi *earth*
gempa bumi *earthquake*

EXERCISE 9

Over to you!

You want to change some money …

CD2, TR 2, 4:40

A *Good afternoon. Can I change dollars into rupiah?*
B Dolar apa? Dolar Amérika?
A *No, Singapore dollars.*
B Ya.
A *What's the rate?*
B Satu dolar sama dengan 1.600 rupiah. Mau tukar berapa?
A *1,000 dollars. I'd like some small change please.*
B Ini uangnya. Silahkan hitung kembali.

Cash, travellers' cheques or plastic?

The rupiah is the standard unit of currency used in Indonesia. Most shops do not accept foreign currency, although some well-established shops and businesses do take credit cards in the major cities and tourist areas. If you plan to travel in areas less frequented by mainstream tourists, you will need to carry cash, as travellers' cheques can be difficult to change and you may find that your credit cards are not accepted. In addition, you may also find that the rates of exchange in such areas are not as competitive as in the cities. Outside tourist areas you may find that money changers, as they are known in Indonesia, are closed on national holidays, which can create difficulties if you are running low on Indonesian currency. In short, as far as money goes, you need to be prepared in advance.

Learning tip

Are you finding some Indonesian words difficult to memorize? If you are, then this approach to memorization that you can use for any foreign language may be just what you need.

Languages that are related to English or that have had a significant influence on English will offer you many natural similarities that you can use as mental hooks or associations. It is easy to learn **Hund**, the German for *dog* because it is related to the English word *hound*. Similarly the French word **mouton** meaning *sheep* gives us *mutton*.

Indonesian, unfortunately, offers virtually no natural associations to the English speaker as the two languages are not related. However, by using your imagination and your unique experience of the world around you, you can create false associations that are just as effective.

Here is how it works: Take a word like **selimut** which means *blanket*. Somehow you have to create an association that will make the word **selimut** and its meaning unforgettable to you. What does it sound like? It sounds very similar to *silly mutt* in English. How are you going to link the words so you not only get the sound, but you also get the meaning? In your mind's eye, see a cartoon dog bound into a room with a slippery floor, a kitchen, for example, come to a flying halt on a brightly coloured blanket, slide uncontrollably across the room on the blanket and crash into the wall on the other side. Only a *silly mutt* would do something like that! An important point to remember when doing this is to include action. Just the image of the blanket with a dog on it will not be as effective as a colourful image that moves and has great sound effects.

The Indonesian for *to jump* is **meloncat** (pronounced **melonchat**). At first glance it offers no apparent associations and it does not readily fit into a known phrase in English. But look again. You have two words there: **melon** which we can take as

(Contd)

melon and **chat** which, if you frequent Indian restaurants, you might know is a kind of salad. Imagine a beautifully dressed Indian waiter taking a flying leap off a springboard into a huge bowl of **chat** made with **melon**. As the waiter lands in the salad with a huge splat, pieces of fresh, ripe juicy melon (savour the smell!) fly everywhere, including over you. This gives you the approximate sound of the word and an action that gives you the meaning within the same image. Just repeat the word a few times with the proper pronunciation and use the image to reinforce it.

You could have taken **chat** as the French for *cat* and made a different image, although you would have to bear in mind the difference in pronunciation. Or you could have taken **chat** to mean the act of talking casually and created an action-filled image around that. The beauty of this memory system is that the choice is yours!

Speaking of chats, *to chat* in Indonesian is **bercakap-cakap**. If you take the **ber-** prefix away, which you know indicates a verb, you are left with four words that sound like *chuck up*, *chuck up!* You might create an image of yourself chatting to someone, a friend perhaps, who then *chucks up* all over you! And then does it again, hence the doubling effect. Remember to put yourself in the image and imagine with all your senses what it would be like. You could even add the **ber-** as a sort of wretching sound before the chucking up to remind you that it is a **ber-** verb. The image is necessarily disgusting. In this case, the more revolted you feel, the more engaged your senses are which, in turn, makes the association more memorable.

Finally, let us take a more obscure association as an illustration. **Dorong** means *push* like a sign you might see on a door. That has started to give it away already!... **Dorong** sounds like *door wrong* which does not make sense. However, imagine you are going up to a door (marked **dorong**), imagine pushing it open gingerly only to find a huge, snarling monster with snapping teeth behind it that scares the living daylights out of you. *Oops!*

Wrong **door!** *Wrong door!* **Wrong** *door!* How many times will you need to repeat that to remember it? Not many!

The mind likes the unusual or anything that stimulates your emotions or senses. Images that are grotesque, hilarious, full of action and colour, sexual, vulgar or rude tend to be the most memorable and, therefore, the most effective for this type of exercise. Each person has a unique life experience, so it is more effective for you to come up with associations based on that rather than associations that someone else can offer.

What about words that you cannot find associations for? There will be some, but you may also find that the focus spent on a word trying to come up with an association may be enough to learn it anyway!

This does not mean that you have to go through the whole process of bringing the image back every time you want to recall a word. That would not be productive. You may need to trace it back to your association a couple of times, but once you have used the word or phrase a few times in different contexts, it will start to come to you naturally. This system is not meant to replace learning the words properly, but it can certainly help your learning along and save you time and effort! Most of the time you can only find approximations or the word stresses might be different, so you still need to refer to the Indonesian words for proper pronunciation.

Some learners frown on this approach, dismissing it as childish or stupid. It is offered here simply as an option to use or not to use, as you see fit.

But try this... without even glancing at our earlier explanations, can you say what the Indonesian word is for *blanket*? How about to *jump*, *to chat* or *push*? If you imagined the images as you read along, you will probably find that you have been 'hard wired' to remember these words. If you know those words now

(Contd)

and you did not know them before you read this learning tip, you may have found something that works for you.

Still sceptical? If so, write the four words in English down on a piece of paper and put it in an envelope to be opened in a month's time. Do not make any effort to recall the words over this time. When you open the envelope, can you recall the Indonesian by using the associations?

Is it better to learn words without this step, if you can? Yes. But if learning vocabulary is proving to be a barrier to your progress in the language then try another way of remembering, such as association.

TEST YOURSELF

1 How would you form hundreds in Indonesian?

2 How would you form thousands?

3 How would you form millions?

4 What prefix is used with numbers to mean *one*, as in *one thousand*?

5 How do you express years in Indonesian?

6 What effect does the suffix **-an** have on numbers words such as **ratus** and **juta**?

7 What further uses of **-nya** did you learn in this unit?

8 In what kind of expressions is **-nya** usually found?

9 When **ber-** is added to a noun base, what is often the resulting meaning?

10 What is the effect of adding **me-** to a noun base?

10

Transport

In this unit you will learn how to
- *buy tickets for journeys*
- *talk about using various modes of transport*
- *use more time expressions*

PART ONE

Dialogue

Ken and his family would like to travel back to Jakarta from Bandung by plane. Ken approaches a taxi driver to take him to the travel agency.

CD2, TR 3, 0:03

Ken	Apa taksi ini pakai méter?
Supir	Ya, Pak.
Ken	Tolong antarkan saya ke Anta Travel di Jalan Supratman.
Supir	Kita sudah sampai, Pak. Apa mau saya tunggu?
Ken	Boléh, saya cuma sebentar, tapi dilarang parkir di sini.
Supir	Saya akan kembali 30 menit lagi.
Di biro perjalanan	
Ken	Saya mau pesan tempat duduk ke Jakarta.
Karyawan	Tikét sekali jalan atau tikét pulang pergi, Pak?

Ken	Tikét sekali jalan. Berapa ongkosnya dari Bandung ke Jakarta?
Karyawan	Kelas apa, Pak, ékonomi atau kelas bisnis?
Ken	Ekonomi saja.
Karyawan	Harganya untuk kelas ékonomi 200.000 rupiah. Untuk berapa orang?
Ken	Untuk empat orang. Apa juga ada tikét spésial yang murah?
Karyawan	Ya, kami ada tikét spésial, dengan masa berlaku satu bulan, tidak bisa mengganti tanggal ataupun rute jika sudah dikeluarkan.
Ken	Apa ada peraturan lainnya?
Karyawan	Ya, uang tidak kembali.
Ken	Berapa kali penerbangan ke Jakarta?
Karyawan	Tiga kali seminggu. Setiap Minggu, Senin dan Rabu.
Ken	Jam berapa saja?
Karyawan	Jam 4.30 dan jam 7.30.
Ken	Berapa jam penerbangan ke sana?
Karyawan	Cuma 45 menit.
Ken	Jam berapa saya harus ke bandara?
Karyawan	Satu jam sebelum keberangkatan.
Ken	Baik. Tolong buatkan réservasi untuk empat orang untuk minggu depan.
Karyawan	Jangan lupa mengkonfirmasikan lagi tikét anda.
Ken	Pasti. Bisa saya minta duduk di dekat jendéla, jika memungkinkan.
Karyawan	Saya coba.
Ken	Terima kasih.

méter *meter*
antarkan saya ke… *take me to…*
sampai *to arrive*
kita sudah sampai *(here) we're there*
Apa mau saya tunggu? *Do you want me to wait?*
sebentar *a moment*
Saya cuma sebentar. *I'll only be a moment.*

dilarang (larang, v**)** *it is forbidden*
30 menit lagi *in 30 minutes*
pesan *to order, (here) to reserve, to book*
tempat duduk *a seat*
tikét sekali jalan *one-way ticket*
tikét pulang pergi *return ticket*
ongkos *cost*
Berapa ongkosnya? *How much is the fare?*
kelas *class*
ékonomi *economy*
bisnis *business*
Berapa orang? *How many persons?*
spésial *special*
masa *period*
berlaku *to be valid*
masa berlaku *validity*
uang tidak kembali *unrefundble*
rute *route*
sudah dikeluarkan *after (it is) issued*
peraturan *restriction, regulation*
tidak bisa diganti dengan uang *unrefundable*
Berapa kali? *How many times? How frequent?*
dua kali *twice*
sebelum *before*
keberangkatan (berangkat, v**)** *departure*
buatkan *to make (for someone)*
réservasi *reservation*
mengkonfirmasikan (konfirmasi, n**)** *to confirm*
Bisa saya minta… *May I have…*
jendéla *window*
duduk di dekat jendéla *a window seat*

TRANSLATION

Ken	Does this taxi use a meter?
Driver	Yes, Sir.
Ken	Please take me to Anta Travel on Supratman Street.
Driver	We're here, Sir. Do you want me to wait?
Ken	OK, I'll only be a moment, but it is forbidden to park here.
Driver	I'll come back in 30 minutes.
Ken	I would like to book a seat to Jakarta.
Employee	A one-way ticket or a return, Sir?
Ken	A one-way ticket. How much is the fare from Bandung to Jakarta?
Employee	What class, Sir, economy or business?
Ken	Just economy.
Employee	The price for economy class is 200,000 rupiah. For how many people?
Ken	For four people. Is there a special cheap ticket?
Employee	Yes we have a special ticket, that is valid for one month, you can't change the date or re-route once (it is) issued.
Ken	Are there any other restrictions?
Employee	Yes, it is unrefundable.
Ken	How frequent is the flight to Jakarta?
Employee	Three times a week. Every Sunday, Monday and Wednesday.
Ken	At what time?
Employee	At 4.30 and at 7.30.
Ken	How many hours is the flight going there?
Employee	Just 45 minutes.
Ken	At what time should I be at the airport?
Employee	One hour before departure.
Ken	OK, please make a reservation for four people next week.
Employee	Don't forget to reconfirm your ticket.
Ken	Sure. Can I reserve a seat by a window, if possible?
Employee	I'll try.

How the language works 1

1 When asking about the cost of travel, it is normal to use the word **ongkos** which means *expenses* or *fare* rather than **harga** which means *price*. So **Berapa ongkosnya?** means *What's the fare?*

Berapa ongkosnya ke Dénpasar?	*What's the fare to Denpasar?*

EXERCISE 1

How would you ask:

a What the fare is to Medan?
b What the fare is from Kupang to Dili?

2 A key phrase to use when asking for anything is **Bisa saya minta...** *May I have...?*

Bisa saya minta tikét pulang pergi?	*May I have a return ticket?*

Two other useful phrases to use when asking for services occur in the dialogue:

Tolong, antarkan saya ke...	*Please take me to...*
Tolong, buatkan saya...	*Please make/do for me...*

Insight

The verbs **antar** (*to take*) and **buat** (*to make*) can both have **-kan** attached to them with the specific meaning of *to do something* **for** *someone*. This will be covered later in the course in more detail so, for now, just notice the verb forms and learn them as set expressions. Notice also that **tolong**, *please*, should be placed before the request as it is polite to do so in Indonesian.

3 Dilarang + verb is used to state that something is forbidden. You will come across it regularly in official signs telling you not to do something:

**DILARANG MELONCAT
DI KOLAM RENANG!**

*DON'T JUMP INTO THE
SWIMMING POOL!*

meloncat *to jump*
kolam renang *swimming pool*

Insight

Meloncat implies a jump in an upward direction; to jump across something is **melompat**.

What do you think this sign means?

pintu *door, gate*

DILARANG
PARKIR DI
DEPAN PINTU

4 Berapa jam? Jam means *hour* and **Berapa jam?** means *How many hours?*

Berapa jam ke Bandung?   *How many hours to Bandung?*

Insight

Do not confuse this with **Jam berapa?**, *What time is it?*

EXERCISE 2

Which question would you ask to get the following answers?

a Jam lima soré.
b Kira-kira dua jam.

5 You have already come across **lagi** meaning *further* or *more* with verbs in Unit 6. With periods of time, it has another important and distinct meaning: it translates *in a certain period of time* where that means *after a certain period of time has passed*. For example:

Saya beritahu kamu sepuluh menit lagi.	*I'll let you know in ten minutes.*
Meréka akan pulang dari pesiar keliling dunia dua bulan lagi.	*They will come back from their world cruise in two months.*

QUICK VOCAB

beritahu *to let (someone) know*
pesiar *cruise*
keliling *around*
dunia *world*
pesiar keliling dunia *world tour*

EXERCISE 3

Form the following time periods:

a in seven months
b in 55 minutes
c in three weeks

English also uses *in* to refer to the time it takes to complete an action, as in *I will complete this exercise in ten minutes*, in other words *It will take me ten minutes to complete this exercise*. Indonesian does <u>not</u> use **lagi** to convey this meaning. In this situation, **dalam waktu** translates *in*:

Saya akan menyelesaikan latihan ini *dalam waktu* sepuluh menit.	*I will complete this exercise in ten minutes. (within the space of ten minutes)*

QV

menyelesaikan (selesai, v) *to finish*
latihan *exercise*

6 Durations of time such as **hari, minggu, bulan** etc. take the prefix **se-** with the specific meaning of *a* as in *once a month* etc.:

minggu *week*	**seminggu** *a week*
Berapa kali seminggu?	*How many times a week?*

bulan *month*
Pulau ini menerima *This island receives 4,000 visitors*
  4.000 turis sebulan.   *a month.*

sebulan *a month*

menerima (terima *v.***)** *to receive, to accept*

EXERCISE 4

Prefix these time expressions with **se-** then make the phrases that follow:

hari   *day*
tahun   *year*
abad   *century*

a twice a year
b three times a day
c once a century

sekali *once*

7 If and when... To make a question with *when?* you already know that you must use **kapan?** In English we also use *when* in sentences where it is not a question such as **When** *I was young I used to eat ice cream* or *Remember to give her this book* **when** *you see her.* You cannot use **kapan** in this type of sentence. When translating *when* you must think whether you are talking about an event in the future or the past.

To express *when* in the past in Indonesian, **waktu** or **ketika** is used. **Waktu** is used more in the spoken language while **ketika** tends to be more used in written language. This usage often corresponds to *while* in English, as in *while I was waiting for the bus...*:

Dia datang ke rumah saya *waktu*   *He came to my house* **when**
  saya sedang menonton TV.   *I was watching TV.*
Ketika **kakaknya menikah, dia di**   *When her brother got married,*
  London.   *she was in London.*
Ibu menélpon saya *ketika* **saya**   *Mother called me when I was*
  sedang makan.   *eating.*

To express *when* in the future, you must use **kalau** or **jika**, both of which also mean *if*:

Tolong beritahu kami *kalau* **sudah sampai.**

Please tell us **when** *we get there.*

Jika **saya lulus ujian, saya akan buat pésta.**

If *I pass the exams, I will have a party.*

Kalau **saya jutawan, saya akan sumbangkan ke orang miskin.**

When *I become a millionaire, I will give charity to the poor.*

lulus *to pass (an exam)*
jutawan *millionaire*
sumbangkan (sumbang, v.) *to give charity*

Insight

A word needs to be said about the tense structure in sentences such as the last one. As **kalau** and **jika** have two meanings (*when* and *if*) this sentence could also *mean If I were a millionaire, I would give charity to the poor.* Note that in *if* sentences of this type, **akan** still needs to be included where it replaces *would* in English.

Understanding Indonesian

EXERCISE 5

Read or listen to the dialogue again and say whether the following statements are true or false.

a Taksi yang ingin Ken naik tidak pakai méter.
b Supir taksi bersedia menunggu Ken.
c Ken dan keluarga membeli tikét kelas bisnis.
d Ken membeli 5 tikét.

e Ken dan keluarga harus tiba di lapangan terbang satu jam sebelum keberangkatan.

f Ken meminta tempat duduk di gang.

bersedia (sedia, *a***)** *to be ready to, to be willing to*
lapangan terbang *airport*
terbang *to fly*
meminta (minta, *v.***)** *to ask for, to request*
gang *aisle*

QUICK VOCAB

EXERCISE 6

The following expressions refer to things you are being told not to do. Look at the signs and write the number of the expression next to the corresponding sign.

a **b** **c** **d**

e **f** **g** **h**

i Dilarang mendahului
ii Dilarang masuk
iii Dilarang bélok kiri
iv Dilarang balik arah

v Dilarang membuang sampah
vi Dilarang parkir
vii Dilarang merokok
viii Dilarang berhenti

mendahului (dahulu, *v***)** *to pass, to overtake*
balik arah *U turn*
membuang (buang, *v***)** *to throw*
sampah *litter, garbage*

QV

PART TWO

Dialogue

Mark and Reza are planning to go to Yogya by train. They are discussing how to get to the railway station.

Mark	Naik apa kita ke stasiun?
Reza	Kita naik angkot saja.
Mark	Di mana kita bisa menunggunya?
Reza	Ada halte di depan gedung itu.
Mark	Tiap berapa menit angkot itu léwat?
Reza	Lima menit.
Mark	Angkot yang mana ke stasiun?
Reza	Angkot nomor 45.
Mark	Apa angkot yang itu?
Reza	Bukan, yang berwarna coklat. Itu dia angkot-nya.

*(On the **angkot**.)*

Mark	Kita sedang di mana sekarang? Tolong beritahu saya kalau sudah sampai.
Reza	Kita ada di Jalan Sudirman 15 menit lagi kita sampai.
Mark	Lihat! Ada kecelakaan.
Reza	Pantas saja macet luar biasa.

*(To the conductor **(kenék)**.)*

Reza	Berhenti, Pak. Kami mau turun di sini. Awas, Mark, hati-hati!

(At the railway station.)

Reza	Ayo, Mark, cepat! Kita ke lokét itu. Kami mau beli tikét keréta ke Yogya. Berapa ongkosnya?
Pegawai	Harganya 100.000 rupiah.
Mark	Berapa lama perjalanannya?
Pegawai	Enam jam. Keréta yang jam berapa?
Reza	Yang jam empat soré.
Mark	Dimana kami harus ganti keréta?
Pegawai	Keréta ini langsung ke Yogya.
Mark	Bisa kami minta tempat duduk di dekat jendéla.

Pegawai	Maaf, sudah terisi.
Mark	Apa nama stasiun di Yogya?
Pegawai	Namanya Stasiun Yogya.
Reza	Baik. Saya senang, semuanya sudah berés.
Pegawai	Jangan sampai ketinggalan keréta, Bu.

stasiun *station*
Naik apa kita ke…? *How do we get to…? (What mode of transport do we take to…?)*
halte *bus stop*
tiap *every*
Tiap berapa menit angkot itu léwat? *Every how many minutes does that angkot pass?*
berapa menit? *how many minutes?*
léwat *pass, to go past*
yang mana? *which (one)?*
nomor *number*
angkot yang berwarna coklat *the brown-coloured angkot*
berwarna (warna, n) *to be coloured*
coklat *brown, chocolate*
Itu dia. *It's that one.*
beritahu *to let (someone) know*
Lihat! *Look!*
kecelakaan (celaka, a) *accident*
Pantas! *It's no wonder!*
macet luar biasa *the traffic is worse than usual*
luar biasa *out of the ordinary*
turun *to get off, get out of (a vehicle)*
Ayo! *Come on!*
Cepat! *Hurry up!*
lokét *ticket window*
keréta *train*
sudah terisi *already taken, already occupied*
terisi (isi, v) *to be occupied*
berés *sorted out*
ketinggalan (tinggal, v) *to miss*
Jangan sampai ketinggalan keréta *Don't miss the train*

TRANSLATION

Mark	How do we get to the station?
Reza	We take the *angkot*, of course.
Mark	Where can we wait for it?
Reza	There is a bus stop in front of that building.
Mark	Every how many minutes does that *angkot* pass?
Reza	(Every) five minutes.
Mark	Which *angkot* goes to the station?
Reza	*Angkot* number 45.
Mark	Is it that *angkot*?
Reza	No, the brown-coloured one. That is the *angkot* there.
Mark	Where are we now? Please let me know when we get there.
Reza	We are on Sudirman Street. Within 15 minutes we will get there.
Mark	Look! There has been an accident.
Reza	It's no wonder there is a big traffic jam.
Reza	Stop. We want to get off here. Watch out, Mark. Be careful!
Reza	Come on, Mark. Hurry up! Let's go to the ticket window.
	We would like to buy a train ticket to Yogya. How much is it?
Employee	It is 100,000 rupiah.
Mark	How long is the journey?
Employee	Six hours. The train at which time?
Reza	At four in the afternoon.
Mark	Where do we have to change trains?
Employee	The (this) train is direct to Yogya.
Mark	Can we have a seat near the window?

Employee	Sorry, they're already occupied.
Mark	What's the name of the station in Yogya?
Employee	It's called Yogya Station.
Reza	OK. I'm happy (that) everything's sorted out.
Employee	Don't miss the train, Madam.

How the language works 2

1 Naik apa ke..., *How shall we go to...* The most common way to express going by some form of transport is by using the verb **naik** + vehicle word.

naik mobil	*to go by car*
naik keréta api	*to go by train*

Some words for vehicles you have not yet met are:

bis	*bus*
motor	*motorbike*
bécak	*pedicab*
bajaj (*pronounced* **bajai**)	*bajai*
bémo	*motorized pedicab*
kapal laut	*ship*
kapal terbang	*plane*
sépeda	*bicycle*

Insight

Kapal terbang is literally *a flying vessel* (**kapal** meaning *vessel*), i.e. *a plane.* You have already met the other word for *plane*, **pesawat**.

Naik is the most common way to say how you are going somewhere, although you can also express it using **dengan**, where we use *by* in English. So you can say, for example:

| Meréka suka pergi ke sana dengan bis. | They like going there by bus. |
| Pagi ini ayah saya datang dari pasar dengan mobil. | This morning my father came from the market by car. |

pasar *market*

In theory, you can add the prefix **ber-** to any form of transport, thus creating a verb meaning *to go by* that mode of transport. So **naik keréta api** would become **berkeréta api**. In practice, however, only two of these forms are common in colloquial language: **berkuda**, *to go by horse*, and **bersepéda**, *to go by bike*, which is very common. For all other forms of transport it is more natural to use **naik**:

| Ratna bersepéda ke universitas setiap hari. | Ratna cycles to university every day. |

Finally, *to go on foot* is expressed by **berjalan kaki** (**jalan kaki**) in Indonesian:

| Mari kita jalan kaki ke bioskop. | Let's walk to the cinema. |

2 The last question word you will meet in this course is **yang mana** meaning *which*. It can be used on its own to ask *Which one?* or it can be used to mean *which* + noun in which case it *follows* the noun it refers to, like an adjective.

EXERCISE 7

Can you now say:

a which bag?
b which idea?

The important thing to note when using **yang mana** is that it is asking about a choice, given a set of alternatives. It differs in usage from noun + **apa** (see Unit 6) which asks about the *type* of something.

Look at these two examples:

Film apa yang kamu tonton?   *What films do you watch?*
                                    (i.e. what kind of films)
Film yang mana yang kamu   *Which film do you like?* (given that
  suka?   you have a choice of two or more)

3 Prefix **me-** with suffix **-i**. Verbs with **me- -i** are created from noun, adjective, adverb and verb bases:

tahu	*to know*	**mengetahui**	*to comprehend*
cinta	*love*	**mencintai**	*to love*
kurang	*less*	**mengurangi**	*to reduce*
paham	*understanding*	**memahami**	*to understand*

Most of these verbs imply an action towards someone or something or a closing of distance between two things. These verbs always take an object. For example:

naik	*to go up*	**menaiki**	*to climb*
dahulu	*previous*	**mendahului**	*to overtake*
dekat	*close*	**mendekati**	*to draw close to*

Using Indonesian

EXERCISE 8

Choose words and phrases from the dialogues in this unit to complete the following:

a Bis _____ ke pusat kota?
b _____ duduk di dekat pintu keluar?

c _____ reservasi untuk dua orang ke Lombok!

d _____ saya ke Jalan Sudirman.

e _____ ongkosnya dari Surabaya ke Bali?

f _____ penerbangannya?

g Jangan sampai_____ pesawat!

h _____ kita ke Bandung?

QV **pintu keluar** exit

EXERCISE 9

Over to you!

You (**A**) are a student called Daniel Johnson. You have gone to the travel agent (**B**) to book a flight to Melbourne.

CD2, TR 3, 3:54

A	_I would like to book a seat to Melbourne. Economy class._
B	Untuk tanggal berapa?
A	_Next week (on) the 15th September. What's the fare?_
B	350 dolar untuk tikét pulang pergi.
A	_How long is the flight to Melbourne from Jakarta?_
B	Sekitar tiga jam.
A	_Good, please make a reservation for me under the name of Daniel Johnson. Can I have an aisle seat?_
B	Saya coba.

QV **duduk di dekat gang** an aisle seat

Getting around

Public transport in Indonesia comes in all shapes and sizes. Apart from trains, you can take buses from city to city. Some of these have air conditioning and some do not. Safety standards and regulations may not be what you are used to in your own country. Buses allow people to pile on, even though there is seemingly no room. In addition to buses, much smaller vehicles, known as **angkot** (short for **angkutan kota**, *city transport*), also follow set routes.

Probably the safest transport for a foreigner to take is a taxi that uses a meter. Other taxis, as well as **bajaj** (little more than a motorbike with a cab behind for passengers) or a **bécak** (a motorless pedicab) or a **bémo** (a motorized **bécak** – **bécak motor**) are also available, as are motorbikes which you hire with a driver and ride behind him! You will have to agree a price in advance with these private forms of transport. Interestingly, if you need to direct a **bécak** driver (**tukang bécak**), or if he needs to confirm the direction you want him to go in, he will use points of the compass rather than *left* and *right*! The points of the compass are: **utara**, *north*, **selatan**, *south*, **timur**, *east*, and **barat**, *west*.

Bajaj   Bécak

As of 1989, **bécak** were no longer permitted to be used on the main roads of Jakarta owing to increasing congestion. In fact, such is the congestion caused by people commuting in the mornings that some roads have been decreed a *Three in one area* between 7 and 10 a.m. This means that cars using these roads must have at least three passengers in them to be able to use the road. These zones are indicated by the sign **KAWASAN THREE IN ONE**, an interesting mix of English and Indonesian!

With Jakarta being as congested as it is, punctuality is not always possible, even with the best will in the world, so it is lucky that Indonesians recognize the concept they call **jam karét** or *rubber time*. It is not considered rude to arrive for an appointment up to an hour late. If you are doing business in Indonesia it is worth bearing this concept in mind to avoid any cultural misunderstandings.

TEST YOURSELF

1 Which word is usually used to talk about fares?

2 How would you say *May I have?* in Indonesian?

3 What should you do if you see a sign with **Dilarang** on it?

4 What does **lagi** mean with time expressions?

5 What is the difference in usage between **lagi** and **dalam waktu**?

6 What does **se-** mean when added to a time word such as **hari**?

7 How do you express *when* to refer to both past and future events?

8 What is the most common way to express *to go* by some form of transport?

9 What prefix can also be used to express *to go* by some form of transport?

10 What does **yang mana** mean?

11

Checking in

In this unit you will learn how to
- *get rooms in a hotel*
- *ask about services*
- *say what you usually do*

PART ONE

Dialogue

Ken and his family have arrived at Ciater, a hot spring and health resort outside Bandung. They have not made a reservation, so Ken is trying to negotiate rooms for his family.

CD2, TR 4, 0:02

Ken	Selamat siang. Apa masih ada kamar kosong?
Pegawai	Sebentar… Ya, masih Pak, untuk berapa kamar?
Ken	Dua. Satu twin bed dan satu double bed untuk saya dan isteri.
Pegawai	Untuk berapa malam?
Ken	Saya belum tahu berapa lama saya menginap di sini.
Pegawai	Baiklah, saya akan tuliskan untuk satu malam dulu.
Ken	Berapa harganya untuk satu malam?
Pegawai	Untuk harga standar 250.000 rupiah.

Ken	Apakah sudah termasuk sarapan pagi?
Pegawai	Betul.
Ken	Apa bisa kasih kamar yang berhubungan satu sama lain, supaya kami bisa mengawasi anak-anak. Apa juga bisa minta kamar yang menghadap ke gunung?
Pegawai	Tentu. Bagaimana dengan pembayaran, Pak, dengan kartu krédit atau kontan?
Ken	Kartu krédit. Bisa kami lihat dulu kamarnya?
Pegawai	Pasti. Tolong diisi formulir ini, Pak. Nama, alamat, nomor paspor dan tanda tangan.
Ken	Baik. Fasilitas apa saja yang ada di sini?
Pegawai	Kolam renang umum dengan air panas buka 24 jam.
Ken	Bagus sekali. Kami sekeluarga biasanya pergi berenang setiap Minggu. Apa ada karaoké? Anak perempuan saya suka menyanyi.
Pegawai	Ya. Setiap malam. Selain itu kami juga menyediakan bufé khusus masakan Sunda setiap malam Sabtu.
Ken	Apa ada yang lain? Seperti pijat? Setiap kali saya ke Indonesia, saya selalu pergi ke panti pijat.
Pegawai	Ada, Pak. Silahkan télpon ke consierge*, dan meréka akan menyiapkan untuk Bapak. Ini kunci kamarnya dan kupon untuk sarapan pagi dari jam 8 sampai 10.30. Selamat beristirahat.

Insight

Consierge is pronounced like *concierge* in French.

kosong *empty*
kamar *room*
kamar kosong *vacancies*
berapa malam *how many nights*
menginap (inap, v) *to stay, to spend the night*
tuliskan (tulis, v) *to write down* (here) *to book* (someone) *in*
Berapa harga untuk satu malam? *How much for one night?*
standar *standard*
sarapan pagi *breakfast*

kamar yang berhubungan satu sama lain *connecting room(s)*
ber hubungan (hubung *a) to be in contact with*
supaya *so that*
mengawasi (awas, *v) to watch over*
menghadap ke (hadap, *v) to face*
pembayaran (bayar, *v) payment*
Bagaimana dengan pembayaran? *How do you want to pay?*
kontan *cash*
diisi (isi, *v) to be filled*
Tolong diisi *Please fill in*
formulir *form*
nomor paspor *passport number*
tanda tangan *signature*
fasilitas *facility*
umum *public*
buka *open*
karaoké *karaoke*
menyediakan (sedia, *v) to provide*
masakan (masak *v.) cuisine, cooking*
pijat *massage*
panti pijat *massage parlour*
menyiapkan (siap, *a) to prepare*
kupon *coupon*
Selamat beristirahat *Have a nice stay*

Insight

Twin bed, double bed? These obviously aren't Indonesian words, but they are in standard use in hotels, to the extent that the Indonesian equivalents would actually seem unnatural. This course unswervingly teaches you Indonesian as it is spoken today, so… note also, unsurprisingly, **single bed!**

TRANSLATION

Ken	Good afternoon. Do you (still) have vacancies?
Employee	Wait a moment... Yes, we do, how many rooms (do you need)?
Ken	Two, one two-bed room and one double room for my wife and me.
Employee	For how many nights?
Ken	I don't know yet how long I will stay here.
Employee	OK, I will book you in for just one night.
Ken	How much is it for one night?
Employee	The standard price is 250,000.
Ken	Is breakfast also included?
Employee	Of course.
Ken	Can you give (us) connecting rooms, so that we can watch over our children. Can you give (us) a view of the mountains?
Employee	Certainly. How would you like to pay, Sir, with credit card or cash?
Ken	Credit card. Can we see the room beforehand?
Employee	Sure. Please fill in this form, Sir. Name, address, passport number and signature.
Ken	OK. What facilities do you have here?
Employee	(We have) a public swimming pool from the hot spring, open 24 hours.
Ken	That's great. My family and I usually go swimming every Sunday. Is there karaoke? My young daughter likes to sing.
Employee	Yes. Every evening. Apart from that we can also provide a buffet of special Sundanese cuisine every Saturday evening.
Ken	Is there anything else, like massage? Every time I (come) to Indonesia, I always go to a massage parlour.
Employee	Yes, there is. Please telephone the concierge and they can arrange (it) for you. These are the keys to the rooms and the coupon for breakfast from 8 to 10.30. Have a nice stay.

How the language works 1

1 Did you notice the use of **minta** in the dialogue? Two more phrases you might find useful when making requests are **Apa bisa minta?**, *May I have...?* and **Apa bisa kasih?**, *May I have...?*

Apa bisa kasih kamar yang menghadap ke kolam renang?

Can I have a room that looks out onto the swimming pool?

Insight

Menghadap ke is also used to express *with a view of* in Indonesian.

---

2 Position of question words. Units 1 to 10 have gradually introduced you to all the question words you will need to know to function in everyday Indonesian. You will have noticed that some question words occur in various positions in the sentence, while others, namely **kenapa** and **mengapa** must *always* occur as the first word in the sentence. **Apa** is also an exception, as you will see.

Although it is quite possible to place the other question words first in the sentence, there is a rule governing where the question word should occur, if you want to mimic authentic Indonesian speech.

To find where the question word should be placed, you first need to think of the question as it would be if it were a statement that already has the answer to the question in it. For example, if you want to ask *Where does she come from?*, one possible answer is *She comes from New York*; in Indonesian **Dia berasal dari New York**. The question word occupies the same position in the question as the thing it asks about in the corresponding statement. Therefore **dari mana** replaces **dari New York** giving you the completed question, **Dia berasal dari mana?**

Look at the following questions:

Siapa **pergi ke London?**　　**Who** *is going to London?*
Yanti pergi *ke mana?*　　　**Where** *is Yanti going?*

These two questions could both be based on the sentence *Yanti* **pergi** *ke London*, *Yanti is going to London*. The first question asks *who* so **siapa** replaces Yanti. The second asks *where* Yanti is going, so **ke mana** replaces **ke London**.

EXERCISE 1

Make four questions in the following sentence based on the underlined and lettered words:

Tahun lalu	Tuti	berlibur	dengan sepupunya	di Lombok.
a	**b**		**c**	**d**

Possible complications arise with **apa** because, as you know from Unit 2, **apa** not only means *what?*, but it also functions as a question marker. As a question marker **apa** *must* occur at the beginning of the sentence.

When you are using **apa** with the intended meaning of *what?*, you need to follow the positioning rules we have just seen, otherwise what you say might be ambiguous. Look at the following examples in which **apa** has different functions:

Apa **anda minum?**　　　*Are you drinking?*
Anda minum *apa?*　　　*What are you drinking?*
Apa **kamu sedang makan?**　*Are you eating?*
Kamu sedang makan *apa?*　*What are you eating?*

Two questions that you learnt in Unit 6 **apa yang** and **siapa yang** are always used at the beginning of the sentence and are exceptional to the rules of question word order. Many questions asking *what?* or *who(m)?* can be expressed both ways:

Dia kenal *siapa?*   *Who(m) does she know?*
Siapa **yang dia kenal?** *Who(m) does she know?*

In addition, when noun + **apa** occurs, as in Unit 6, it is treated as a single unit and is not subject to the positioning rules.

EXERCISE 2

Translate the following pairs of questions paying particular attention to how the different position of **apa** affects the meaning.

1 a Apa dia makan?
 b Dia makan apa?

2 a Apa mau pesan?
 b Mau pesan apa?

3 a Apa kamu membaca?
 b Kamu membaca apa?

_____

Understanding Indonesian

EXERCISE 3

Using the dialogue, say whether the following questions are true or false.

a Hotel Ciater masih mempunyai kamar yang kosong.
b Harga hotél belum termasuk sarapan pagi.
c Ken membayar dengan uang tunai.
d Kolam umum air panas buka 24 jam.
e Ken meminta kamar yang menghadap ke pantai.
f Sarapan pagi mulai dari jam tujuh sampai jam 10.30.

EXERCISE 4

Read and fill in the following form. Try to work out what the form is asking before checking with the vocabulary section beneath it. Some words you already know have been included again to help you fill in the form.

```
Nama ..............................................................................
Alamat ............................................................................
Tanggal lahir ...................................................................
Tempat lahir ....................................................................
Umur ..............................................................................
Jenis kelamin ...................................................................
Status perkawinan ............................................................
Kebangsaan .....................................................................
Agama ............................................................................
Pekerjaan ........................................................................
Nomor paspor ..................................................................
Maksud kunjungan ...........................................................
Lama tinggal ....................................................................
Tanda tangan ...................................................................
```

alamat *address*
tanggal lahir *date of birth*
tempat lahir *place of birth*
jenis kelamin *sex*
pria *male*
wanita *female*
status perkawinan *marital status*
belum kawin *not married*
kawin *married*
cerai *divorced*
janda *widow*
duda *widower*
maksud *purpose, intention*
maksud kunjungan *reason for visit*
bisnis *business*
liburan *holiday, vacation*

kunjungan keluarga *visiting relatives*
belajar *study*
lama tinggal *length of stay*
tanda tangan *signature*

PART TWO

Dialogue

Reza and Mark are checking in to a hotel at which they have already booked rooms by telephone.

CD2, TR 4, 2:10

Mark	Selamat soré, kami mau cék-in atas nama Mark Spencer dan Reza Septianingrum yang kami pesan kemarin.
Pegawai	Tunggu sebentar. Saya periksa di komputer. Betul sekali, dua single. Atas nama Bapak Mark Spencer dan Ibu Reza Septianingrum.
Mark	Terima kasih. Apa di sini ada pusat kebugaran? Saya biasanya senam setiap soré.
Pegawai	Ada, juga kolam renang, sauna dan mandi uap.
Mark	Menarik sekali. Saya biasanya bangun jam delapan pagi. Lalu kita berenang, sauna dan sarapan pagi.
Reza	Rencana yang bagus. Apa yang bisa kita lakukan di malam hari?
Pegawai	Di sini ada bar dan diskotik. Setiap Minggu ada band khusus dengan penyanyi ibu kota.
Mark	Saya di Inggeris biasanya setiap minggu ke bar.
Reza	Saya bisa lihat, kamu sudah tidak sabar untuk ke sana.
Mark	(tertawa) Bagaimana dengan makanan? Saya sudah lapar sekali.
Pegawai	Malam ini ada bufé masakan Indonesia. Buka dari jam delapan malam.
Mark	Terima kasih.
Pegawai	Ini kuncinya dan kupon sarapan pagi untuk bésok. Selamat istirahat.

cék-in *check in*
atas nama *under the name(s) of*
tunggu sebentar *just a moment*
periksa *to check*
betul sekali *quite right*
pusat kebugaran (hugar a) *fitness centre*
senam *aerobics, to do aerobics*
sauna *sauna*
uap *steam vapour*
mandi uap *steam bath*
ibu kota *capital city*
di malam hari *in the evening*
sabar patient *patience*
tidak sabar untuk *cannot wait to*
bar *bar*
lapar *hungry*
bufé *buffet*
istirahat *stay*

Insight

Note the expression **di malam hari** *in the evening*, literally 'in the eve of the day'. Note also **di eiang hari, di soré hari** and **di pagi hari**, depending on the timeframes discussed in Unit 1.

TRANSLATION

Mark	Good afternoon. We would like to check in under the names Mark Spencer and Reza Septianingrum. We (were the ones who) reserved yesterday.
Employee	Wait a moment... I will check on the computer. That's correct, two single rooms under the name Mark Spencer and Reza Septianingrum.
Reza	Thank you. Is there a fitness centre here? I usually go to the gym every afternoon.
Employee	There is, also there is a swimming pool, sauna and steam bath.
	(Contd)

Mark	Very interesting. I usually get up at eight o'clock. Then we go swimming, take a sauna and have breakfast.
Reza	That's good planning. Well done. What can we do here in the evening?
Employee	There is a bar and disco. Every Sunday night there is a special band with a singer from the city.
Mark	In England I am used to going to the bar every week.
Reza	I can tell, you cannot wait to go there.
Mark	What about the food? I'm really hungry.
Employee	Tonight there is an Indonesian buffet. It's open from eight o'clock in the evening.
Mark	Thank you.
Employee	Here are the keys and these are the breakfast coupons for tomorrow. Have a nice stay.

How the language works 2

1 In this unit you have met **biasanya** which means *usually*. The base word **biasa** and a prefixed form **terbiasa** are both used to mean *used to* or *accustomed to*:

Saya biasa berbahasa Indonesia   *I am used to speaking Indonesian*
  dengan teman-teman.   *with friends.*
Adik Tuti sudah terbiasa   *Tuti's little brother is already used*
  menggunakan komputer.   *to using a computer.*

When **biasa** and **terbiasa** are used with verbs, as in the examples, they can be used just as they are. When they are used with a noun, **dengan** must be inserted:

Dia belum biasa *dengan*   *He is not yet used to the heat in*
  kepanasan di Indonesia.   *Indonesia.*

kepanasan (panas, *a*) *heat*

Remember that where *used to* has a different meaning, such as that in the sentence *We used to live here*, either the tense marker **dulu** or **dahulu** must be used.

Dahulu kami tinggal di sini.   *We used to live here.*

Insight
Dahulu sounds very formal in speech; **dulu** is more natural in normal conversation.

2 The combination of the prefix **ke-** and the suffix **-an**, when attached to an adjective base, produces a certain type of noun:

baik	*good*	ke-**baik**-an = **kebaikan**	*goodness*
indah	*beautiful*	ke-**indah**-an = **keindahan**	*beauty*
sulit	*difficult*	ke-**sulit**-an = **kesulitan**	*difficulty*

Insight
This usage creates what is known as an abstract noun, that is, a noun that usually refers to a general quality or concept, not something concrete like people, animals or material objects.

EXERCISE 4

Form abstract nouns from the following adjectives with **ke- -an** and, in each case, state what you think the noun you created means.

a séhat *healthy*
b aman *safe*
c bersih *clean*
d mudah *easy*
e jelék *ugly*
f nyaman *pleasant*
g bodoh *stupid*
h senang *happy*

Ke- prefix combined with **-an** suffix is used to create certain nouns from verbs:

datang	*to come*	**kedatangan**	*arrival*
pulang	*to return home*	**kepulangan**	*return*

Ke- -an with a noun base produces a new noun which often extends the meaning of the base noun, but the resulting meaning is not always as easy to deduce as with the adjective bases. They can often refer to places or institutions. Study the following:

hidup	*life*	**kehidupan**	*way of life*
bangsa	*nation*	**kebangsaan**	*nationality*
menteri	*minister*	**kementerian**	*ministry*
duta	*ambassador*	**kedutaan**	*embassy*

Using Indonesian

EXERCISE 5

Use the sentences that follow to make a question replacing the words in bold in each case.

a Meréka akan berangkat ke Inggeris **pada hari Selasa**.
b Yanti pergi **ke bioskop** dengan Siti.
c Pagelaran Ramayana mulai **jam delapan**.
d Penerbangan dari Jakarta ke Bali **sekitar dua jam**.
e **Minggu depan** meréka akan pergi berlibur ke Medan.
f Orang tuanya sudah datang **dari luar negeri**.
g Kita bisa pergi **dengan bis** ke pusat kota.
h Keréta Jakarta-Surabaya ada **dua kali** sehari.

pagelaran (gelar, *v*) *performance*
sehari *a day, per day*

EXERCISE 6

Over to you!

You are booking a room …

A	Selamat soré, Pak. Ada yang bisa saya bantu?
B	*Yes. I would like to stay here for a couple of days. Are there still vacancies?*
A	Masih.
B	*How much for one night?*
A	450.000 rupiah.
B	*Is breakfast included?*
A	Ya. Sampai tanggal berapa Bapak tinggal di sini?
B	*Until the 10th December. Can I pay with another currency apart from US dollars?*
A	Bisa. Maaf, bisa saya lihat paspornya, Pak?
B	*Sure. Just a moment.*
A	Tolong isi formulir ini dan tanda tangan Bapak di sebelah kanan.
B	*OK. Is there a sauna here?*
A	Ada, juga kolam renang di lantai tiga. Pusat kebugaran ada di sampingnya.
B	*What time is it open?*
A	Jam sembilan pagi sampai jam 8.30 malam.
B	*Thank you.*
A	Selamat istirahat. Ini kunci kamar dan kupon untuk sarapan pagi.

Where to stay

In the towns, cities and major tourist areas such as Bali, you can find plenty of luxury hotels that can cater to your every need. If you are looking for a more authentic experience, or if you would like to sample Indonesian hospitality, there are several options open to you. You could try a **wisma** which is an Indonesian-style hotel but quite comfortable. If you want something more homely, then a **losmén** is what you seek. A **losmén** tends to be family run and, more often than not, you will find yourself eating meals with the family too, more like a paying guest than a client. Finally, if you are on a very tight budget, you could try a **penginapan**, *inn*, which provides all the very basic comforts but little else.

If you do go off the beaten track and are contemplating staying in a remote village or town, it is considered polite to consult with the village head (**kepala désa** or **lurah**) and ask for permission. Your manners and sensitivity will mark you as a person who has respect for the local culture and will endear the villagers to you.

If you ever have to make a complaint about anything while you are in Indonesia you may feel that your complaint is being brushed aside by the one you are addressing. He or she may appear to make light of your problem by saying something like **Tidak apa-apa**, *It's OK*, **Tidak ada masalah**, *It's not a problem*, **Biar saja**, *Let it be*, or something similar. Although this may appear, at face value, to be an indication of disinterest to a westerner, it is not to be taken as one. Different cultures deal with a potentially awkward situation, such as making a complaint, in different ways. Preferring the indirect approach, Indonesians tend to hide their embarrassment behind such an attitude as these phrases imply, but this does not mean that they do not take your complaints seriously. Furthermore, in any dealings you have with Indonesians, you should avoid an outward display of anger as this is regarded as childish and will almost certainly result in your wishes being ignored.

TEST YOURSELF

1 How would you make a polite request in Indonesian?

2 What does **menghadap ke** mean?

3 How do you work out the correct position of a question word within a sentence?

4 Which question word do you need to be particularly careful with in order to avoid ambiguity?

5 How would you express *to be accustomed to* in Indonesian?

6 What do you need to add to the above expression when a noun follows it?

7 What effect do the prefix **ke-** and suffix **-an** have on adjectives?

8 What effect does **ke- -an** have on certain verbs?

9 What effect does **ke- -an** have when attached to a noun?

10 What should you be aware of when making a complaint in Indonesia?

12

Beautiful batik

In this unit you will learn how to
- *go shopping for clothes*
- *talk about sizes, colours, and what things are made of*
- *barter with a street seller*

PART ONE

Dialogue

Jamilah is doing a spot of clothes shopping with her two children.

CD2, TR 5, 0:03

Ibu Jamilah	Saya mau membelikan suami saya keméja batik. Apa ada ukuran yang paling besar, warna biru?
Pelayan	Sebentar saya cari… Maaf Bu, Warna biru sudah habis terjual. Tinggal warna abu-abu. Warna biru ukuran S.
Ibu Jamilah	Itu kekecilan untuk suami saya. Dia tidak suka warna abu-abu. Ada yang lain?
Pelayan	Ya tetapi bahannya berbéda.
Ibu Jamilah	Mengapa ini lebih murah daripada yang tadi?
Pelayan	Oh, karena itu batik asli dan ini batik cap.
Ibu Jamilah	Hm… saya lebih suka yang itu. Sayang! Tidak ada warna biru.

Calvin	Ma, aku suka celana batik itu. Kelihatan nyaman dan coraknya unik.
Ibu Jamilah	Itu terbuat dari bahan katun. Apa ukuranmu?
Calvin	M, sebesar itu saja.
Ibu Jamilah	Celana itu cocok sekali untuk kamu. Silvia, kamu mau apa?
Silvia	Aku mau baju yang berwarna mérah itu.
Ibu Jamilah	Terlalu seksi untuk mu. Pilih yang lain saja!
Pelayan	Ini bonnya. Silahkan bayar di kasir.
Ibu Jamilah	Terima kasih.
Pelayan	Untuk celana panjang 15 persén diskon. Totalnya 825.000 rupiah. Ini uang kembalinya.

membelikan (beli, v) to buy (something for someone)
ukuran size
paling besar the biggest
warna colour
biru blue
keméja shirt
ma mum, mom
batik batik
habis (here) completely
terjual (here) sold out
tinggal there remains
abu-abu grey
kekecilan too small
bahan material
berbéda different
lebih murah cheaper
daripada than
tadi the last one, the one before
asli original
cap printed
lebih suka prefer
Sayang! What a shame!
aku I
celana trousers
corak pattern, design

terbuat dari *made from*
bahan katun *cotton*
sebesar itu *as big as these, (here) the same as these*
cocok untuk *to suit (someone)*
baju *dress*
baju yang berwarna mérah *a red-coloured dress*
séksi *sexy*
pilih *to choose*
bon *bill*
kasir *cashier*
celana panjang *(long) trousers*
persén *per cent*
diskon *discount*
total *total*
uang kembali *change*

TRANSLATION

Jamilah	I want to buy a batik shirt for my husband. Do you have the biggest size in blue?
Shop assistant	Just a moment, I'll look for (one). We're right out of the blue one. We only have grey left. We (only) have the blue (one) in a 'small'.
Jamilah	It is too small for my husband. He doesn't like grey. Are there any other ones?
Shop assistant	Yes, but they are a different material.
Jamilah	Why are these cheaper than the last ones?
Shop assistant	Oh, because those are genuine batik and these are printed batik.
Jamilah	I prefer those. What a shame! You don't have them in blue.
Calvin	Mum, I like those batik trousers. They look comfortable and the design is special.
Jamilah	They are made from cotton. What's your size?
Calvin	Medium, the same size as those (trousers).
Jamilah	Those trousers really suit you. Silvia, what do you want?
Silvia	I want that red dress.

Jamilah	It's too sexy for you. Choose a different one.
Shop assistant	Here is your bill. Please pay at the cashier.
Jamilah	Thank you.
Shop assistant	There is a 15% discount on these trousers. All together that comes to 825.000 rupiah. Here is your change.

How the language works 1

1 Terlalu, which you have already met briefly in Unit 11, is one way of saying *too* in Indonesian. It is used in the same way we use *too* in English:

terlalu besar *too big*
terlalu kecil *too small*

In addition to **terlalu** certain nouns can also be modified to mean *too* by placing the adjective between the prefix **ke-** and the suffix **-an.** Here are some you may find useful when shopping:

kebesaran *too big*
kekecilan *too small*
kemahalan *too expensive*
kepéndékan *too short*
kepanjangan *too long*

EXERCISE 1

Make *too…* expressions using **ke- -an** with these adjectives, then translate them.

a dingin
b panas
c penuh
d asin
e cepat
f tinggi

dingin *cold*
asin *salty*

2 Making comparisons. When you wish to compare the qualities
of one thing with another, i.e. when you want to say something
is *more... than something else*, use **lebih** before the adjective or
adverb:

lebih **mahal**	*more expensive*
lebih **murah**	*more cheap* (or *cheaper*)
Pakaian itu *lebih* **mahal di**	*These clothes are more expensive*
Amérika.	*in America.*

To express *than* as in *more... than* **daripada** is used:

lebih **mahal** *daripada*	**more** *expensive* **than**
lebih **murah** *daripada*	**more** *cheap* **than** (or *cheaper* **than**)
Batik di Yogya *lebih* **murah**	*Batik in Yogya is cheaper than*
daripada **di Jakarta.**	*in Jakarta.*
Dia datang *lebih* **sering**	*He comes more often than before.*
daripada **sebelumnya.**	

sebelumnya *formerly, previously*

EXERCISE 2

Add the missing words to the Indonesian sentences so that the
meaning corresponds to the ones in English.

a *Amir goes to the cinema more often than Jani.*
  Amir pergi ke bioskop _____ sering _____ Jani.
b *She is more diligent than her brother.*
  Dia _____ rajin _____ kakaknya.
c *This house is bigger than that house.*
  Rumah ini _____ besar _____ rumah itu.

One way to express the *most...* or *the... -est*, as in *the biggest* is
formed by placing **paling** before the adjective instead of **lebih**.

Compare:

besar *big*   *lebih* **besar** *bigger*   *paling* **besar** *biggest*
énak   *tasty*   *lebih* **énak** *tastier*   *paling* **énak** *tastiest*

EXERCISE 3

How do you form these expressions in Indonesian?

a better
b the cheapest
c the most difficult
d prettier
e more crowded
f spicier
g thirstiest
h hotter
i dirtier
j the smallest

Adding **paling** to an adjective is not the only way to express *the most…* in Indonesian. The alternative form you need to be aware of is formed with the prefix **ter-** which is attached to the adjective to form exactly the same meaning as **paling**.

baik   *good*   *ter* **baik** → **terbaik**   *the best*
besar   *big*   *ter* **besar** → **terbesar**   *the biggest*
bodoh *stupid*   *ter* **bodoh** → **terbodoh** *the most stupid*

3 To say what something is made of, **terbuat dari** (or just **dari**) is used in Indonesian:

Cincin ini terbuat dari pérak.   *This ring is made of silver.*
Kué ini terbuat dari tepung beras.   *This cake is made from rice flour.*
Jakét saya terbuat dari kulit.   *My jacket is leather.*

pérak *silver*
tepung beras *rice flour*
kulit *leather*

EXERCISE 4

Can you form these sentences in Indonesian?

a That statue is made of marble.
b This vase is made of clay.
c This ball is made of rubber.

patung *statue*	**tanah liat** *clay*
marmer *marble*	**bola** *ball*
jambang *vase*	**karét** *rubber*

4 The last personal pronoun we shall be looking at in this course is **aku**, an informal word for *I* which Silvia and Calvin use in the dialogue. It is highly informal and should only be used between family members or to those with whom you are on very familiar terms (i.e. good friends) and with whom you share equal social standing. It would be highly inappropriate to use this when talking to a stranger. In fact, it might be taken as a sign of arrogance or lack of respect for someone if you use it inappropriately. You may hear it used, so you need to know what it means, but the best advice for a foreigner is: if in doubt, use **saya!**

It can also be used as a possessive pronoun whereby it is added to the noun in question as a suffix, like **-mu** in Unit 2. Before it is added to the noun, the **a** drops, leaving you with **-ku** which means *my*:

rumahku   *my house*
mobilku   *my car*

5 There are two ways to express *to wear* in Indonesian. One way employs the verb **pakai** (or less colloquially **memakai**) which means *to use* as well as *to wear*.

Gadis itu memakai pakaian tradisional.

That girl is wearing traditional dress.

Saya biasa pakai sarung di rumah.

I'm used to wearing a sarong at home

sarung *sarong*

The second way uses the **ber-** prefix to create a verb from the item of clothing being worn. In just the same way as the noun becomes the base for the transport words in Unit 10 (Part Two), the item of clothing becomes the base in this instance:

baju	*dress*
berbaju	*to wear a dress*
kebaya	*kebaya*
berkebaya sutera	*to wear a silk kebaya*

sutera *silk*

Insight

A **kebaya** is a traditional, ceremonial outfit for women that is worn with batik and a **seléndang**, a long scarf that is draped over one shoulder. The first of the four illustrations in Unit 3, Forms of address section shows a lady wearing one.

EXERCISE 5

Select words from the clothes vocabulary section beneath this exercise.

a to wear a tie
b to wear gloves
c to wear a skirt
d to wear a raincoat
e to wear black trousers
f to wear sunglasses
g to wear a rattan hat

Colours and Clothes
topi *hat*
keméja *shirt*
dasi *tie*
jakét *jacket*

rok *skirt*
celana (panjang) *(long) trousers*
celana péndék *short trousers*
blus *blouse*
jas *suit*
jas hujan *raincoat*
kacamata gelap *sunglasses*
sarung tangan *glove(s)*
kaos kaki *sock(s), stocking(s)*
sepatu *shoe(s)*
sepasang sepatu *a pair of shoes*
ikat pinggang *belt*
gelang *bracelet*
anting-anting *earrings*
kalung *necklace*
rotan *rattan*
mérah *red*
putih *white*
hitam *black*
hijau *green*
kuning *yellow*
biru *blue*
ungu *purple*
marun *maroon*
mérah jambu *pink*
coklat *brown*

Insight

Anting-anting refers to *dangle earrings*, whereas *stud-type earrings* are **giwang**.

Colours can be made *light* or *dark* by adding **muda** and **tua** respectively:

biru muda *light blue*
hijau muda *light green*
coklat tua *dark brown*
mérah tua *dark red*

> **Insight**
>
> This is a figurative use of **muda** and **tua**, which you already know mean *young* and *old*, respectively.

6 To express *to suit (someone or something)* Indonesian uses **cocok untuk**:

Keméja itu cocok sekali untuk adikmu.   *That shirt really suits your brother.*

Note that the Indonesian version requires **untuk**, *for*. Such words are known as *prepositions*. Although prepositions are basically location words *on, in, around* etc., they often occur as an integral part of certain set phrases. In some cases, a preposition may be required in one language but not in the other to express a similar concept, as with **cocok untuk**, and sometimes the preposition is different in each language. For example, in English we say *to spend money on something*, but the Indonesian equivalent uses **untuk** – **menghabiskan uang untuk**:

Kamu sungguh-sungguh sudah menghabiskan semua uangmu untuk pakaian?   *Did you really spend all your money on clothes?*

sungguh-sungguh *really*
menghabiskan (habis, a) *to spend (money or time)*

7 The prefix **ter-** used with verbs can sometimes creates a form that is similar to a past participle in English. The *past participle* is the form that you can place after *to be* to indicate that something has happened, for example *I am lost*. The emphasis in using the **ter-** verbs in Indonesian is on the state of completedness of an action. Treat them like adjectives:

terkenal *famous*
tersedia *available*
tertarik *interested*

Some **ter-** prefixed verbs can also imply an accidental occurrence or a misfortune:

terpaksa *forced (to), obliged (to)*
tersesat *lost*
terjebak *stuck*

Understanding Indonesian

EXERCISE 6

Answer the following true/false questions based on the dialogue.

a Jamilah ingin membelikan celana batik untuk suaminya.
b Jamilah mencari ukuran paling besar, warna abu-abu.
c Silvia membeli baju warna mérah yang séksi.
d Batik asli harganya lebih mahal dari harga batik cap.
e Calvin memilih celana batik yang nyaman dan unik.
f Pelayan memberi diskon 15% untuk semua belanjaan.

memilih (pilih, *v*) *to choose*
belanjaan (belanja, *n*) *purchases, items purchased*

EXERCISE 7

Label the pictures using the clothes vocabulary in Exercise 5.

PART TWO

Dialogue

Reza has taken Mark to a traditional market so he can look for presents to take back to England.

Mark	Saya mau mencari oléh-oléh untuk teman dan keluarga saya. Kalung ini bagus sekali. Terbuat dari apa?
Penjual	Ini dari pérak.
Mark	Berapa harganya?
Penjual	50.000 rupiah.
Reza	Kamu bisa tawar. Ini bukan harga pas.
Mark	Bisa kurangi harganya? 30.000 rupiah?
Penjual	Tidak bisa, Mas. Saya rugi.
Reza	35.000 saja Pak. Kalau boléh.
Penjual	Boléhlah. Rugi sedikit tidak apa-apa asal mbak datang lagi kapan-kapan. Mau beli berapa buah?
Mark	Saya beli tiga buah.
Reza	Mark, kenapa kamu beli yang itu? Yang ini lebih mengkilap.
Mark	Tidak apa-apa. Cuma untuk oléh-oléh.
Penjual	Itu harganya lebih mahal, karena pérak asli dan buatan tangan.
Mark	Apa ini?
Reza	Itu kain sarung. Kamu bisa pakai di rumah pengganti celana panjang. Itu biasa di sini.
Mark	Saya mau beli satu.
Penjual	Saya juga ada kipas dari batik. Bisa dipakai untuk hiasan dinding.
Mark	Ya, tapi ukurannya besar sekali dan berat. Lain kali saja. Terima kasih.

oléh-oléh *souvenirs*
kalung *necklace*
tawar *to bargain, haggle*
harga pas *fixed price*
kurangi (kurang) *to reduce*
Bisa kurangi harganya? *Can you lower the price?*
rugi *lose out*
asal *as long as, provided that*
kapan-kapan *sometimes*
Berapa buah?* *(here) How many?*
tiga buah* *(here) three (of them)*
mengkilap (kilap, v) *to shine*
buatan tangan *hand made*
kain sarung *sarong*
pengganti (ganti, v) *instead of*
Itu biasa di sini. *It's usual here.*
dipakai (pakai, v) *to be used*
bisa dipakai *it can be used*
pengganti *instead of*
kipas *fan*
hiasan *decoration*
dinding *wall*
lain kali *another time*

Insight

Buah has a special meaning that will be discussed in Unit 14.

TRANSLATION

Mark	I want to look for some presents for my friends and family. This necklace is very beautiful. What's it made of?
Seller	Silver.
Mark	How much is it?
Seller	50,000 rupiah.
Reza	You can haggle. The price isn't fixed.
Mark	Can you lower the price? 30,000 rupiah?
Seller	I can't. I'll make a loss.

Reza	Just 35,000. If you can.
Seller	OK. I'll make a small loss, as long as you come again sometimes. How many do you want?
Mark	I want three.
Reza	Mark, why did you buy those? This one's more shiny.
Mark	It's OK. (They're) just for presents.
Seller	Those are more expensive because they are made from real silver and they are hand made.
Mark	What's this?
Reza	That's a sarong. You can wear it at home instead of trousers. It's usual here.
Mark	I want to buy one.
Seller	I also have a batik fan. You can use it as a wall decoration.
Mark	Yes, but it's too big and heavy. Another time, maybe. Thank you.

How the language works 2

1 Comparisons of equality. Indonesian has two ways of saying something is *as... as* something else, for example, *She is **as rich as** her brother*.

Add **se-** to the adjective that describes the quality you are comparing:

kaya *rich*
Dia se**kaya kakaknya.**
mahal *expensive*
Kalung ini semahal gelang itu.

*se-**kaya** → **sekaya** as rich as*
She is as rich as her brother.
*se-**mahal** → **semahal** as expensive as*
This necklace is as expensive as that bracelet.

gelang *bracelet*

EXERCISE 8

Form these comparisons:

a as cheap as
b as heavy as
c as shy as

Use the construction **sama** *adjective* **-nya dengan**:

kaya *rich*
Dia *sama* **kayanya** *dengan*
  kakaknya.

sama kayanya dengan *as rich as*
She is as rich as her brother.

mahal *expensive*

sama mahalnya dengan *as*
  expensive as

Kalung *sama* **mahalnya** *dengan*
  gelang itu.

This necklace is as expensive as
  that bracelet.

> **Insight**
> **Sama dengan** on its own means *the same as*. So you can say,
> for example: **Rumah dia** *sama dengan* **rumah kita**, *His house*
> *is the same as our house.*

EXERCISE 9

Check you can form the following using the **sama** *adjective* **-nya**
dengan construction:

a as poor as
b as bald as
c as flirtatious as

botak *bald*
genit *flirtatious, coquettish*

> **Insight**
> The word **genit** is common in Indonesia but doesn't have the
> same negative connotations as it does in English.

As we have seen **sama dengan** in Indonesian means *the same as* in English. As you know **dengan** means *with*, so Indonesians think of it as *the same with*. The word **dengan** features in several very common expressions where we use other prepositions, or no preposition, in English. It is worth learning the following list now, noting the difference between the two languages.

sama *dengan*	*the same **as***
berbéda *dengan*	*different **from***
penuh *dengan*	*full **of***
kawin *dengan*	*to get married **to***
dengan **télpon**	***by** phone*
dengan **mobil**	***by** car*
dengan **bis**	***by** bus*
bercakap *dengan*	*to chat **to***
berbicara *dengan*	*to talk **to***
kenal *dengan*	*to know*
berteman *dengan*	*to be friends **with***

Examples:

Saya akan menghubungi dia dengan télpon.	*I'm going to contact her by phone.*
Ruangan itu penuh dengan asap rokok.	*That room is full of smoke.*
Meskipun harganya sama, kualitas tas ini berbéda dengan tas itu.	*Although the price is the same, the quality of this bag is different from that bag.*

menghubungi (hubung, *v***)** *to contact*
ruangan (ruang, *n***)** *room*
asap rokok *cigarette smoke*
asap *smoke, fumes*
meskipun *although*
kualitas *quality*

2 Me- prefix with -kan suffix. Some base words carry the prefix **me-** coupled with the suffix **-kan**. In many cases this combination is simply needed to create a verb from a noun base with no particular distinct meaning.

For example:

merencana**kan**   *to make plans (from **rencana**, plans)*
menggambar**kan**   *to portray (from **gambar**, picture)*

When **me- -kan** is attached to certain adjectives, the result is a verb in Indonesian that corresponds to an *-ing* adjective in English. For example:

*me**lelah**kan*   tiring (formed from the adjective base **lelah**
        meaning *tired*)

Insight

As **me- -kan** often creates a verb that indicates that something has been caused to be in a certain state, the thinking is – it makes me (or someone else) tired, so it is *tiring*.

EXERCISE 10

Can you work out what the following **me- -kan** verbs are in English, by looking at the base adjectives on the left?

a **malu** *embarrassed* **memalukan**
b **senang** *pleased* **menyenangkan**
c **puas** *satisfied* **memuaskan**
d **cemas** *worried* **mencemaskan**
e **bosan** *bored* **membosankan**
f **takut** *frightened* **menakutkan**

When **me- -kan** is attached to a verb base, a new verb is created that can have one of two basic meanings according to context. The first is a type of verb that we do not have in English. This type of verb stresses that the action is performed for the benefit of someone or something else which is why it is known as a *benefactive* verb. You can see an example of such a verb in the first dialogue – **membelikan**, *to buy something for someone*.

Saya memberikan dia bunga. *I gave him a flower.*

As benefactive verbs automatically carry the meaning of doing something for someone **untuk**, *for* is not required. However, it is not incorrect to use **untuk** with these verbs and many Indonesian speakers do!

Saya mau membelikan sesuatu *I want to buy something for*
  untuk teman.   *a friend.*

me- -kan creates a new verb from certain verb bases that changes the focus of the action from something that you do yourself into a related verb. You will notice that these base verbs are specifically those which have no receiver of the action. Therefore the **me- -kan** creates a related verb that allows you to do that action to something or someone else.

In English, too, we have verbs that perform both functions. You can say *I returned* or you can use the same verb in a different way with a receiver of the action and say *I returned the book to the library*. Although the form of such verbs is often the same in English, Indonesian needs to create a further verb around the original verb as a base with **me- -kan**.

Take the example with **kembali**, *to return*. You can say:

Saya kembali. *I returned.*

To make the other form, **me-** and **-kan** are added to the base word **kembali** creating **meng*embali*kan** (sound change rules will be covered later in the course). The new verb means *to return (something)*:

Saya mengembalikan buku itu ke *I returned the book to the public*
  perpustakaan umum.   *library.*
Dia sudah mengeluarkan sampah. *She's already put the trash out.*

···
Insight
> **Mengeluarkan**, *to put something out*, comes from the verb **keluar**, *to go out*.
···

Using Indonesian

EXERCISE 11

Answer these questions using the corresponding pictures as a guide:

a Yang mana lebih tinggi, jerapah atau kuda?

b Yang mana lebih cepat, kapal terbang atau keréta api?

c Siapa yang lebih muda, Budi atau Iwan?

d Yang mana lebih luas, Pulau Kalimantan atau Pulau Sumatra?

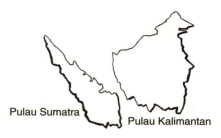

Pulau Sumatra

Pulau Kalimantan

Arab Saudi 45°

Malaysia 32°

e Yang mana lebih panas,
Malaysia atau Arab Saudi?

jerapah *giraffe*
kuda *horse*

EXERCISE 12

This exercise takes the form of a short general knowledge quiz
to test your geography as well as your Indonesian! See if you
can answer the questions.

a Negara apa yang paling luas di dunia?
b Benua apa yang paling besar di dunia?
c Negara apa yang paling padat penduduknya di dunia?
d Sungai apa yang paling panjang di dunia?
e Gunung apa yang paling tinggi di Indonesia?

negara *country*
benua *continent*
padat *dense*
padat penduduknya *densely populated*

EXERCISE 13

Choose suitable phrases to complete the Indonesian sentences so that they mean the same as the English ones.

a Pantai Kuta di Bali _____turis setiap hari.
Kuta Beach in Bali is full of tourists every day.

b Minggu depan Santi akan _____ pengusaha muda di hotél Sahid Jaya.
Next week Santi will get married to a young businessman at the Sahid Jaya Hotel.

c Saya melihat dia sedang _____ pimpinannya di kantor.
I see her talking to her boss in the office.

d Cara berjalannya _____ ibunya.
The way she walks is the same as her mother.

e Karena jalannya berbatu kami harus pergi _____.
Because of the stone road we have to go by jeep.

f Apakah kamu _____tetangga baru itu?
Do you know that new neighbour?

g Saya _____nasi goréng untuk sarapan pagi.
I am used to fried rice for breakfast.

h Dia suka musik klasik semenjak _____Syariffudin.
She likes classical music since she has become friends with Syariffudin.

QUICK VOCAB

pimpinan (pimpin, v) *boss*
cara berjalan *way of walking, gait*
berbatu (batu, n) *stoned, built with stones*
klasik *classical*
semenjak *since*

EXERCISE 14

Look at the pictures. Complete the sentences that refer to each one and answer all the questions in each section.

a Saya mau membeli ___

Terbuat dari apa ____ itu? ____

BAMBU
RP 65.000

BATIK
24
150.000 RP

b Saya mau membeli ____ ____.

Berapa harganya? ____ ____
Apa ukurannya? ____

c Saya mencari ____

Terbuat dari apa? ____

PERAK
RP 100.000

d Saya mau mencari ____

Berapa harganya? ____ ____
Terbuat dari apa? ____

WAYANG
KAYU
RP 75.000

pérak silver
bambu bamboo

EXERCISE 15

Over to you!

You (**A**) are shopping for a present for your elder brother. You approach the sales assistant (**B**) for help.

A	*I want to buy something for my elder brother.*
B	Di sini ada topi, dasi dan keméja.
A	*What's this tie made of?*
B	Dari batik sutera.
A	*How much is it?*
B	80 ribu rupiah.
A	*Is the price fixed?*
B	Ya. Tetapi ada diskon 10 %.
A	*OK. I'll take two which have different designs.*

ambil to take
motif design, pattern
yang motifnya berbéda which have different designs

About batik

If you are interested in the arts and crafts traditions of Indonesia, then you will certainly find the **batik** work of Central Java a delight! The word **batik** is thought to come from the Javanese word **ambatik** which means *drawing* or *writing*. Yogyakarta and Solo are the traditional homes of Indonesian batik where the craft has been honed to a fine art over the centuries.

In the traditional batik-making process, wax is applied to the cloth by hand, with a tool called a **canting**, or by using a copper stamp, known as a **cap**. When the wax becomes hard, the cloth is dyed, dried and the waxing/dying process is repeated with a different colour. The wax renders certain areas of the cloth resistent to the dyes which only colour the exposed areas.

Batik that has been entirely produced in the traditional way, by a master-artisan using a **canting** can take months to complete depending on the intricacy of the pattern being created. For this reason, an item made from genuine **batik tulis** (literally *written batik*) can cost the equivalent of several hundred pounds. If you are shopping for the genuine article, and you want to be sure that you are not being offered imitation batik at a vastly inflated price, here is a tip that might help: Genuine **batik tulis** has exactly the same pattern on both sides of the material so if it is not fully reversible, it is definitely not genuine. If it is reversible there's a good chance that it is.

Printed batik is exquisite, nonetheless, and the range of different batik products available means that you will never be at a loss for something authentic and unusual to take back as a souvenir or present from your trip. In major cities you will find shops devoted entirely to batik goods, where you can buy sarongs, fans, wall hangings, traditional clothing and much more. If you can bear to tear yourself away from the beaches of Bali and Lombok, a visit to the batik factories of Java would be well worth the ride.

Learning tip

If you have Indonesian friends, have you noticed any recurring mistakes they make when speaking English? When people learn a new language they sometimes try to fit the foreign language into the pattern of their own language, especially in areas of the foreign language that they have not yet mastered. For example, in this unit we have looked at some common expressions where the preposition is different in both languages, such as **kawin dengan** where Indonesians say *to get married **with*** rather than *get married **to*** which we use in English. Such an error does not impede the goal of communication, as you can easily see what the speaker means; however, it is even better to get it perfect! Such clues can help you to improve your Indonesian and, indeed help your friends improve their English! If you notice recurring differences such as an Indonesian saying *the same **with*** where he or she should say *the same **as*** check in your textbook or a dictionary to see why this is happening, as the answer could be a fundamental difference between the two languages and knowing about it can help you to improve your command of Indonesian, even if it is only in a small way.

TEST YOURSELF

1 What are the two ways to say *too (big*, etc.) in Indonesian?

2 How would you express *more...than* in Indonesian?

3 How would you express *the most...* or *the ...-est*?

4 What does **terbuat daripada** mean?

5 What happens to **aku** when added to a noun to show possession?

6 What are the two ways to express *to wear* in Indonesian?

7 What prefix often expresses an accidental occurrence?

8 In which two ways does Indonesian form comparisons of equality?

9 What effect do the prefix **me-** and suffix **-kan** have on certain adjectives?

10 What is a benefactive verb, and how do you form one?

13

Eating out

In this unit you will learn how to
- *understand an Indonesian menu*
- *order food in restaurants and from street vendors*

PART ONE

Dialogue

Ken and his family are having dinner in a restaurant in Jakarta.

CD2, TR 6, 0:02

Pelayan	Selamat malam, untuk berapa orang, Pak.
Ken	Untuk empat orang.
Pelayan	Silahkan, ini daftar makanannya. Mau pesan apa?
Ibu Jamilah	Saya mau pesan soto ayam, gado-gado, capcai, saté kambing dan ayam goréng Kalasan.
Ken	Tolong jangan pakai saos kacang, saya alérgi kalau makan kacang.
Pelayan	Baiklah. Sotonya berapa porsi?
Ibu Jamilah	Satu porsi. Hm... berapa banyak satu porsi?
Pelayan	Bisa untuk berdua. Ada lagi yang mau dipesan?
Ken	Apa di sini punya makanan khusus? Bisa anda rékoméndasi?
Pelayan	Ya. Ikan bakar dengan saos tiram.
Ken	Apa itu pedas?

Pelayan	Kami bisa buatkan yang tidak pedas. Mau pesan minuman apa?
Silvia	Saya mau és kelapa muda.
Calvin	Apa ada és campur?
Pelayan	Maaf kami tidak punya, tapi kami punya és kacang.
Calvin	Saya mau coba.
Ken	Untuk saya tolong segelas air putih tanpa és, dan saya juga mau pesan pencuci mulut és krim.
Ibu Jamilah	Berapa lama makanan itu siap?
Pelayan	Kira-kira 15–20 menit.
Ken	Tidak apa-apa. Terima kasih.
Pelayan	Maaf agak terlambat, kami sangat sibuk setiap malam Minggu.
Pelayan	Bagaimana makanannya, Bu?
Ibu Jamilah	Sotonya énak sekali, tapi saténya agak mentah.
Ken	Bisa tambah lagi segelas air. Saya kehausan.
Pelayan	Baik, Pak.
Ken	Bisa saya minta bonnya?
Pelayan	Ini bonnya.

daftar makanan *menu*
Mau pesan apa? *What would you like to order?*
ayam *chicken*
saté kambing *goat satay*
ayam goréng *fried chicken*
saos *sauce*
kacang *peanut*
saos kacang *peanut sauce*
alérgi *allergic*
porsi *portion*
Berapa porsi? *How many portions?*
dipesan (pesan v) *to be ordered*
Ada lagi yang mau dipesan? *Is there anything else you'd like to order?*
rékoméndasi *to recommend*
bakar *to grill, grilled*
tiram *oyster*

és *ice*
kelapa *coconut*
kelapa muda *young coconut*
campur *mix*
és campur *ice with mixed fruits and coconut milk*
és kacang *red beans with coconut milk and ice*
air putih *drinking water*
pencuci (cuci, v) *someone or something that washes*
mulut *mouth*
pencuci mulut *dessert (literally something to clean the palette)*
krim *cream*
és krim *ice cream*
siap *ready*
mentah *raw, undercooked*
tambah *extra amount*
Bisa tambah lagi ... *May I order some more ...*
kehausan (haus a) *very thirsty*
bon *bill, check*

Insight

Be careful with **pedas**. It means *hot* as in *spicy*, whereas **panas** means *hot to the touch*, and they can easily be confused when talking about food.

Translation

Waiter	Good evening, (a table) for how many, Sir?
Ken	(For) four people.
Waiter	Here's the menu. What would you like to order?
Jamilah	I would like (to order) chicken soto, gado-gado, capcai and goat satay, and fried chicken Kalasan.
Ken	Please don't use peanut sauce – I am allergic to peanuts.
Waiter	All right. How many portions of soto?
Jamilah	One portion. Hmm... how big is one portion?

Waiter	It's enough for two people. What else would you like to order?
Ken	Do you have a speciality? What can you recommend?
Waiter	Yes… grilled fish with oyster sauce.
Ken	Is it spicy?
Waiter	We can make it not spicy for you. What drinks would you like to order?
Silvia	I'd like young coconut ice.
Calvin	Do you have *és campur*?
Waiter	Sorry, we don't have (it here), but we do have *és kacang*.
Calvin	I want to try (it).
Ken	Can I have a glass of water without ice, and I would like to order dessert – ice cream.
Jamilah	How long before it's ready?
Waiter	Around 15 to 20 minutes.
Ken	That's no problem. Thank you.
Waiter	Sorry it took so long. We are very busy every Sunday night.
Waiter	How was the food, Madam?
Jamilah	The soto is delicious but the satay is rather undercooked.
Ken	Could I have one more glass of water, please? I'm so thirsty.
Waiter	OK, Sir.
Ken	Could I have the bill, please?
Waiter	Here you are, Sir.

How the language works 1

1 To order food in a restaurant simply use the phrase **Saya mau pesan**, *I would like to order*, or **Bisa minta…** *Could I have…*, followed by the dishes you would like to order. Notice also the phrase **Bisa tambah lagi**, *Could I have some more…*:

Saya mau pesan satu porsi gado-gado.

I'd like (to order) a portion of gado-gado.

Bisa kami minta rendang daging dan nasi kuning untuk bertiga.   *Could we have beef rendang and nasi kuning for three.*

> ### Insight
> Notice the use of **berdua**, **bertiga** etc, when ordering portions of food for more than one person.

EXERCISE 1

Look at the list of Indonesian foods in 2, choose three things that appeal to you and make sentences using the phrases just seen once each.

2 Indonesian food – understanding the menu

bubur ayam	*rice porridge with tofu or chicken*
capcai	*vegetable stir-fry*
gado-gado	*vegetables with peanut sauce*
sayur asam	*vegetables in a sour sauce*
gudeg	*chicken, egg and jackfruit with coconut and herbs*
lodéh	*vegetables in coconut milk and herbs*
semur daging	*beef cooked in a sweet sauce*
rendang daging sapi	*beef cooked in coconut milk and spices*
rendang daging ayam	*chicken cooked in coconut milk and spices*

> ### Insight
> If you just ask for **rendang** it usually just refers to beef rendang.

gulai daging	*Indonesian-style beef curry*
gulai ayam	*Indonesian-style chicken curry*
saté	*meat grilled on a skewer served with peanut sauce and/or sweet soy sauce*
saté ayam	*chicken satay*
saté kambing	*goat satay*
saté babi	*pork satay*

saté daging	*beef satay*
bakso/baso	*noodles and meatballs in a broth*
bakmi/mie	*noodles*
kwétiau	*flat noodles*
nasi goréng	*fried rice*
nasi uduk	*steamed rice with coconut and herbs*
nasi kuning	*steamed rice with turmeric and herbs*
nasi rames/campur	*steamed rice with vegetables and fish*
nasi tumpeng	*a mixture of rice and sticky rice served in a cone shape*
soto	*soup, usually chicken*
pecel lélé	*catfish with chilli sauce*
sambal	*a type of salsa with chilli and shrimp paste*
pémpék	*fish cake in tamarind sauce*
telur dadar	*omelette*
telur mata sapi	*fried egg, sunny side up (**mata sapi** literally means bull's eye!)*
bala-bala	*fried vegetable with flour*
bubur kacang hijau	*mung bean porridge*
pukis	*a cake in the shape of a crescent*
tahu isi	*tofu with a vegetable filling*
rujak	*mixed fruit salad with a spicy sauce*
lumpia	*spring roll*
kelepon	*a green rice ball with a sweet centre*
biskit	*biscuit*
dodol	*a chewy sweet wrapped in a dried leaf*
putu	*steamed rice in a cylinder shape with brown sugar inside*
és kopyor	*coconut in fruit syrup and with fruit*
és kacang	*red beans with coconut milk and ice*
és kelapa	*young coconut pulp and ice*
és cendol	*rice jelly with coconut, sugar and ice*
és cincau	*cincau leaves, jelly and ice*
és jeruk	*citrus juice and ice*
és alpukat	*avocado, syrup and ice*
téh jahé	*ginger tea*
bubur ketan hitam	*sweet black rice and coconut milk*

Understanding Indonesian

EXERCISE 2

Read or listen to the dialogue in Part One and say whether the following statements are true or false.

a Jamilah alérgi dengan kacang.
b Ikan bakar dengan saos tiram, makanan spésial di restoran.
c Restoran tidak menyediakan és campur.
d Ken memesan és krim untuk pencuci mulut.
e Saté yang dipesan terlalu matang.
f Makanan siap dalam sepuluh menit.

alérgi dengan *allergic to*　　**terlalu matang** *over-cooked*
memesan (pesan *v***)** *to order*　　**matang** *cooked*

EXERCISE 3

◀) **CD2, TR 6, 2:00**

An Indonesian couple, Pak Agus and Ibu Ratih, are dining out in a traditional Indonesian restaurant in the countryside. Familiarize yourself with the menu that follows and with the words in the vocabulary section before you listen to the conversations in the restaurant.

Part 1: Listen to the dialogue, paying attention to what the couple order. Write **A** next to the items Pak Agus eats or drinks and **R** next to the items his wife, Ibu Ratih, eats or drinks.

Part 2: After you have listened enough times to understand the order, listen again and answer the questions.

Part 1

Daftar Makanan	Makanan Pencuci Mulut
Makanan Utama	*és kacang*
capcai	*és alpukat*
gado gado	*és kelapa*
semur daging	
rendang	**Minuman**
gulai	*air putih*
nasi goréng	*bir*
nasi kuning	*anggur mérah*
nasi rames	*anggur putih*
saté ayam	
saté kambing	
soto	
lumpia	
sambal	

Part 2

a Why does Pak Agus want to sit by the window?
b What does Ibu Ratih ask the waiter after she has eaten the chicken satay?
c How much does the bill come to?

makanan utama *main dishes*
méja *table*
pemandangan (pandang n) *view, scenery*
berseléra untuk *to have an appetite for*
seléra *appetite*
habis *run out of, finished*
lezat *delicious*
resép *recipe*
benar-benar *really*
yakin *sure, convinced*
kepingin *to long for*
Itu saja? *Is that it?*

QUICK VOCAB

Apa makanannya diberi...? *Does the meal come with...?*
terpisah (pisah *a) separate*
diberi terpisah *to be brought (i.e. ordered) separately*
sayang *(here) darling*
berubah (ubah *n.)* **pikiran** *to change one's mind*
merasakan (rasa, *n)* *to taste*
rahasia *secret*
koki *chef*
kenyang *full (of food)*

> ### Insight
> **Sayang!** can have two meanings in Indonesian, one meaning
> *What a shame!* and the other, as you'll hear in the conversation
> in the listening exercise, as a term of endearment.

PART TWO

Dialogue

Mark and Reza are enjoying the relaxed atmosphere at a **warung tenda**.

CD2, TR 6, 4:30

Reza	Ini tempat langganan saya.
Mark	Itu masakan apa?
Penjual	Itu namanya pémpék. Terbuat dari ikan dan tepung. Masakan spésial dari Palémbang.
Mark	Hm... Harum sekali, mengundang seléra.
Penjual	Mau pesan apa, Mas?
Mark	Itu nasi goréng?
Penjual	Betul, mie goréng atau mie rebus juga ada.
Mark	Saya mau pesan nasi goréng saja. Berapa harganya sepiring?
Penjual	4.500 rupiah.
Mark	Tolong jangan pakai vétsin.

Penjual	Néng, mau pesan apa?
Reza	Seperti biasa, saya mau kwétiau yang pedas dan siomay.
Mark	Kwétiau? Masakan itu apa isinya?
Reza	Itu mie goréng dicampur dengan makanan laut seperti cumi-cumi, udang dan sayur-sayuran.
Mark	Apa itu pakai telur?
Reza	Ya.
Penjual	Maaf, mau pesan minuman apa?
Mark	Coca-Cola pakai és.
(Then the food is ready.)	
Penjual	Ini pesanannya. Silahkan!
Mark	Bisa minta garpu sama séndok?
Reza	O, ini keasinan, bisa minta kécap manis?
Penjual	Boléh.
Reza	Terima kasih. Saya mau pesan satu lagi dibungkus untuk nénék saya? Tolong jangan pakai cabé.

langganan *customer*
tepung *flour*
harum *to smell nice*
mengundang (udang *v.***) seléra** *to make one's mouth water*
rebus *to boil*
mie rebus *boiled noodles*
vétsin *monosodium glutamate*
Makanan itu apa isinya? *What does it (this food) have in it?*
isi *contents*
telur *egg*
pesanan (pesan *v***)** *order*
Ini pesanannya. *Here is your order.*
garpu *fork*
sama *with, and*
séndok *spoon*
keasinan (asin, *a***)** *too salty*
kécap manis *sweet soya sauce*
dibungkus *to be put in a container, to take away*
cabé *chilli*

QUICK VOCAB

TRANSLATION

Reza	I'm a regular here.
Mark	What food is it?
Vendor	It's called *pémpék*. It's made from fish and flour. It's a speciality of Palembang.
Mark	Hm... It smells really nice, it makes my mouth water.
Vendor	What would you like to order, Sir?
Mark	Is that nasi goréng?
Vendor	Yes, there are also fried noodles and boiled noodles.
Mark	I would just like to order *nasi goréng*. How much is it per serving (plateful)?
Vendor	4,500 rupiah.
Mark	Please don't use monosodium glutamate.
Vendor	Miss, what would you like to order?
Reza	As usual, I would like a spicy *kwétiau* and *siomay*.
Mark	*Kwétiau?* What does it have in it?
Reza	It's fried noodles mixed with seafood like squid, shrimp and vegetables.
Mark	Is there egg in it?
Reza	Yes.
Vendor	Excuse me, would you like anything to drink?
Mark	Coca-Cola with ice.
Vendor	This is your order. Please (enjoy your food).
Mark	Can I have a fork and spoon?
Reza	Oh, it's too salty, can I have sweet sauce?
Vendor	Yes, of course.
Reza	Thank you. Can I order one more to take away for my grandma? Please don't use chilli.

Insight
While it originally refers to a thick, sweet soy sauce, the word **kécap** has been borrowed into English and now refers to the tomato sauce we all know as *ketchup!*

How the language works 2

1 In English we are used to talking about *a **packet** of cigarettes*, *a **bottle** of milk*. These are mostly words that count things or put them into a category based on the type of container the thing comes in. These are some you will find useful:

piring *plate*
mangkuk *bowl*
botol *bottle*
gelas *glass*
cangkir *cup*
kotak *box*
bungkus *packet, parcel*
potong *piece, slice*

When you talk about *one* of something or *a*, the counting word, if you are using one, should be prefixed with **se-**, for example:

sepiring kari   *a plate of curry*

However, when ordering food etc., you may also say:

satu piring kari   *one plate of curry* (as opposed to two, three etc., to make your order clear)

For any number of items above one, the counting word is used after the number, without the **se-**:

dua mangkuk soto   *two bowls of soup*

Generally speaking, if you are ordering a portion of some type of food, from a street vendor, for instance, you would do so according to what it comes in or on. **Nasi goreng** comes on a plate and **bakso** comes in a bowl, so you would use the appropriate counting word in your order. However, there is an even simpler option. You can use **porsi** which means *portion* and can be used to order anything.

| **Bisa saya minta satu porsi mie goréng?** | *Can I have a portion of fried noodles?* |

2 Sometimes the **ke-** prefix **-an** suffix combination occurs with adjectives, nouns and verbs creating an expression that means that something unplanned and, in particular, unpleasant, has happened. It is rather like the use of **ter-** mentioned in Unit 12. The following are very common, so learn them as set expressions:

QUICK VOCAB

ketinggalan *to miss (e.g., a form of transport)*
kesiangan *to oversleep*
kecopétan *to be pickpocketed*
kemalaman *to stop out at night* (with unpleasant results, e.g., missing the last bus home, getting home late with the prospect of being scolded)
kehujanan *to be caught in the rain*
kekenyangan *to over-eat (to the point of discomfort)*

The meaning of some **ke- -an** expressions have become idiomatic in use. Two that are appropriate to talking about food and drink are:

kelaparan   *to be famished, starving*
kehausan   *to be parched, really thirsty*

Using Indonesian

EXERCISE 4

Can you form the questions and expressions you might need in dealing with various street vendors?

A I would like to order *bakso*. How much for one bowl?
Not too hot.

B I would like to order tea.
How much for one bottle?
Please don't use ice.

C I would like to order *nasi goréng*. How much for one plate? Don't use eggs. To take away, please.

D I would like to order *saté kambing*. How much for one plate? Could I have it rare?

setengah matang *rare*

EXERCISE 5

Write a suitable **ke- -an** expression under each of the following pictures. You may need to create expressions from adjectives using what you learnt in Unit 12. There are sample answers in the key.

a

b

c

d

e

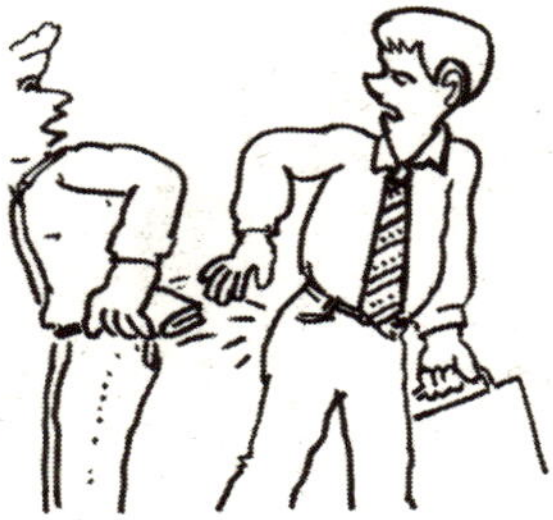

f

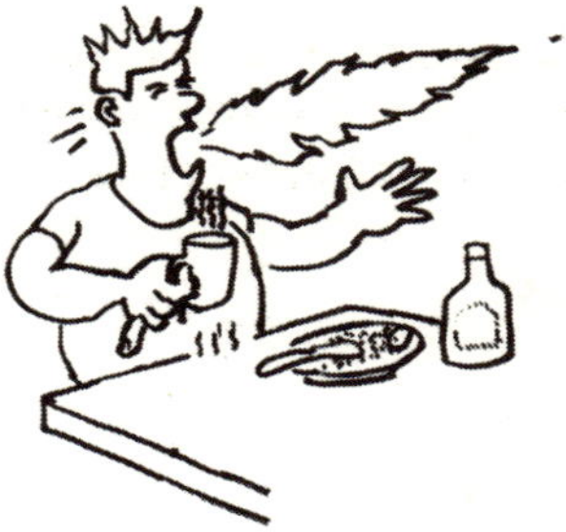

g

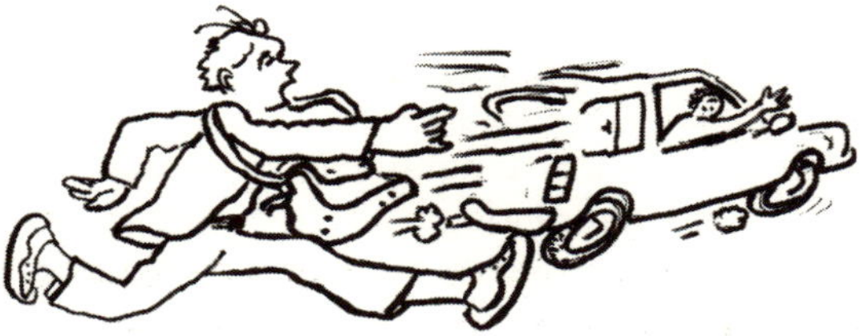

EXERCISE 6

Over to you!

You (**B**) are Ibu Tyler. You have decided to go to a restaurant for dinner. The waiter (**A**) greets you.

A Selamat siang, Bu. Untuk berapa orang?
B *For one person.*
A Ini daftar makanannya. Mau pesan makanan apa?
B *I would like to order mie goréng. Does it contain shrimp?*
A Ya, tapi kami bisa buatkan tanpa udang.
B *That's good. I am allergic to shrimp.*
A Mau pesan minuman apa?
B *Do you have és campur?*
A Ya.
B *I would like* és campur *without tapé.*
A Mau pesan apa lagi, Bu?

(Contd)

CD2, TR 6, 6:08

B *That's all. How long (before) the food's ready?*
A Sekitar 15 menit.
B *No problem. Thank you.*
A Silahkan menunggu sebentar.

mengandung (kandung, n) *to contain*
udang *prawn, shrimp*
tapé *fermented cassava*
Cukup itu saja. *That's all.*

> **Insight**
> The words **tanpa,** *without* and **tambah,** *add* are virtual
> opposites when it comes to ordering food. If you want
> something without a certain ingredient, be sure to be clear
> with your pronunciation.

Eating out – Indonesian style

If you like spicy food, then you will love Indonesian cuisine! Be
careful when you order 'extra hot' because your idea of what is
extra hot might be where Indonesian spiciness leaves off!

There are many ways to sample authentic Indonesian food. For
the more formal experience try a **rumah makan Padang**, *Padang
restaurant*. Rice is always served at Padang restaurants, but the
main feature is the variety of dishes you can try. Ten or so dishes of
the customer's choice are served in small portions, so you can try
many different types of cooking at one time. The plates are usually
expertly piled one on top of the other in the shop window so that
you can see what you can choose from. Indonesians may choose to
eat with their fingers, which is why there is often a bowl of water
and lemon present, to refresh their hands after eating. Eating in this
way is not compulsory, so if none is provided, do not hesitate to
ask for cutlery, if you need it!

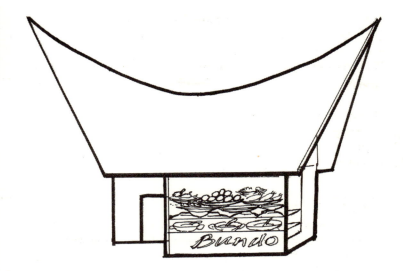

Rumah makan Padang.

A lot of food is sold on the street by vendors who wander the streets with their extremely narrow and compact mobile food stalls. They make their presence known in the area by banging on a pan or ringing a bell and announcing what they are selling. These vendors are quaintly known as **kaki lima**, *five legs*. The two wheels of the stall plus the stand make three 'legs' and the vendor's own make five! The vendor will serve you with the food and wait until you have finished it before moving on, as it tends to be served on real crockery rather than disposable plates.

You can also experience the Indonesian culinary atmosphere at a **warung ténda**, *tent shop*, also known as a **warung gaul**, *socializing shop*. These are open shops, usually with tables and some sort of makeshift tent (hence the name). Obviously they are static, unlike the wandering vendors, but the atmosphere is much less formal than a restaurant. Several vendors may operate at such a place, so you can sample a variety of foods. As the other name **warung gaul** implies, these shops are not just for eating but for socializing, so, not only will you get well fed there, you will have a genuine, local atmosphere to soak up and, hopefully, an opportunity to practise your Indonesian.

Indonesians are very fond of their snacks (**makanan ringan**) and eat them at breakfast time or when serving coffee or tea. Another word you might hear for snacks is **cemilan**. This is a native Javanese word that the Indonesians will be delighted to hear you using!

Although they are called **minuman,** many Indonesian drinks are more like desserts than drinks and are often served as such after meals: **és kacang,** and other drinks that are made with ice, are very refreshing in the hot climate.

Finally, a word on tipping! In big restaurants you are expected to tip, but only if a service charge (usually 10%) has not been applied to your bill. If no service charge has been applied, it is generally recommended to tip between 5 and 10% of the total bill. At small shops or street vendors, you are not expected to tip.

TEST YOURSELF

1 What two ways do you know to order food in Indonesian?

2 Which word means *hot* as in *spicy*, **pedas** or **panas**?

3 What expression would you use to order some more of something?

4 What word could you use when ordering for five people?

5 If unspecified, what would you expect to receive if you asked for **daging**?

6 What two ways could you use to order a plate of something?

7 How do you know which counting word to use when you order something?

8 What effect can the **ke- -an** combination have on meaning?

9 What other way do you know of to express this?

10 What's a Javanese word for *snacks*?

14

At the supermarket

In this unit you will learn how to
- *shop for food at a shop or supermarket*
- *understand an Indonesian recipe*

PART ONE

Dialogue

Jamilah and her two children, Calvin and Silvia, are shopping at a big supermarket.

CD2, TR 7, 0:03

Calvin	Kita perlu berapa kilo kentang?
Jamilah	Kira-kira satu kilo. Kita juga perlu setengah kilo wortel dan beberapa bawang bombay.
Calvin	Kita juga kehabisan bawang putih.
Jamilah	Ya kita perlu setengah kilo, juga seikat daun bawang dan sélédri. Tolong masukkan ke dalam plastik untuk ditimbang. Silvia, jangan ambil jeruk yang itu. Tolong ambil yang di sebelah sana! Berapa harga seékor ayam?
Pramuniaga	Harganya 35.000. Itu beratnya sekilo setengah.
Jamilah	Saya juga mau beli lima potong daging bistik. Berapa harga satu potongnya?
Pramuniaga	Satu potong harganya 15.000 rupiah.
Jamilah	Kenapa mahal sekali?

Tukang daging	Ya, karena diimpor dari Australia.
Silvia	Aku mau ke bagian minuman? Aku mau membeli beberapa kaléng Coca-Cola dan dua kaléng bir dan satu botol wiski untuk papa.
Calvin	O, ya saya juga mau beli makanan ringan. Tiga bungkus kerupuk kentang dan biskuit.
Jamilah	Pergilah, tapi jangan terlalu banyak. Saya kelupaan bumbu-bumbu dapur, merica, kunyit, jahé, seré dan daun jeruk.

In the above dialogue, **plastik** refers to *plastic bag* where *bag* is understood. As we have seen this is characteristic of Indonesian speech. The full form is **kantong plastik** – *plastic bag*.

kilo *kilo*
kentang *potato*
wortel *carrot*
bawang bombay *onion*
kehabisan (habis, v) *run out of*
bawang putih *garlic*
seikat *bunch*
daun *leaf*
seikat daun *a bunch of leaves*
daun bawang *spring onion*
sélédri *celery*
masukkan (masuk, v) *put in*
plastik *plastic*
ditimbang (timbang, v) *to be weighed*
seékor *one (of animals)*
seékor ayam *one chicken*
beratnya *it weighs*
sekilo setengah *one and a half kilos*
daging *meat*
bistik *steak*
diimpor dari *to be imported from*
impor *to import*
bagian *section, part*
kaléng *can*

wiski *whisky*
papa *dad, daddy*
kerupuk *crackers*
kerupuk kentang *crisps* (or *chips* in US English)
biskuit *biscuit*
jangan terlalu banyak *not too many*
kelupaan (lupa, v) *to forget (accidentally)*
bumbu-bumbu *spices*
merica *pepper*
kunyit *turmeric*
jahé *ginger*
seré *lemon grass*
jeruk *citrus fruit, orange*
daun jeruk *lemon leaves*

Insight

Daun jeruk are called *lemon leaves* in English, but in fact,
jeruk means *orange* in Indonesian. However it also means
citrus fruit, so how can you tell the difference? If unspecified,
you can take it that **jeruk** refers to *orange*, but if another type
of citrus fruit is being referred to, this will follow **jeruk**, i.e.
jeruk nipis, *lemon*; **jeruk limau**, *lime*; **jeruk bali**, *pomelo* etc.

TRANSLATION

Calvin	How many kilos of potatoes do we need?
Jamilah	About one kilo. We also need half a kilo of carrots and some onions.
Calvin	We are running out of garlic.
Jamilah	Yes, we need a half of a kilo, also a bunch of spring onions and celery. Please put them into a plastic (bag) to have them weighed. Silvia, don't take those oranges. Please get the ones over there. How much is one chicken?
Shop assistant	35,000. It weighs a kilo and a half.
Jamilah	I would also like five pieces of steak. How much is one piece?
Shop assistant	15,000 rupiah per piece.

Jamilah	Why is it so expensive?
Butcher	Because it is imported from Australia.
Silvia	I want to go to the drinks section. I want to buy some cans of cola, two cans of beer and one bottle of whisky for dad.
Calvin	Oh yes I also want to buy snacks too. Three packets of crisps (and) biscuits.
Jamilah	Go (and get them then), but not too many. I've forgotten the spices – pepper, turmeric, ginger, lemon grass and lemon leaves.

How the language works 1

1 **Sedikit** means *a little* or *some* but it can only be used with things that you cannot count, such as *sugar*, *knowledge* etc. For things that you can count you cannot use **sedikit**. Instead, you must use **beberapa** meaning *a few* or *several*. **Banyak** *(a lot of)*, however, can be used with either.

EXERCISE 1

Look at the following nouns with **banyak** and the meanings. Write the words out again replacing **banyak** with **sedikit** or **beberapa** as appropriate.

a banyak kopi *a lot of coffee*
b banyak nasi goréng *a lot of fried rice*
c banyak resép *a lot of recipes*
d banyak pengetahuan *a lot of knowledge*
e banyak porsi nasi goréng *a lot of portions of fried rice*

pengetahuan (tahu, v) *knowledge*

Note that *how much?* is rendered by **berapa banyak?** in Indonesian.

2 In Unit 13 you were introduced to counting words that categorize things according to the container they come in etc. This probably seemed very natural to you, as English categorizes such things in just the same way. In Indonesian, however, there are more counting words that are used for things you might not expect from an English point of view. In Unit 4 you came across **seorang** which is often used with jobs. This literally means a person and it acts like *a/an* in English. There are more such counting words called *classifiers*, because they *classify* different sets of nouns according to certain inherent characteristics:

> **buah** is used for fruit, large objects such as TVs, refrigerators, computers, books, clothes, cassettes etc.
> **butir** is used for eggs and other small, round objects
> **ékor** is used for animals. **Ékor** means *tail*, therefore animals are counted in *tails*. This also includes animals with no tail!
> **lembar** is used for paper, photographs and other flat objects
> **orang** is used for people
> **pucuk** is used specifically for letters
> **tangkai** is used for long, thin objects such as flowers

Insight

Letters used to be rolled up into a tube, which is why they fall into the same category as firearms: because of the shape.

It will come as no surprise by now that to say *one* or *a/an* the classifier must be prefixed by **se-**:

| **seékor babi** | *a pig* |
| **dua ékor tikus** | *two mice* |

EXERCISE 2

Try some counting!

a eight sheets of paper
b a paw-paw
c a rose

d four birds
e three dictionaries

papaya *paw-paw*
bunga mawar *rose*

QV

···

Insight

Classifiers are entirely optional. **Sebuah rumah** means a *house*, but so does **rumah** without the classifier! You do need to be aware of classifiers, however, as some speakers do use them in certain situations, such as when talking about jobs.

···

Understanding Indonesian

EXERCISE 3

Say whether the following questions, based on the dialogue, are true or false.

a Jamilah perlu satu setengah kilo kentang.
b Kentang harus dimasukkan ke dalam plastik untuk ditimbang.
c Harga satu ékor ayam dengan berat satu kilo, 35 ribu rupiah.
d Silvia membeli tiga kaléng bir dan satu botol wiski untuk Ken.
e Calvin hanya membeli dua bungkus kerupuk kentang dan biskuit.
f Jamilah kelupaan membeli jahé dan seré.

dimasukkan (masuk v) *to be put (into)*

EXERCISE 4

Read this recipe for beef *rendang* then answer the questions.

Bahan-bahan

1 kg daging sapi
2 buah kelapa untuk diambil santannya

15 batang cabé (menurut seléra)
6 siung bawang mérah
6 siung bawang putih, ketumbar 1 séndok jahé 4 cm, laos 4 cm
2 batang seré
1 lembar daun kunyit
4 lembar daun salam
5 lembar daun jeruk

Cara membuat

1 Potong daging dengan ukuran 5 × 4 × 1 cm.
2 Haluskan semua bahan-bahan kecuali, daun salam, daun jeruk dan daun kunyit.
3 Masukkan daging, santan dan bumbu-bumbu yang telah dihaluskan ke dalam wajan. Masak hingga daging lembut, tambahkan garam secukupnya, daun jeruk, daun salam serta daun kunyit ke dalam wajan. Tunggu sampai airnya menyusut. Kira-kira 1 jam masakan siap disajikan.
(Recipe supplied by Tapsiah Kemas of Bekasi, Java)

QUICK VOCAB

bahan-bahan *ingredients, provisions, 'stuff'*
diambil (ambil *v***)** *to be taken*
untuk diambil santannya *(from which) to get out the coconut milk*
santan *coconut milk*
batang *stick*
menurut seléra *to taste (not as a verb, but as in a cooking recipe)*
siung *slice*
bawang mérah *shallot*
séndok *(here) spoonful*
ketumbar *coriander*
laos *galangal*
daun kunyit *saffron*
daun salam *bay leaf*
potong *to cut into pieces*
dengan ukuran___ cm *(here) into___ cm sized pieces*
cara membuat *method, directions*
haluskan (halus, *a***)** *to grind, to mill*
kecuali *except for*

dihaluskan (halus *a*) *to be ground up*
wajan *wok*
hingga *until*
lembut *soft*
tambahkan (tambah, *v*) *to add*
garam *salt*
secukupnya *sufficient*
tambahkan garam secukupnya *add salt to taste*
serta *along with*
tunggu sampai airnya *wait until it is absorbed*
menyusut (susut, *v*) *to reduce, to simmer down*
disajikan *to be served up*

a Sebutkan bahan-bahan untuk membuat rendang?
b Berapa buah kelapa yang diperlukan?
c Berapa kilo daging sapi untuk resép di atas?
d Apakah daun jeruk harus dihaluskan?
e Berapa jam dibutuhkan supaya daging menjadi lembut?

sebutkan (sebut, *v*) *to mention, (here) to list*
dibutuhkan (butuh *n.*) *to be needed*

QV

PART TWO

Dialogue

Reza wants to cook Mark her Indonesian speciality, beef rendang, so they go off to the market together to buy what they need.

Reza	Berapa harga satu kilo daging?
Penjual	Satu kilo 25.000 rupiah.
Mark	Mau beli berapa kilo?
Reza	Dua kilo cukup.
Mark	Apa lagi yang harus kita beli? Apa kita juga butuh kelapa?
	(Contd)

CD2, TR 7, 1:34

Reza	Ya kita butuh dua buah kelapa, untuk diperas santannya.
Mark	Bumbu apa yang kamu butuhkan?
Reza	Saya perlu cabé dan bumbu-bumbu yang segar, seperti laos, tiga batang seré, dua buah kunyit, setengah kilo bawang mérah.
Mark	Di mana kita bisa dapatkan bahan-bahan itu?
Reza	Di bagian bumbu-bumbu.
Mark	Buah apa itu yang ada durinya?
Reza	Oh, itu buah durian. Kamu beruntung, sekarang musim buah-buahan. Ada buah belimbing, duku, cempedak dan jambu. Kamu bisa mencicipi semuanya.
Mark	Buah durian. Bagaimana rasanya?
Reza	Rasanya manis dan agak pahit, tapi baunya sangat tajam.
Mark	Boléh saya coba?
Reza	Tentu. Rasanya agak anéh, tapi siapa tahu kamu doyan.
Mark	Bisa saya bawa ke Inggeris?
Reza	Saya kurang yakin, mungkin kalau dikemas dengan baik, sehingga baunya tidak kemana-mana. Lebih baik kamu coba dulu.
Mark	Berapa sekilonya?
Reza	Sekitar 12.000 rupiah.
Mark	Mari kita beli.

untuk diperas santannya *to extract the coconut milk*
diperas (peras, *v*) *to be extracted*
butuh *necessity*
butuhkan (butuh, *v*) *to need*
segar *fresh*
bagian bumbu-bumbu *condiments and spices section*
dapatkan (dapat, *v*) *to get*
durian *durian*
duri *spike*
yang ada durinya *which is spiky*
sekarang musim buah-buahan *now the fruits are in season*
musim *season*
buah belimbing *star fruit*
duku *lanseh fruit*

cempedak *bread fruit*
jambu *guava*
mencicipi (cicip, v) *to taste, to sample (food)*
rasa *taste*
Bagaimana rasanya? *What does it taste like?*
manis *sweet*
pahit *bitter*
anéh *weird*
Siapa tahu, kamu doyan! *Who knows, you may love it!*
doyan *to like, to love (slang)*
saya kurang yakin *I'm not so sure*
dikemas (kemas, v) *to be packed, to be put into a container*
sehingga *so that*
bau *to smell bad, to stink*
kemana-mana *everywhere*
Lebih baik kamu coba. *You'd better try it.*
berapa sekilonya? *how much per kilo?*

Insight

Kemana – mana means *everywhere* when movement is impiled. If no movement is impiled **dimana – mana** is used.

TRANSLATION

Reza	How much is one kilo of meat?
Vendor	25,000 per kilo.
Mark	How many kilos do you want to buy?
Reza	Two kilos are enough.
Mark	What else should we buy? Do we need coconut too?
Reza	Yes, we need two coconuts to extract the milk.
Mark	What spices do you need?
Reza	We need chillis, fresh spices such as *galangal*, three sticks of lemon grass, turmeric and half a kilo of red onions.
Mark	Where can we get that stuff?
Reza	In the condiments section.
Mark	What's the fruit with the spikes?

(Contd)

Reza	Oh, it's a *durian*. You are lucky. Now the fruits are in season. There is star fruit, *lanseh* fruit, bread fruit and guava. You can try them all.
Mark	Durian. What does it taste like?
Reza	It tastes sweet and a little bit bitter but it has a strong smell.
Mark	Can I try it?
Reza	Sure, it tastes a little bit weird but who knows, you may love it!
Mark	Can I take it to England?
Reza	I'm not sure, maybe (you can) if it is well packed so the smell does not leak out everywhere. You'd better try (it) first.
Mark	How much for one fruit?
Reza	Around 12,000.
Mark	Let's buy (one)!

Insight

In case you were wondering, Mark would not have been allowed to take a durian to England. In fact, so pungent is the small that durians are banned in many hotels in SE Asia!

How the language works 2

1 Look at the following sentences in English:

A *We boiled the prawns.*
B *The prawns were boiled by us.*

Both sentences have the same meaning but each is expressed in a different way. Sentence **A** is known as *active* in that it stresses that someone or something is carrying out an action, but sentence **B** is known as *passive* because it stresses that something happened to someone or something not necessarily with the agent of the action (that is, the person or thing that carries out the action) being expressed. It is the *passive* we shall look at in this section.

The prefix **di-** indicates a passive.

The passive is mainly formed from verbs beginning with the **me-** prefix. The prefix (**me-, men-, mem-** or **meng-**) is removed so you are left with the base verb* and **di-** is added to this base:

to take **men**gambil → **meng**-ambil → ambil → **di**-ambil → **di**ambil
  to be taken
to give **mem**beri → **mem**-beri → beri → **di**-beri → **di**beri *to be given*

Saya diberi uang. *I was given money.*

Certain other verbs that do not begin with **me-** prefixes can also be made passive such as **minum** and **makan**, simply by adding the **di-** prefix to them:

minum *to drink*   **diminum** *to be drunk*
makan *to eat*   **dimakan** *to be eaten*

Kué akan dimakan.   *The cake will be eaten.*

EXERCISE 5

Write the passive form of these verbs:

a mencari
b memeriksa
c menulis
d mengirim
e mengantar
f menjemput

memeriksa (periksa, *v***)** *to examine*

When you make a passive form in English, it is not always necessary to express the agent of the action – you can just say, for instance, *The prawns were boiled*, but you do not need to say by whom. You can do the same in Indonesian. If you do want to express who the action was done by, you can use **oléh** plus a personal pronoun, although the use of **oléh** is optional. Note that the person the action was done by with or without **oléh** must follow the passive verb. Note further that *by him* or *by her* can both be rendered by **oléh***nya*:

Dia diperiksa oléh dokter.
Dia diperiksa dokter.
} *She was examined by the doctor.*

Anda akan dijemput oléh Sari di bandara.
Anda akan dijemput Sari di bandara.
} *You will be met at the airport by Sari.*

EXERCISE 6

Change these sentences from active into passive ones.

a Dia sedang mendengar lagu.
b Meréka menonton TV.
c Kami harus minum obat tiga kali sehari.
d Dokter menyuntik pasién.

lagu *song*
obat *medicine, medication*
menyuntik (suntik, v) *to inject*
pasién *patient*

Using Indonesian

EXERCISE 7

Look at each of these pictures and write a suitable classifier under each. Use the **se-** form.

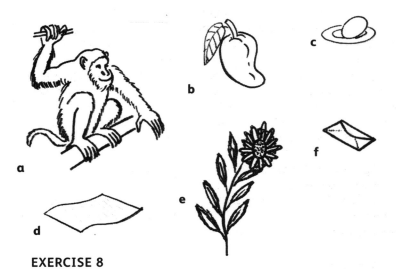

EXERCISE 8

Use the pictures to create a sentence and a question as in the example. Ask how much a kilo of each product costs, except for **d**, where you should ask how much a bottle costs.

a Example: Saya mau beli telur.
Berapa harga sekilonya?

EXERCISE 9

Over to you!

Take the part of Jamilah (**A**) who is shopping for meat.

> **A** *I would like to buy (some) beef.*
> **B** Berapa kilo, Bu?
> **A** *Two kilos. How much is that?*
> **B** Tiga puluh ribu rupiah.
> **A** *Please cut (it) into pieces.*
> **B** Baik. Ini dagingnya.
> **A** *Thank you.*

dipotong-potong *to be cut into pieces*

Supermarkets; four words for 'rice'

The **pasar swayalan**, literally *self-service market*, is how Indonesians refer to the supermarket. In such places you can buy all manner of produce, including a selection of imported items.

Rice is the staple diet in Indonesia and features at all three meals of the day. If you are staying in Indonesia and you are cooking for yourself, when you go shopping for rice you need to be aware that **nasi** is probably not what you want! East Asian countries tend to take their rice seriously so their languages often have two words for rice, depending on whether it is the cooked variety or the raw variety that you want. **Nasi** only refers to *cooked rice*. *Raw rice* in Indonesian is **beras**. To take it one stage further, *sticky rice* is **ketan** and the rice that you see in the process of growing in the **sawah** (*rice field*) is known as **padi,** a term that we have adopted into English from Indonesian/Malay.

TEST YOURSELF

1 What is the difference in usage between **sedikit** and **beberapa**?

2 What can you do with **banyak,** that you can't do (grammatically speaking) with **sedikit**?

3 How would you say *how much?* when asking about a quantity of something?

4 How are classifiers used in Indonesian?

5 What classifier would you use for a Manx cat?

6 What prefix is used to mean *one* of such and such a classifier?

7 Is the usage of classifiers compulsory?

8 What prefix indicates a passive verb?

9 The passive prefix usually replaces which verbal prefix?

10 How do you express *by* with a passive verb?

15

Hobbies

In this unit you will learn how to
* *talk about likes, dislikes and favourites in detail*
* *say what your hobbies are and what sports you do*
* *say how long something has been happening*

PART ONE

Dialogue

Jamilah is catching up with an old friend she has not seen since she moved to New Zealand.

Ibu Rika	Apa yang ibu (kamu*) lakukan di waktu luang di Sélandia Baru?
Ibu Jamilah	Saya biasanya masak, baca novel dan nonton film.
Ibu Rika	Film apa yang paling kamu suka?
Ibu Jamilah	Film kegemaran saya drama, komédi dan sejarah. Apa ibu juga suka menonton?
Ibu Rika	Ya kalau acara TV tidak bagus, kami suka menyéwa vidéo. Saya paling suka film drama dan petualangan. Sedangkan suami saya suka film laga dan film yang mengerikan.
Ibu Jamilah	Saya tidak begitu suka film yang mengerikan.
Ibu Rika	Kegiatan apa lagi selain itu?

Ibu Jamilah	Saya mengantar anak perempuan saya kursus balét dua kali seminggu, setiap hari Selasa dan Jumat soré. Dia ingin menjadi seorang pemain piano juga penari balét.
Ibu Rika	Sibuk sekali Silvia.
Ibu Jamilah	Ya. Ibu hobinya apa?
Ibu Rika	Dulu sewaktu masih gadis, saya suka sekali menyelam, snorkling dan hiking. Tapi sekarang tidak pernah lagi. Hanya érobik dua kali seminggu.
Ibu Jamilah	Saya kurang suka menyelam, juga saya benci berkémah. Tapi saya kadang-kadang suka érobik.
Ibu Rika	Suami ibu hobinya apa?
Ibu Jamilah	Dia suka komputer dan fotografi. Hampir seluruh waktu dihabiskan main komputer. Dia juga pintar main ténis.
Ibu Rika	Sama, suami saya juga paling suka komputer sama nonton bola kaki.

*Kamu was recorded in error and should not be part of the text.

waktu luang *free time, spare time*
luang *free, vacant*
baca *to read*
novel *novel*
film *film*
kegemaran (gomar *v.) favourite*
drama *drama*
komédi *comedy*
sejarah *history*
acara TV *TV programme*
menyéwa (séwa, *v) to rent*
vidéo *video*
petualangan *adventure*
sedangkan *whereas, but*
film laga *action film*
film yang mengerikan *horror film*
kegiatan (giat, *a) activity*
kursus *course*

balét *ballet*
pemain piano *pianist*
pemain (main, v) *player*
juga *(here) and*
penari balét *ballet dancer*
hobi *hobby*
sewaktu masih gadis *while I was still a maiden, before I was married*
sewaktu (waktu, n) *at the time when...*
menyelam (selam, v) *dive*
snorkling *snorkeling*
hiking *hiking*
tidak pernah lagi *not since, never since (then)*
érobik *aerobics*
saya kurang suka *I don't really like*
benci *to hate*
berkémah (kémah, v) *camping*
fotografi *photography*
hampir seluruh waktunya *almost all the time*
hampir *almost*
dihabiskan (habis, v) *to be spent*
dia pintar main ténis *he is good at tennis*
pintar *clever, good at*
bola kaki *football, soccer*

Insight

Gadis is specifically an unmarried girl, a maiden.

TRANSLATION

Rika	What did you do in your free time in New Zealand?
Jamilah	I usually cooked, read novels and watched films.
Rika	What kind of film do you like the most?
Jamilah	My favourite films are drama, comedy and history. Do you like watching films too?
Rika	Yes, if what's on TV is not good. We like to rent a video. I like drama and adventures the most but my husband likes action and horror.

Jamilah	I don't really like horror films.
Rika	What other activities did you do?
Jamilah	I take my daughter to ballet school twice a week, every Tuesday and Friday afternoon. She wants to be a pianist as well as a ballet dancer.
Rika	Silvia's very busy.
Jamilah	What's your hobby?
Rika	Before I was married, I loved diving, snorkeling and hiking but I haven't done those things since. I only do aerobics twice a week.
Jamilah	I don't really like diving, I hate camping too. But sometimes I do aerobics.
Rika	What's your husband's hobby?
Jamilah	He loves computers and photography. Almost all his time is spent on playing the computer. He is good at playing tennis too.
Rika	The same as my husband. He loves computers and watching the football.

How the language works 1

1 From previous units, you already know that to talk about what you like you can use **suka** and to talk about what you do not like **tidak suka. Saya suka mendaki gunung,** *I like climbing mountains.* Another good word for *like* is **gemar** which is less colloquial and tends to sound more formal than **suka** but will give the listener a good impression of your Indonesian. It is important to note that **gemar** cannot be used to refer to people or animals:

Saya gemar main kartu.   *I like playing cards.*

To say that you love doing something Indonesian uses **suka sekali:**

Saya suka sekali komédi.   *I love comedy.*

To express what you do not like, you can simply use **tidak suka**:

Saya tidak suka tiram.   *I don't like oysters.*

In English, we tend to use the word *hate* in a fairly casual way
when we talk about out likes and dislikes: *I hate washing up!* etc.
In Indonesian *hate* is rendered by **benci**:

Saya benci masak.   *I hate cooking.*
Saya benci sekali berenang. *I hate swimming so much.*

However, it is generally much better to express oneself in a less
extreme way in Indonesian when talking about negative things.
Therefore you (and the Indonesians you speak to) might find the
phrase **tidak begitu suka** a more acceptable alternative.
It corresponds to *do not really like* in English.

Saya tidak begitu suka baso.   *I don't really like baso.*
Saya tidak begitu suka masak. *I don't really like cooking.*

A similar and very common expression uses **kurang**:

Saya kurang suka pisang goréng.   *I don't really like fried bananas.*

Gemar acts as a root to give us **kegemaran** which means *favourite*
and follows what it refers to, like other adjectives.

film kegemaran saya   *my favourite film*
alat musik kegemaran saya *my favourite musical instrument*

Kegemaran can be used to talk about hobbies and activities that
you like doing. As with **gemar** it cannot be used to talk about
people or animals. Instead, either **kesayangan** or **kesukaan** must
be used:

| Dia pemain bola kaki kesayangan saya. | *He's my favourite football player.* |

Yet another word for *favourite* is **favorit** which is of foreign origin and popular among young people. The usage of **favorit** is not restricted so it can be used with anything, as in English:

| **film favorit saya** | *my favourite film* |
| **pemain bola kaki favorit saya** | *my favourite football player* |

EXERCISE 1

Use the correct form of **kegemaran** or **kesukaan/kesayangan** with the following words. Use each one at least once.

a olah-raga
b bintang film
c guru
d sandiwara
e binatang

bintang *star*
sandiwara *play (at the theatre)*

Another useful word derived from **gemar** is **penggemar** which expresses a *real fan of...* in Indonesian. As in English it does not just refer to sports, but can be used with anything.

| **Saya penggemar musik jazz.** | *I'm a real fan of jazz music.* |
| **Ayah saya penggemar baseball.** | *My dad's a real baseball fan.* |

EXERCISE 2

Are you a real fan of these sentences?

a My girlfriend is a real fan of Leonardo di Caprio.
b They are real fans of Chinese food.
c Jani's sister is a real soap opera fan.
d You're a real soccer fan, aren't you?

sinétron *soap opera*

Understanding Indonesian

EXERCISE 3

Read or listen to the dialogue again and say whether these statements are true or false.

a Pada waktu luang Jamilah biasanya suka menonton film horor.
b Jamilah mengantar Silvia kursus balét dua kali seminggu.
c Setelah menikah Rika masih suka pergi menyelam.
d Suami Jamilah menghabiskan waktunya dengan bermain komputer.
e Suami Rika hobinya fotografi.
f Jamilah tidak pintar main tenis.

 film horor *horror film(s)*

EXERCISE 4

Without referring back to the dialogue, see if you can complete the sentences with the correct information by selecting 1, 2 or 3 in each case.

a Di Sélandia Baru Ibu Jamilah biasanya
   1 masak, baca koran dan nonton film
   2 masak, baca novel dan nonton film
   3 masak, baca novel dan nonton sinétron

b Ibu Rika dan Ibu Jamilah gemar menonton film
   1 drama
   2 petualangan
   3 komédi

c Ibu Jamilah harus mengantar putrinya ke sekolah balét
   1 hari Jumat dan Selasa

2 hari Selasa dan Rabu

3 hari Kamis dan Selasa

d Suami Ibu Jamilah dan Ibu Rika penggemar
    1 tenis
    2 bola kaki
    3 komputer

PART TWO

Dialogue

Mark and Reza are talking about what they do in their free time.

Mark	Reza, apa yang kamu kerjakan di waktu luang?
Reza	Saya suka jalan-jalan dengan teman-teman dan belanja. Kadang-kadang saya berenang. Dan kamu?
Mark	Saya suka membaca buku, masak dan mendengar musik.
Reza	O, ya saya juga suka musik. Tiada hari tanpa musik. Musik memberi saya semangat dan inspirasi. Musik apa yang paling kamu suka?
Mark	Saya suka semua musik, khususnya musik klasik.
Reza	Saya juga suka jazz, pop dan dangdut.
Mark	Apa itu dangdut?
Reza	Dangdut, musik traditional yang digabung dengan tarian. Mirip musik India.
Mark	Apa lagi hobi kamu?
Reza	Saya senang menyanyi dan menari. Kita bisa pergi ke karaoké bésok, kalau kamu mau.
Mark	Tapi saya tidak bisa menyanyi. Saya pemalu!
Reza	Saya tidak percaya.
Mark	O, ya olahraga apa yang paling kamu suka?
Reza	Saya suka bola voli dan ténis méja. Kamu?
Mark	Karaté. Di Inggeris setiap minggu saya selalu latihan.

(Contd)

CD2, TR 8, 2:00

Reza	Wow. Berapa lama kamu sudah latihan karaté?
Mark	Saya sudah latihan selama tiga tahun. Saya tertarik dengan karaté sejak saya pergi ke Jepang lima tahun yang lalu.
Reza	Tadi kamu bilang, suka masak. Masakan apa yang paling kamu suka?
Mark	Masakan India, terutama kari. Saya tidak pernah bosan makan kari setiap hari.
Reza	Saya tidak suka masak, tetapi saya suka makan.

QUICK VOCAB

kerjakan (kerja, v) to do
jalan-jalan to go for a leisurely walk, to hang around
Tiada hari tanpa musik. There's no day without music.
tiada not, to not exist
semangat motivation
inspirasi inspiration
khususnya especially
pop pop (music)
dangdut traditional Indonesian music and dancing
digabung (gabung, n) to be combined
mirip to resemble, to be like
tarian (tari, v) dance
pemalu (malu, a) a shy person
percaya to believe
bola voli volleyball
ténis méja table tennis
karaté karate
latihan (latih, v) practice, exercise
latihan karaté karate practice
selama for (with time expressions)
tertarik dengan to be interested in
sejak since
tadi a moment ago, earlier
bilang to mention
terutama (utama, n) especially
bosan to get bored
Saya tidak pernah bosan I never get bored

TRANSLATION

Mark	What do you do in your spare time?
Reza	I like hanging around with my friends and shopping. Sometimes I go swimming. And you?
Mark	I like reading books, cooking and listening to music.
Reza	Oh yes, I like music too. (There's) no day without music. Music gives me motivation and inspiration. What kind of music do you like the most?
Mark	I like all music, especially classical music.
Reza	I like jazz, pop and *dangdut*.
Mark	What's *dangdut*?
Reza	*Dangdut* is traditional music which is combined with dancing. It is like Indian music.
Mark	What other hobbies do you have?
Reza	I am fond of singing and dancing. We can go to karaoke tomorrow if you want.
Mark	But I can't sing. I'm a shy person.
Reza	I don't believe (you).
Mark	By the way, what sports do you like?
Reza	I like volleyball and table tennis. You?
Mark	Karate. In England I always do karate every week.
Reza	Wow. How long have you been doing karate?
Mark	I've been doing it for three years. I've been interested in karate since I went to Japan five years ago.
Reza	A moment ago you said (you) like cooking. What food do you like the most?
Mark	Indian food, especially curry. I never get bored of eating curry every day.
Reza	I don't like cooking, but I like eating.

How the language works 2

1 When we talk about sports in English, we use a variety of verbs to express them. We say, for example, *I **play** tennis*, but *I **go** skiing*.

In Indonesian, you will be glad to hear, one verb, **main**, is used for them all.

main tenis	*to play tennis*
main ski	*to go skiing*

Main is also used to talk about playing musical instruments:

main trombon	*to play the trombone*
main piano	*to play the piano*

qv

terompét *trumpet*	**suling** *flute*
biola *violin*	**gitar** *guitar*
célo *cello*	**tambur** *drums*
klarinét *clarinet*	

2 **Berapa lama kamu (sudah)...?**, *How long have you been...?*
To say how long you have been doing something **selama** translates *for* in the Indonesian version:

Dia tertarik dengan ténis méja *selama* **dua tahun.**	*She's been interested in table tennis for two years.*
Saya sudah main piano *selama* **enam tahun.**	*I've already been playing the piano for six years.*

You could also say that you have been doing something *since...* In this case **sejak** is used:

Saya tertarik dengan wayang kulit *sejak* **saya melihat pertunjukan di Jawa.**	*I have been interested in shadow puppets since I saw a performance in Java.*
Adik Budi mencari pekerjaan *sejak* **dia tamat.**	*Budi's brother has been looking for a job since he graduated.*
Meréka belajar pencak silat *sejak* **meréka kecil.**	*They've been studying pencak silat since they were children (literally: since they were small).*

wayang kulit *leather shadow puppet*
pencak silat *an Indonesian martial art*

EXERCISE 5

Can you form these sentences?

a I have been studying *pencak silat* for three weeks.
b He has been interested in karate since he went to Japan.

2 The prefix **pe-** indicates nouns that refer to a person
who performs an action. Thus, **pe-** nouns are often connected with
jobs and sports. Many, but not all, are derived directly from
ber- and **me-** prefixed verbs, with the **pe-** replacing the **ber-** or
the **me-**:

penari *dancer* (from **menari,** *to dance*)
perenang *swimmer* (from **berenang,** *to swim*)
pemain *player* (from **main,** *to play*)

EXERCISE 6

See if you can work out the meanings of these *performer* nouns
using some of the verbs you have met already in the course.
Remember to think of them in their prefixed form!

a penulis
b pembantu
c pembeli
d penjual
e penjaga
f pengajar
g pekerja
h pelari

berlari (lari, *v) to run*

Using Indonesian

EXERCISE 7

Match the words to the pictures by writing in the letter of each picture. Choose, and indicate with the symbols shown in brackets, two activities that you love doing (✓✓), two activities that you like doing (✓) and two that you do not like doing (✗). Make up six sentences based on this information.

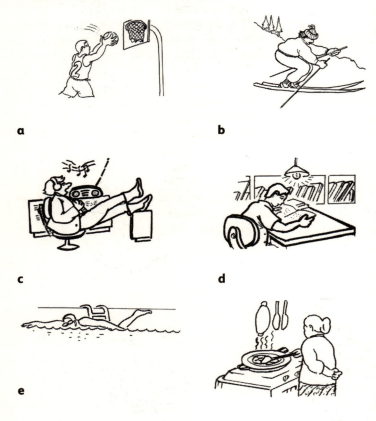

a

b

c

d

e

f

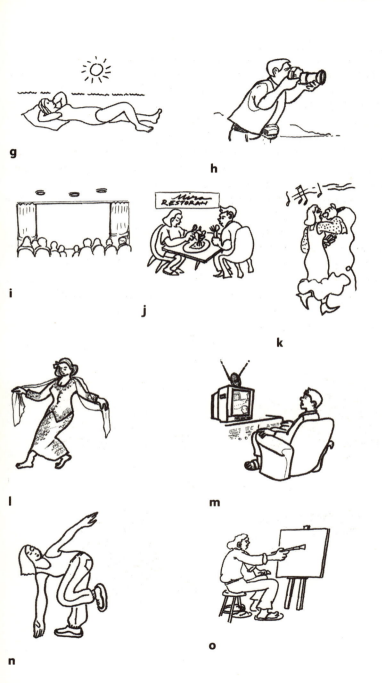

g

h

i

j

k

l

m

n

o

p

q

 i ___érobik.
 ii ___berkebun.
 iii ___main bola baskét.
 iv ___main ski.
 v ___berjemur.
 vi ___nonton.
 vii ___mendengar musik.
viii ___masak.
 ix ___menari.
 x ___bepergian/jalan-jalan.
 xi ___melukis.
 xii ___menyanyi.
xiii ___membaca.
xiv ___berenang.
 xv ___fotografi.
xvi ___makan di réstoran.
xvii ___nonton di bioskop.

bola baskét *basketball*
ski *ski*
berjemur (jemur, *v***)** *sunbathing*

bepergian (pergi, *v.***)** *travelling*
berkebun (kebun, *n***)** *gardening*

EXERCISE 8

Over to you!

You (**B**) are having a conversation with your Indonesian friend (**A**) about your likes, dislikes and hobbies.

◉ CD2, TR 8, 3:42

A Apa hobi kamu?
B *I like reading and travelling most.*
A Buku apa yang paling kamu suka?
B *Psychology, culture and history books.*
A Apa kamu juga suka novel?
B *Not really, but I like the novels of Agatha Christie a lot.*
A Tadi kamu bilang suka bepergian. Negara apa yang sering kamu kunjungi?
B *Countries in Asia, especially Indonesia, Malaysia, China and so on.*
A Apa kamu juga suka olahraga?
B *Hmm, I don't really like (them).*
A Bagaimana dengan berenang?
B *I don't like (it) either.*

psikologi *psychology*   **sangat suka** *to like a lot*
budaya *culture*   **sering** *often*
tidak begitu *not really*   **dan lain-lain** *and so on*

QV

Entertainment – Indonesian style

On your travels around Indonesia you might get the chance to see a **wayang kulit** (*leather shadow puppet*) performance. Such shows often retell the Hindu epic, the Ramayana, which plays such an important part in Indonesian culture, especially in the chiefly Hindu areas of the archipelago such as Bali. In fact, the Balinese dance, the **Kecak** is also based on the Ramayana. Although performances of **wayang kulit** and **wayang golék** (*wooden puppets*) have become a quaint tourist attraction, they have roots that are steeped in ancient tradition.

It would be a great injustice to refer to the **dalang** as mere puppeteers. They are highly trained and gifted performers who maintain a position of respect within Indonesian society. Not only do the **dalang** have to captivate the audience by telling the story and act out the voices of the puppets as well as the movements, but they also have to direct the **gamelan** orchestra, which always accompanies the show, from backstage. Performances are usually given in a local language such as Balinese, Sundanese or Javanese, so do not be surprised if the language does not sound like what you have learnt in this book!

A **gamelan** orchestra consists of a collection of various bowls and gongs that resonate at different frequencies, which, when combined with the drums, tend to have a rather meditative effect.

Another form of music that you cannot miss in Indonesia is **dangdut**. It is a kind of folk music that grew up in rural areas, and is loved and danced to by people today, old and young, alongside the usual pop music. It was derived from the musical traditions of India, Portugal and Arabia that came to Indonesia, thanks to the spice trade over many centuries. **Dangdut** did not always enjoy popularity as the lyrics were considered rather risqué and the dancing was considered indecent by some. All big towns and cities should have a **dangdut** bar somewhere, so why not give it a try? Do not be too surprised if you find yourself addicted to it before long!

Pencak silat is to Indonesia and Malaysia what karate is to Japan and kung fu is to China. Although there are many different styles of the art throughout Indonesia and Malaysia, the traditional roots of the art remain the same. As well as promoting health and strength, the art is a system of self-defence that grew out of a need to protect oneself and one's family and loved ones from man and beast.

TEST YOURSELF

1 What are the two ways to say *like* in Indonesian?

2 What restriction is placed on the usage of **gemar**?

3 How would you express *to hate* in Indonesian when talking about likes and dislikes? (Be careful!)

4 How do you express *favourite* in Indonesian?

5 How do you express *favourite* when talking about animals?

6 What does **favorit** mean, and is its usage restricted?

7 How do you say *a real fan of* in Indonesian?

8 What verb is used with all sports in Indonesian?

9 How do you express *for* and *since* with time expressions?

10 What does the prefix **pe-** indicate?

16

At the doctor's

In this unit you will learn how to
- ***talk about your body***
- ***say how you feel***
- ***talk about various common ailments***
- ***deal with a visit to the doctor***

PART ONE

Dialogue

Ken is not feeling well, so he has made an appointment at the private clinic his company uses. He is in the consulting room with an Indonesian doctor.

CD2, TR 9, 0:02

Dokter	Sakit apa, Pak?
Ken	Sesak nafas saya kambuh lagi. Saya tidak bisa tidur tadi malam, susah bernafas. Jantung saya berdebar cepat sekali.
Jamilah	Tangannya dingin dan menggigil.
Dokter	Sudah berapa lama merasa begini?

Ken	Saya sakit sudah dua tahun. Kadang-kadang sembuh, kadang-kadang datang lagi. Saya biasanya selalu joging setiap pagi sebelum berangkat ke kantor. Tapi, dalam seminggu ini saya sangat sibuk, jadi tidak ada waktu.
Dokter	Apa anda sedang pakai obat?
Ken	Ya, ini obat saya.
Dokter	Apa ada penyakit lain?
Ken	Ya, saya menderita tekanan darah tinggi.
Dokter	Apa anda merokok atau minum minuman keras.
Ken	Saya tidak merokok, tapi saya minum minuman keras.
Dokter	Mari saya periksa. Saya beri resép obat yang dapat anda beli di apoték. Jangan lupa teruskan obat anda dan banyak istirahat.
Ken	Terima kasih.
Dokter	Mudah-mudahan cepat sembuh.

Sakit apa? *What seems to be the trouble?*
sesak nafas *asthma*
kambuh lagi *to come back (of an illness)*
susah *difficult*
bernafas (nafas, n) *to breathe*
jantung *heart*
berdebar (debar, n) *to beat*
tangan *hand*
menggigil (gigil, v) *to shiver*
Sudah berapa lama merasa begini? *How long have you been feeling like this?*
merasa (rasa, n) *to feel*
begini *like this, in this way*
sembuh *to get better*
joging *jogging*
Apa anda sedang pakai obat? *Are you on any medication?*
pakai obat *to take medicine*
obat *medicine, medication*

penyakit (sakit, *a*) *illness*
menderita (derita, *n*) *to suffer from*
tekanan darah tinggi *high blood pressure*
tekanan (tekan, *n*) *pressure*
darah *blood*
periksa *(here) to examine*
minuman keras *hard drinks (i.e. alcohol)*
resép obat *prescription*
apoték *pharmacy*
teruskan (terus, *v*) *to keep going, to keep taking*
istirahat *to rest*

TRANSLATION

Doctor	What seems to be the trouble?
Ken	My asthma is coming back. I couldn't sleep last night and I had trouble breathing. My heart was beating so fast.
Jamilah	His arm was cold and shivering
Doctor	How long have you been feeling like this?
Ken	I have been ill for two years. Sometimes it gets better, sometimes it comes back. I used to go jogging every morning before I went to the office but this week I have been busy so I haven't had the time.
Doctor	Are you taking any medication?
Ken	Yes, this is my medication.
Doctor	Do you have any other illnesses?
Ken	Yes, I suffer from high blood pressure.
Doctor	Do you smoke or drink?
Ken	I don't smoke but I do drink.
Doctor	Let me examine you. I'll give you a prescription that you can buy from the pharmacy. Don't forget to keep taking your own medication and take a lot of rest.
Ken	Thank you.
Doctor	I hope you're better soon.

How the language works 1

1 Sakit means *ill* or *sick*. It is also used to express which part of the body feels painful or aching, or ill. The body part follows **sakit**:

Saya sakit perut.   *I have a stomach ache.*

QUICK VOCAB

badan *body*
kepala *head*
rambut *hair*
mata *eye(s)*
alis mata *eyebrow(s)*
dahi *forehead*
telinga *ear*
hidung *nose*
pipi *cheek(s)*
mulut *mouth*
bibir *lips*
dagu *chin*
léhér *neck*
tenggorokan *throat*
bahu *shoulder(s)*
dada *chest*
perut *stomach*
tangan *hand(s)*
jari *finger(s)*
jempol *thumb*
paha *thigh(s)*
betis *calf/calves*
kaki *leg/legs, foot/feet*

Insight

Indonesian does not make a distinction between legs and feet!

EXERCISE 1

How are we feeling?

a He has a headache.
b Do you have an earache?
c My hand hurts.

Some other words for ailments you may find useful are:

QUICK VOCAB

maag *indigestion*
batuk *cough*
demam *feverish*
pusing *dizzy*
muntah *to vomit*

2 In English, we always say *to **take** medicine* but in Indonesian you usually say *to **drink** medicine*, **minum obat** or, as in the dialogue, you can say **pakai obat**, literally *to use medicine*.

3 This section deals with how to give commands in Indonesian. There are two types of commands: one tells someone to do something, *positive command*, and the other tells someone not to do something, *negative command*.

To give someone a positive command simply state the verb for the action you wish completed:

Makan itu!   *Eat that!*

There are certain factors to take into account regarding the form of the verb when giving commands. This is where an awareness of verb bases comes in useful. If the verb you want to make a command from is a **ber-** or a **me-** verb with a verb base, then the **ber-** or **me-** drops leaving just the base to use as the command form:

308

bermain *to play*   **ber-***main*
Main di sana!   *Play over there!*
mencari *to lookfor*   **men-***cari*
Cari pekerjaan!   *Look for a job!*

If you make a command from a verb with prefix **me-** combined with suffix **-kan** then just the **me-** is removed leaving verb base + **-kan** as the command form. You have already met this form in expressions such as:

Tolong, buatkan saya réservasi   *Please make me a reservation*
   untuk bésok.   *for tomorrow.*

This comes from **membuatkan,** *to do something for someone.*

Masukkan jeruk di tas ini!   *Put the oranges in this bag!*

This is from **memasukkan,** *to put (something) int*o.

Jangan, which means *don't*, is used to form the negative command to tell someone not to do something. In the negative command, however, the prefixes **me-** and **ber-** are retained when using **jangan**:

Jangan bermain di rumah!   *Don't play in the house!*
Jangan menghidupkan (hidup, *v*) TV! *Don't turn on the TV!*

menghidupkan *to turn on (an appliance)*

EXERCISE 2

Try some commands!

a Take out the garbage!
b Run faster!
c Don't work all day long!
d Don't buy too much chocolate!

sepanjang hari *all day long*
sepanjang *all, whole*

In informal spoken style, with both positive and negative commands only the base of the verb (with any suffixes like **-kan**) can be used:

Jangan main di sini!   *Don't play here! (standard form*
                                  Jungan bermain di sini)

Note that this is <u>only</u> possible with verbs with verb bases. Otherwise prefixed forms must be used, for example:

Jangan merokok di kamar   *Don't smoke in the living room,*
  tamu, ya?   *OK?*

rokok is a noun base of the verb.

As in the last example, you can add **ya?** to a command to soften it. Another way to reduce the force of a comand is to add **-lah** to the verb. It is added directly to the verb or the adjective as a suffix. You should be aware that without it, your commands will have a distinctly forceful tone to them.

Bacalah!   *Read!*

The suffix **-lah** is especially useful when making positive commands using adjectives. If you want to say *Be happy!*, you will remember that there is no verb to be in Indonesian so you just add **-lah** to the adjective.

Gembiralah!   *Be happy!*

Indonesian often uses the passive form of the verb when making commands. This is due to a cultural necessity to avoid directness if possible, even when giving an explicit instruction:

Jangan dibuka pintu itu.   *Don't open the door. (Literally: Don't let*
  Dingin!   *the door be opened!) It's cold!*

Understanding Indonesian

EXERCISE 3

Answer the following true/false questions based on the dialogue.

a Bila sesak nafasnya kambuh, Ken tidak bisa tidur dan susah bernafas.
b Ken menderita penyakit sesak nafas selama tiga tahun.
c Ken mempunyai obat sendiri yang selalu diminumnya.
d Ken tidak merokok dan tidak minum minuman keras.
e Ken masih menderita tekanan darah tinggi.

bila *when* (similar in usage to **kalau** and **jika** – see Unit 10)
diminumnya *(here) to be taking (it)*

EXERCISE 4

Match the number of the body part below to those indicated in the picture using the letters.

1 perut
2 telinga
3 kepala
4 paha
5 dada
6 jari
7 léhér
8 mata
9 mulut
10 tangan

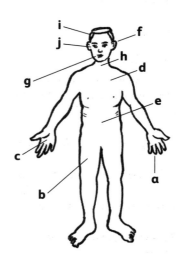

PART TWO

Dialogue

Mark is not feeling well.

Reza   Mark... Kamu kelihatan pucat. Ada apa? Apa kamu sakit?

Mark   Ya... saya sakit perut dan rasanya mual.

Reza   Badan kamu panas, kamu demam. Mari kita ke dokter di klinik 24 jam.

Mark   Tidak usah.

Reza   Apa kamu salah makan?

Mark   Saya kira tidak.

Reza   Kita harus ke sana. Kalau kamu sakit kita tidak bisa pergi bésok.

Mark   Terserah kamu. Saya ikut nasihatmu saja tapi saya pusing, tidak bisa berjalan.

Reza   Saya akan panggil taksi.

(The taxi arrives and takes Mark to the doctor's. Mark has just entered the doctor's surgery.)

Dokter   Selamat malam! Sakit apa?

Mark   Perut saya sakit dan saya muntah terus.

Dokter   Apa yang kamu makan atau minum.

Mark   Saya cuma makan nasi goréng dan minum air dari keran.

Dokter   Hm... air dari keran harus dimasak dulu. Sudah berapa lama merasa begini?

Mark   Dari tiga jam yang lalu.

Dokter   Apa lagi keluhan anda?

Mark   Saya buang air terus. Saya lemah.

Dokter   Mari saya periksa. Maaf. Apa anda alérgi terhadap obat?

Mark   Ya saya alérgi terhadap Augmentin.

Dokter	Baik, saya kasih obat pengganti. Diminum tiga kali sehari.
Reza	Bagaimana keadaan kamu sekarang?
Mark	Ya saya merasa lebih baik.
Dokter	Mudah-mudahan lekas sembuh dan jangan minum air dari keran lagi.

pucat *pale*
ada apa *what's wrong*
sakit perut *stomach ache*
rasanya *to feel like*
mual *(to) feel like vomiting*
klinik *clinic*
demam *(to) have a temperature*
tidak usah *there's no need*
salah makan *to eat the wrong thing*
saya kira tidak *I don't think so*
kira *to estimate, to guess*
terserah kamu *it is up to you*
nasihat *advice*
pusing *dizzy*
muntah terus *to keep vomiting*
terus *to keep on (doing something)*
keran *tap*
dimasak *to be boiled*
keluhan (keluh, n) *symptom*
buang air *to go to the toilet*
lemah *weak*
Apa anda alérgi terhadap obat? *Are you allergic to any medicines?*
alérgi terhadap *to be allergic to*
Bagaimana keadaan kamu sekarang? *How do you feel now?*
keadaan (ada, v) *condition*
saya merasa lebih baik *I feel better*
merasa (rasa, n) *to feel*
lekas *quick*

QUICK VOCAB

TRANSLATION

Reza	Mark, you look pale. What's wrong? Are you sick?
Mark	I've got stomach ache and I feel like (I'm going to) throw up.
Reza	You have a temperature and a fever. Let's go to see a doctor at the 24-hour clinic.
Mark	There's no need to.
Reza	Did you eat something that disagreed with you?
Mark	I don't think so.
Reza	You should go there. If you are sick we cannot go tomorrow.
Mark	It's up to you. I'll just follow your advice but I feel dizzy and I can't walk.
Reza	I'll call a taxi.
Doctor	Good evening. What seems to be the trouble?
Mark	I've got stomach ache and and I keep vomiting.
Doctor	What did you eat and drink?
Mark	I only ate fried rice and I drank the water from the tap.
Doctor	Hmm, the water from the tap should be boiled first. How long have you been like this?
Mark	For three hours.
Doctor	What other symptoms do you have?
Mark	I keep going to the toilet and I am weak.
Doctor	Let me examine (you). Excuse me. Are you allergic to any medicines?
Mark	Yes, I'm allergic to Augmentin.
Doctor	OK, I'll change the medicine. This medicine should be taken three times a day.
Reza	How do you feel now?
Mark	Yes, I feel better now.
Doctor	Hopefully, you'll be better soon and don't drink water from the tap again.

How the language works 2

1 **Tidak usah,** or more colloquially **tak usah** (**tak** is an alternative to **tidak** often used in set expressions such as this one) means *There's no point in* or *there's no need to.*

Tak usah kuatir.	*There's no need to worry.*
Tak usah mencampuri urusan orang lain.	*There's no need to interfere in someone else's business.*
Kami tak usah memakai seragam padi hari Sabtu.	*We don't need to wear a uniform on Saturdays.*

A related expression is **tak perlu** also meaning *there's no need to.*

Tak perlu mengajari orang tua.   *There's no need to educate parents.*

mencampuri (campur, *v) to interfere*
urusan (urus, *n) affairs, business*
seragam *uniform*
mengajari (ajar, *v) to educate, to teach*

QV

···

Insight
In Jakarta you'll hear **Nggak usah** – we'll look at the usage of some Jakarta slang in the last unit of this course.

···

2 You already know that **terus** means *direct,* but as a verb it can also mean *to keep on doing something,* as follows:

Terus belajar sampai cita-citamu tercapai.	*Keep studying until you reach your goal.*
Santi terus menunggu pacarnya yang masih belajar di luar negeri.	*Santi keeps on waiting for her boyfriend who is still studying abroad.*

cita-cita *goals, ambitions, dreams*
tercapai (capai, *v) to be reached*

QV

3 Throughout the course you will have noticed that there are many expressions where a word is doubled, sometimes with a prefix added and sometimes with a vowel change in the second word. This is technically known as *reduplication*. So far, the only usage we have looked at gave you the information that the doubling of a noun is sometimes required to create a plural form (refer back to Unit 5).

Although there is no particular reason why reduplication occurs in certain expressions, such as **kupu-kupu**, *butterfly*, there are three broad catergories of (added) meaning that reduplicated expressions fall into:

▶ Expressions of time

pagi-pagi	*early in the morning*
malam-malam	*late at night*
kadang-kadang	*sometimes*
sebentar-sebentar	*now and again*
sekali-sekali	*once in a while*
tiba-tiba	*suddenly*
kapan-kapan	*one of these days*

▶ doing something in a leisurely way or with no particular goal in mind

duduk-duduk	*to sit about (relaxing)*
jalan-jalan	*to go out for a stroll, to 'hang around'*
lihat-lihat	*to browse*
omong-omong	*to chat* (this also means *by the way* in certain contexts)

▶ emphasis

keras-keras	*loudly*
lekas-lekas	*hurry up!*
tergesa-gesa	*to be in a hurry*
terburu-buru	*to be in a hurry*

bermacam-macam	*different kinds of*
bersama-sama	*together*
cepat-cepat	*very quickly*
satu-satu	*one by one*
dua-dua	*two by two etc.*

4 Prefix/suffix pe -an and per -an. In some cases pe- -an (per- -an) nouns that are created from verb bases correspond to what are known as *verbal nouns* in English. That is, they end in *-ing* but are not expressing a continuous tense:

baca	*to read*	**pembacaan**	*reading*
jual	*to sell*	**penjualan**	*selling*
beli	*to buy*	**pembelian**	*buying*

Formed from a concrete noun, the **pe- -an** (**per- -an**) combination often creates a new noun that extends or augments the meaning of the original noun, which now becomes the base. Look at the following examples noting the meanings of the original noun and the corresponding modified nouns:

gunung	*mountain*	**pegunungan**	*mountain range*
bukit	*hill*	**perbukitan**	*hilly region*
kota	*city*	**perkotaan**	*urbanized area*
pustaka	*book*	**perpustakaan**	*library*

Insight

Pustaka is an archaic word for book and **perpustakaan** is a collection of books, i.e. *a library*.

Some of the nouns created by **pe- -an** (**per- -an**) carry meanings that can be a little difficult to relate directly to the original base verb. When the meaning of both the base verb and the created noun are known, however, the link is easy to see, even if it sometimes requires a little lateral thinking as to how the meaning evolved. Examples:

| **menginap** | *to spend the night (somewhere)* | **penginapan** | *inn* |
| **membangun** | *to build* | **pembangunan** | *construction* |

| **terbit** | *to appear* | **penerbitan** | *publishing house* |
| **main** | *to play* | **permainan** | *game* |

Penginapan derives its meaning from *a place to spend the night*, i.e. *an inn*.

In Unit 8 we met a few verbs that have different meanings when the prefix **me-** is attached, one of which was **bangun** which, when the prefix is added, means *to build*. The meaning of **pembangunan** is the noun derived from the prefixed verb **membangun**.

Insight

If you think of **penerbitan** as a place which makes things appear, i.e. be published, then the link between the verb and the noun becomes clear.

EXERCISE 5

Using what you know about **pe- -an (per- -an)** type nouns from the information just given, see if you can work out the meaning of the nouns in the right-hand column created from the noun (**a–d**) and verb (**e–i**) bases in the left-hand column.

a	toko *shop*	**pertokoan**
b	désa *village*	**pedésaan**
c	rumah *house*	**perumahan**
d	kebun *garden*	**perkebunan**
e	cakap *to chat*	**percakapan**
f	periksa *to examine*	**pemeriksaan**
g	umum *to announce*	**pengumuman**
h	juang *to fight*	**perjuangan**
i	coba *to try*	**percobaan**

Using Indonesian

EXERCISE 6

Look at the pictures and write the word(s) for each illness.

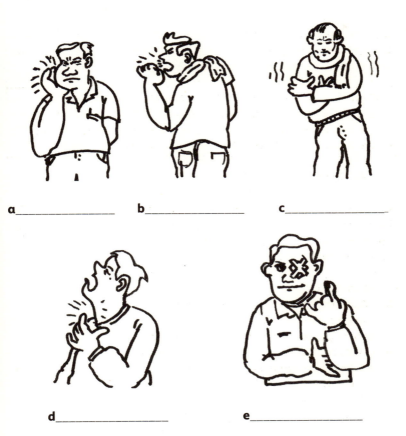

a_____

b_____

c_____

d_____

e_____

EXERCISE 7

Over to you!

You (**B**) have gone to see a doctor (**A**) because you are having trouble with your eyes.

CD2, TR 9, 3:02

A	Silahkan duduk, Pak. Sakit apa dan apa keluhannya?
B	*My eyes are itching and smarting.*
A	Sudah berapa lama?
B	*(Already) two days, since Sunday.*
A	Kenapa bisa begini?
B	*I have a dust allergy, Doctor. In the beginning my eyes were just red but after that (they became) swollen.*
A	Mari saya periksa. Baiklah, tidak terlalu serius, tetapi saya beri Bapak dua macam obat, satunya obat tétés. Ditétés tiga kali sehari. Mudah-mudahan bapak lekas sembuh.
B	*Thank you, Doctor.*

QUICK VOCAB

keluhan *complaint*
gatal *itching*
perih *smarting*
debu *dust*
mulanya *in the beginning*
bengkak *swollen*
serius *serious*
macam *kind, sort*
satunya *one of them*
obat tétés *drops (eye drops)*
tétés *drop, to drop*

Herbal medicines; drinking water

Many Indonesians prefer to put their trust in what we in the west would call 'alternative medicine', rather than go and see a doctor. Indonesia's herbal medicine tradition goes back for centuries, and many recipes are made from herbs that you can find only in the archipelago. You can buy a herbal drink called **jamu** which is a mix of herbs and spices, either from a **jamu** shop or from a **tukang jamu,** a lady who makes varieties of the drink and wanders the street selling it from a basket she carries on her back or on the back of a bicycle.

Mark's mistake in the dialogue is one that all visitors should take heed of. The tap water in Indonesia is not safe to drink. Instead, you can buy bottled water known as **air putih**. This literally means *white water* and it refers to all water that you can drink safely.

TEST YOURSELF

1 How do you say *sick*, *ill* or *it hurts* in Indonesian?

2 What verbs are possible in Indonesian, where we use *to take* (of medicine) in English?

3 When making a positive command, what must be removed from the verb?

4 What happens to the suffix **-kan** when making a positive command?

5 How do you form a negative command?

6 What does the suffix **-lah** do to a command?

7 What kind of verb form does Indonesian often use to soften a command?

8 What three broad meanings does reduplication create?

9 What kind of noun do **per- -an** and **pe- -an** create in Indonesian?

10 How does Indonesian refer to water that is safe to drink?

17

A phone call

In this unit you will learn how to
- *make a phone call*
- *talk about the weather*
- *understand some of the features of street Indonesian*
- *use a dictionary*

PART ONE

Dialogue

During the Knights' stay in Indonesia, Silvia has been making friends. She has been invited to go to Rusli's house in Bandung where he is planning to have a barbecue. While she is shopping for something to take with her to Rusli's it starts to rain, so Sylvia goes to a **warung télpon** to check with Rusli about the afternoon's plans.

Silvia	Selamat pagi, bisa saya pakai télpon?
Karyawan	Ya, kamar nomor tiga, Néng.
Silvia	Maaf, saya mau menélpon Bandung, berapa kode areanya?
Karyawan	Dua-dua.
Silvia	Berapa biayanya per menit?
Karyawan	Satu menitnya 3.000 rupiah, Ada diskon dari jam 9 malam sampai jam 6 pagi.

(Contd)

Silvia	Terima kasih.
	(Rusli's sister Rani answers the phone.)
Silvia	Halo... bisa bicara dengan Rusli?
Rani	Maaf dia tidak ada. Dari siapa ini?
Silvia	Ini Silvia, temannya.
Rani	Dia pulang sebentar lagi.
Silvia	Bisa titip pesan?
Rani	Tentu.
Silvia	Tolong télpon saya di 842 8423. Atau saya nanti télpon lagi.
Rani	Baik, nanti saya sampaikan.
	(Silvia rushes back home and, having not received a call from Rusli for an hour, she decides to phone him again, as it is still raining, and she is not sure whether it is going to be worth going to Bandung.)
Silvia	Halo... bisa bicara dengan Rusli?
Rani	Tunggu sebentar.
Rusli	Halo, Silvia... Ini Rusli, maaf saya belum nélpon, baru sampai.
Silvia	Tidak apa-apa.
Rusli	Bagaimana dengan rencana kita malam ini?
Silvia	Saya pikir lebih baik kita tunda dulu, karena hujan deras.
Rusli	Bagaimana kalau bésok. Mudah-mudahan cuacanya bagus.
Silvia	Baik, sampai bésok.

QUICK VOCAB

télpon *telephone*
berapa kode areanya? *what's the area code?*
kode *code*
Berapa biaya per menit? *What's the rate per minute?*
biaya *cost*
Halo! *Hello!*
Dari siapa ini? *Who's this?*
titip pesan *leave a message*
titip *to leave*
pesan *message*
Nanti saya sampaikan. *I will pass your message on.*

sampaikan (sampai, v) *to convey, pass on (a message etc.)*
nélpon (short for menélpon) *to telephone*
rencana *plan(s)*
tunda *to delay, put off*
Hujan deras. *It's raining heavily.*
cuaca *weather*

Insight

Halo! is usually used for *Hello!* when picking up a ringing phone in Indonesia.

TRANSLATION

Silvia	Good morning. Can I use the telephone?
Employee	Yes, booth number three.
Silvia	Excuse me. I would like to call Bandung. What's the area code for Bandung?
Employee	Two-two.
Silvia	What's the rate per minute?
Employee	For one minute (it) is 3,000 rupiah. There is a discount from 9 p.m. until 6 in the morning.
Silvia	Thank you.
Silvia	Hello. Can I speak to Rusli?
Rani	I'm sorry, he's out. Who's speaking?
Silvia	This is Silvia, his friend.
Rani	He'll be back home soon.
Silvia	Can I leave a message?
Rani	Sure.
Silvia	Could you ask him to call me on 842 8423. Or I will call back again.
Rani	Ok, I'll pass it on.
Silvia	Hello, can I speak to Rusli?
Rani	Just a moment, please.
Rusli	Hello, Silvia. This is Rusli. I'm sorry I didn't call you before. I just got in.

(Contd)

Silvia	No problem.
Rusli	How about the plans for this afternoon?
Silvia	I think we'd better call it off because it's raining heavily.
Rusli	How about tomorrow? I hope the weather will be fine.
Silvia	OK, see you tomorrow.

Insight

You can make local, national or even international calls from the **warung télpon** or *telephone kiosks* you will find in any city. Unlike coin phone booths that you might find elsewhere there is an attendant in the kiosks.

How the language works 1

1 Talking about the weather. **Bagaimana cuacanya?**, *How's the weather?*

berawan	*cloudy*
berkabut	*foggy*
panas	*hot*
cerah	*bright*
banyak badai	*stormy*
berangin	*windy*
basah	*wet*
mendung	*overcast*
lembab	*damp/humid*
hujan	*raining*

You may also find these words useful:

| **banjir** | *flood* |
| **topan** | *typhoon* |

musim is used to refer to seasons in Indonesian:

musim semi	*spring*
musim panas	*summer*
musim gugur	*autumn*
musim dingin	*winter*
musim panas	*dry season*
musin hujan	*rainy season*

Insight

Indonesia, however, only really has two seasons, dry and hot or wet and hot!

2 Sound changes. You will have noticed that, when you encounter words with the **me-** or **pe-** prefixes, the base words these words are derived from sometimes look different from the base words themselves. This is because some base words undergo changes when they have the **me-** or **pe-** prefixes attached to them.

The rules are as follows:

▶ When **me-** or **pe-** are used as prefixes before c, d and j they become **men-** and **pen-** respectively:

cuci	→	**mencuci**	*to wash*
jemput	→	**menjemput**	*to pick up*
jual	→	**penjual**	*seller*
daki	→	**pendaki**	*climber*

▶ These prefixes also become **men-** and **pen-** before bases beginning with t but in this case, the t disappears:

terima	→	**menerima**	*to receive*
tangis	→	**menangis**	*to cry*
terjemah	→	**penerjemahan**	*translating*
tari	→	**penari**	*dancer*

▶ me- and pe- become **mem-** and **pem-** before **b**:

buang	→ **membuang**	*to throw*
bungkus	→ **membungkus**	*to wrap up*
bantu	→ **pembantu**	*helper*
berita	→ **pemberitaan**	*announcement*

▶ They also become **mem-** and **pem-** before **p** but the **p** disappears:

pinjam	→ **meminjam**	*to borrow*
pijat	→ **memijat**	*to massage*
pilih	→ **pemilihan**	*election*
pandu	→ **pemandu**	*guide*

▶ me- becomes **meng-** and pe- becomes **peng-** before **g** or **h**:

ganti	→ **mengganti**	*to replace*
hidup	→ **menghidupkan**	*to turn on (an appliance)*
ganggu	→ **pengganguan**	*annoying*
habis	→ **penghabisan**	*conclusion*

▶ **meng-** and **peng-** are also used before **k** which disappears:

kira	→ **mengira**	*to guess*
kirim	→ **mengirim**	*to send*
kenal	→ **pengenalan**	*identification*
kemudi	→ **pengemudi**	*driver*

▶ me- and pe- become **meng-** and **peng-** before a vowel:

isi	→ **mengisi**	*to fill in*
obrol	→ **mengobrol**	*to chat*
urus	→ **pengurus**	*manager*
alam	→ **pengalaman**	*experience*

▶ me- becomes **meny-** and pe- becomes **peny-** before bases beginning with **s** but note that the **s** disappears:

sombong	→	**menyombongkan**	*to boast*
sebut	→	**menyebut**	*to mention*
seberang	→	**penyeberangan**	*crossing*
séwa	→	**penyéwaan**	*renting out*

EXERCISE 1

How do you think these words will appear when the prefix in the left-hand column is added? (For some of the words a suffix has already been added to create a useful word, the meaning of which is given in the right-hand column. The root appears in bold.)

a me-	**terjemahkan**	=	*to translate*
b me-	**usik**	=	*to tease*
c me-	**sisir**	=	*to comb*
d me-	**bantah**	=	*to argue*
e pe-	**bangunan**	=	*construction*
f pe	**serang**	=	*attacker*
g pe-	**segar**	=	*stimulating*
h pe-	**imporan**	=	*importation*

3 Using a dictionary. A knowledge of sound changes is particularly useful because Indonesian dictionaries list words alphabetically according to their bases. This means that, when you come across an unknown word that you want to look up, you need to be able to identify the base of the word you are looking for. In other cases where there are several possibilities, you may need to look for the root under more than one letter. For example, looking at the sound change rules, you know that, if the word sought begins with **meng-** then the base word will be one that begins with a vowel, **g-**, **h-**, or **k-**. You might need to look under all of these before you find the corresponding base word.

You do not necessarily need to sit down and memorize the rules as explained earlier, although doing so would be of benefit. As you use a dictionary, you will need to refer to them so often that you will soon acquire a sense of how this happens naturally.

In keeping with the approach we have taken in this course, vocabulary is listed in alphabetical order just as it appears in the text to make it more user friendly for English speakers.

Using Indonesian

EXERCISE 2

Over to you!

You (**B**) are Julia. You are trying to get hold of your friend Lina.

A (Kriing) ... Halo?
B *Good morning, can I speak to Lina?*
A Lina? Maaf, tidak ada nama Lina di sini.
B *Is this 769 1254?*
A Maaf, Ibu salah sambung.
B *Sorry, thank you.*
(You try again.)
C (Kriing) ... Halo?
B *Is this 769 1254?*
C Betul. Dari siapa?
B *This is Julia. Can I speak to Lina?*
C Tunggu sebentar. Maaf dia sedang keluar. Mau titip pesan?
B *Just tell her that I called.*
C Pasti. Télpon saja sekitar satu jam lagi. Dia pasti sudah pulang.
B *OK, thank you.*

QV

salah sambung *to dial the wrong number*
sambung *to dial*
Sampaikan saja salam saya untuk dia. *Just tell her that I called.*
  (literally, send her my regards.)

PART TWO

In this course we have opted to introduce you to Indonesian the way it is really spoken. In addition, you will no doubt encounter a highly informal spoken form of the language on the streets of Jakarta that might make you wonder what language you are actually hearing! While we have concentrated on standard spoken Indonesian throughout this course, this brief guide to informal speech (bahasa gaul) will help to make you more streetwise, linguistically at any rate. Although you need not imitate such a spoken style, unless you want to, of course, you will find it vital to understanding the informal Indonesian that the locals use between themselves.

Dialogue

Reza and Weni are close friends and they haven't met each other for a long time. One day they meet in a shopping mall.

Reza	Gimana kabar lu sekarang? Lagi ngapain di sini?
Weni	Eh… lu, Reza. Lama nggak ketemu. Gué lagi jalan-jalan aja. Ke mana aja selama ini?
Reza	Gué cuma nganter temen bulé belanja. Dia mau beli oléh-oléh untuk nyokapnya.
Weni	Pacarlu, ya!
Reza	Bukan! Dia cuma temen kok. Eh ngomong-ngomong, kenalin dulu ini Mark. Mark, ini Weni.
Mark	Senang berkenalan dengan kamu.
Weni	Dari mana asalnya?
Mark	Dari Inggeris.
Weni	O, ya, hari Minggu ini nyokap gué bikin pésta. Kalo nggak ada acara datanglah ke rumah, ajak aja Mark.
Reza	Pasti dong, kami datang. Rumah lu masih di Pondok Indah, kan?
Weni	Hm, sudah pindah ke Kemang. Jangan kuatir nanti gué jemput.
Reza	Iya déh. Makasih, Weni.
Weni	Sampé ketemu lagi.

(In this list, all standard Indonesian follows the 'street' word for comparison, where possible.)

QUICK VOCAB

gimana [bagaimana] *how*

lu [kamu] *you*

Lagi ngapain di sini? *What are you doing here?*

Lama nggak ketemu. *Long time, no see.*

nggak [tidak] *no, not*

gué [saya] *I (am)*

aja [saja] *just*

nganter [mengantar] *to take*

temen [teman] *friend*

bulé *westerner*

nyokap [ibu] *mother*

ngomong-ngomong [omong-omong] *by the way*

Kenalin dulu ini... *This is... (to introduce a person)*

bikin [membuat] *to make*

kalo [kalau] *if*

Makasih. [Terima kasih.] *Thank you.*

Iya déh *Ok, then.*

sampé [sampai] *until*

Insight

Bulé is a very common word used to refer to Caucasians in particular. It started as a somewhat derogatory term, but its usage has become so widespread in Indonesia that its original force of meaning has become lost, and **bulé** just means *white Westerner*. If someone refers to you as **bulé**, as Reza does in the dialogue, there is no reason to take offence.

TRANSLATION

Reza	How are you? What are you doing here?
Weni	Hey, you, Reza. Long time no see. I am just off for a walk. Where have you been?
Reza	I'm just taking my western friend shopping. He wants to buy some souvenirs for his mother.
Weni	Your boyfriend, right?

Reza	No! He's just a friend. Hey, by the way, this is Mark. Mark, this is Weni.
Mark	Pleased to meet you.
Weni	Where are you from?
Mark	England.
Weni	By the way, my mum's throwing a party this Sunday. If you're free, come along, Mark, too.
Reza	Of course we'll come. Your house is still in Pondok Indah, isn't it?
Weni	Hm, I've already moved to Kemang. Don't worry, I'll pick you up.
Reza	OK then. Thanks, Weni.
Weni	See you then.

How the language works 2

Street Indonesian takes the concept of being economical with words and sounds to the extreme. Unfortunately for foreign learners this makes Indonesian speech even faster than it already is! The following is by no means an exhaustive explanation of street Indonesian but it serves as an introduction.

1 A feature of the spoken language that is not just confined to slang, and that you have already come accross in the course, concerns verbs beginning with the **me-** prefix. With some verbs this form becomes a **ng** as you can see when **mengantar** becomes **nganter** and **mengomong** becomes **ngomong**.

2 Certain standard Indonesian sounds are reduced in street Indonesian:

▶ **au** changes to **o**
  kal*au* → kal*o*

▶ **ai** changes to **é**
  samp*ai* → samp*é*

▶ **a** sometimes changes to **e**
  tem*a*n → tem*e*n

3 Some words have become shortened and/or run together:

▶ **bagaimana → gimana**
  terima kasih → makasih

4 Informal, street language (i.e. slang) makes use of various non-standard vocabulary words. Some common ones are:

gué in place of **saya** (*I*)
lu instead of **kamu** (*you/your*)
nyokap instead of **ibu** (*mother*)
nggak instead of **tidak** (*no, not*)

And a special word for a foreigner and, specifically a westerner, **bulé**!

5 You may also have noticed in the sample dialogue the usage of certain extra words in the sentences such as **dong**, **kok**, **déh** and **ya**. These are commonly added to utterances as tags which are mainly used to convey various shades of emphasis:

▶ **dong** is used to reinforce a statement:

  Pasti dong, kita datang!   *Of course we're coming!*

It can also be used with commands and requests:

  Tolong dong.   *Please.*
  Diam dong!   *Please be quiet!*

▶ **kok** is used to reinforce statements, too:

  Dia cuma temen kok!   *No, he's just a friend!*

Kok can also be used at the beginning of a sentence with the meaning of *How come...?*

Kok dia tidak tahu?   *How come he doesn't know?*

▶ **déh** corresponds to *then* in such phrases as:

Iya déh.   *OK, then.*
Minum aja déh!   *Well, drink it then!*

▶ **ya?** is a question tag, like **bukan?** or **kan?** It is very common in Indonesian speech. It is used to confirm the content of the statement or question:

Pacar lu, ya?   *Your boyfriend, right?*
Sukar, ya?   *It's difficult, isn't it?/It's difficult, right?*

As you saw in Unit 16, it is often added to commands:

Jangan lupa, ya?   *Don't forget, OK?*

For more information on street Indonesian visit
http://www.speakbahasaindonesia.com

Taking your Indonesian further

RECOMMENDED BOOKS

If you are considering buying a dictionary, there are a couple of points to look for if you want to choose one that is useful and effective. What you really need, especially in the development stages of learning, is a dictionary that not only gives you the equivalent word in the foreign language, but also gives you example phrases showing you how to use the various translations in context. A dictionary that does not include adequate examples of contextual usage will only really help you understand Indonesian, but may be unsuitable if you want to put your English into Indonesian!

Another point to look for is whether the dictionary has been designed for Indonesian learners or for foreign learners of Indonesian. If it is designed for Indonesians learning English, you may find that it is not as useful as it could be for your needs. We recommend:

Wendy Sahanaya and Albert Tan, *The Oxford Study Indonesian Dictionary*, Oxford University Press, 2001 (available through OUP Australia: www.oup.com.au)

This is an excellent starter dictionary and as up to date as you will find anywhere. It contains a wealth of indispensable examples of usage and is also fairly compact, which makes it easy to use if you are travelling.

If you are serious about studying the language to a high level and especially if you are working with advanced texts or you would like to study the finer points of the language, you will need a good reference grammar. An excellent choice is:

James Neil Sneddon, *Indonesian, A Comprehensive Grammar*, Routledge, 1996.

THE INTERNET

You can find a list of links to Indonesian newspapers online that you can download at:
http://www.onlinenewspapers.com/indonesi.htm

Some other sites you may find useful for learning more about Indonesian language and culture are:

http://www.seasite.niu.edu/Indonesian/
http://indonesia.elga.net.id/
http://www.goethe-verlag.com/tests/EJ/EJ.HTM
http://hsc.csu.edu.au/indonesian/
http://web.uvic.ca/hrd/indonesian/

For more information and advice about learning languages go to

http://www.languagelearning.ws
http://www.languagelearningsecrets.com

MULTIMEDIA

DVDs can be a great source for language learning! With most DVDs you can change the soundtrack and subtitles to suit your preferences. If you get a DVD of an Indonesian film, you could turn on the subtitles so that you can study the utterances that you do not catch or understand. It does not matter if the DVD is not an Indonesian film, as long as you can opt for an Indonesian-dubbed soundtrack and subtitles in Indonesian and/or English. It would be a great idea to see if you can get your favourite films with an optional Indonesian soundtrack, so that you already know what is being said and so that you will be even more motivated to 'study'. You can learn a great deal by comparing the way in which something is expressed in Indonesian with how it is expressed in English. You also have the option of turning on the subtitles so that you can check the written form of the language being used.

Of course, videos are also useful, but they do not have the flexibility of DVDs. The beauty of the DVD is that you can listen to the film in Indonesian and have English subtitles to help you, listen to the English and read the Indonesian subtitles, or combine subtitles and soundtrack however you want.

OTHER SUGGESTIONS

With the grounding that this course provides, you will find that any opportunity to use your Indonesian will help you to expand your knowledge of the language, so seeking out opportunities to speak the language should be a priority if you are intent on taking your knowledge to new heights.

Carry a small notebook with you in which you can record any new phrases or words that you find interesting or useful. Make a point of learning these phrases and putting them into practice as soon as possible, either in conversation or in writing. You could also note down the new vocabulary that you acquire from reading and keep the notebook with you to use during those times in the day you usually reserve for commuting etc.

An important principle that applies to any language you learn is 'use it or lose it'! If you do not keep on using the language by speaking, listening, reading or writing, then you will find that you start to lose active use of the language as your brain tends to put skills you are not using 'on the back burner'. If this does happen, you will still have a passive knowledge and your active command of Indonesian can be brought back with a few hours of dedicated study. However, it is much better to keep the learning going, once you start.

A dictionary can be a good source of vocabulary expansion. As you know, Indonesian words are built on roots. You could flick through the dictionary and select a root word that looks useful or common, then learn all the various meanings the prefixes and affixes provide to that root, and, if you use a dictionary with plenty of example phrases, such as the one recommended here, you should learn some of those too, as you are learning structures that use the new vocabulary in context. You could keep an alphabetical filing system of flash cards with the root at the top and vocabulary and usage examples below. You could add to these as your knowledge expands and refer to them regularly to test yourself on your retention and keep the language alive in your mind.

Get hold of a magazine in Indonesian on a subject that interests you such as cars, fashion or cooking... whatever happens to be your hobby. Go through the articles noting down and learning new words and phrases that you come across. Do not be concerned that the vocabulary may be specific to a certain subject area, because you will still be exposing your mind to the patterns of the language. This will reinforce structures already in place, as well as expanding your existing knowledge.

You can access a list of updated Indonesian learning resources at the authors' dedicated website http://www.speakbahasaindonesia.com

TEST YOURSELF

1 How would you say *Hello!* on the phone in Indonesian?

2 How would you say *stormy* in Indonesian?

3 Under what circumstances do **me-** and **pe-** become **men-** and **pen-**?

4 Under what circumstances do **me-** and **pe-** become **meng-** and **peng-**?

5 Under what circumstances do **me-** and **pe-** become **meny-** and **peny-**?

6 What does **bahasa gaul** use in place of **tidak**?

7 In **bahasa gaul** what does **dong** mean?

8 How does **bahasa gaul** express **ibu**?

9 What does **terima kasih** become in street Indonesian?

10 What does street Indonesian use as a question tag?

The Indonesian alphabet

🔊 **CD1, TR4, 2:36**

You may need to spell your name while you are in Indonesia. This guide will show you how to pronounce the names of the letters:

a as in father
b like the word **bay**
c pronounced **chay** or as in **Che** Guevara
d like the word **day**
e as in d**ay**
f same as in English
g like the word **gay**
h pronounced **hah** with a puff of air on the last **h**
i as in j**ee**p
j like the word **jay**
k pronounced **kah** with a puff of air on the **h**
l same as in English
m same as in English
n same as in English
o as in h**o**t
p like the word **pay**
q like the word **key**
r like the (English) word **air** but with a trilled **r**
s same as in English
t pronounced **tay** but with a soft **t**
u as in p**oo**l
v like the word **fey**
w like the word **way**
x same as in English
y pronounced **yay**
z pronounced **zep**

Key to the exercises

PRONUNCIATION GUIDE

1 Down 1 enam 2 satu 3 tujuh 5 delapan 6 asyik 7 tolong 10 empat 11 lima 13 haus 16 baru 18 sepuluh 20 énak 21 tiga **Across** 4 warna 5 dua 8 sekolah 9 senang 12 meréka 14 tidak 15 sembilan 17 khusus 19 tempat

UNIT 1

1 a Saya John. Saya (berasal) dari Amérika. **b** Saya Kylie. Saya (berasal) dari Australia. **c** Saya Suzie. Saya (berasal) dari Kanada.

2 Muhammad – Sumatra – mahasiswa; Sutrisno – Jawa – pengusaha; Tuti – Bali – penari Bali; Endang–Sulawési – pelancong **3 a** true **b** false **c** true **d** false **4 a** Selamat datang di Sydney. **b** Selamat datang di Washington. **c** Selamat datang di London. **d** Selamat datang di (your home town). **5 a** Ini kamus. **b** Dia pengusaha. **c** Itu kopi. **d** Ini toko. **e** Dia guru. **f** Ini air. **6 a** Apakah ini kamus? **b** Apakah dia pengusaha? **c** Apakah itu kopi? **d** Apakah ini toko? **e** Apakah dia guru? **f** Apakah ini air? **7** Maaf... Apakah and/a Bapak Pranoto dari Indonesia?//Ya betul.// Selamat datang di Inggeris. Kenalkan, saya Robert Davies.// Apakah anda dari perusahaan BRITIMPORT?//Ya betul. Senang berkenalan dengan and/a.//Senang berkenalan dengan anda juga. **8** Maaf. Apakah anda Ibu Nasution?//Saya dari perusahaan ANGLOTRANS. Kenalkan, nama saya (*your name*).// Senang berkenalan dengan anda juga.

Test yourself 1 Selamat siang. **2** Selamat pagi. **3** Nama saya *your name.* (*or just* Saya *your name.*) **4** Kenalkan, saya *your name.* **5** Saya dari Java. *or* Saya berasal dari Java. **6** Selamat datang di Inggeris. **7** Kita. **8** Ini Ibu Walters. **9** Apakah. **10** Senang berkenalan dengan anda juga.

UNIT 2

1 a foto dia **b** hadiah meréka **c** jam tangan saya **d** gambar kita
(*or* kami) **2 a** Mari kita berbicara bahasa Indonesia! **b** Mari kita
pergi ke Bandung! **c** Mari kita menunggu di luar! **3 a** false **b** true
c false **d** false **4** Dia sudah **menulis** surat. *He has written a letter.*
Meréka sedang **membaca** koran. *They are reading a newspaper.*
Dia **mengajar** bahasa Indonesia. *She teaches Indonesian.* Saya
sedang **minum** téh. *I am drinking tea.* Kami sedang **menonton** TV.
We are watching TV. **5 a** kaméramu **b** kacamatamu **c** kuncimu
d paspormu **6 a** Apa ini semua kopor-kopormu? (**kopor-kopor
kamu**) **b** Apa dia (sedang) menunggu di luar? **c** Apa dia terjebak
macet? **d** Apa kami terlambat? **7 a** 2 **b** 1 **c** 1 **d** 1 **8** Maaf. Saya
sibuk.//Ya.//Bagus kalau begitu.

Test yourself 1 Terima kasih banyak. **2** Terima kasih kembali/
Kembali/Sama-sama. **3 Saya guru** means *I am a teacher*; **guru** saya
means *my teacher*. **4 Bahasa kami** refers to one's native language,
but not that of the person to whom you are speaking; **bahasa kita**
is inclusive, and refers to the language you share with the person
you are speaking to. **5** Mari. **6** Because the form remains the same
no matter what the time-frame referred to. **7** Maaf. **8** It becomes
shortened to **mu** and it is added to the word it refers to. **9** Apa.
10 Say the statement with a rising intonation.

UNIT 3

1 a orang Spanyol **b** bahasa Cina **c** orang Skotlandia **d** orang
Malaysia **e** bahasa Belanda **f** orang Amérika **g** orang Sélandia
Baru **h** bahasa Malaysia (bahasa melayu) **i** orang Singapura **j**
bahasa Jepang **2 a** kopor-kopor berat **b** pakaian olahraga **c** tempat
tidur **d** teman guru bahasa Indonesia saya **e** guru bahasa Indonesia
teman saya **3 a** false **b** true **c** true **d** false **4 a** Dutch **b** fluently **c**
English **d** It's too fast. **5 a** Dia <u>tidak</u> sopan. **b** Meréka <u>tidak</u> buta.
c Kami <u>tidak</u> tinggal di Denpasar. **d** Itu <u>bukan</u> mobil saya. **e** Dia
<u>tidak</u> gembira. **6 a** bukan **b** tidak **c** tidak **d** tidak **7 a** Dari
mana dia masuk? **b** Di mana dia belajar? **c** Ke mana meréka
membawa kopor itu? **d** Dari mana kami datang? **8 a** Berapa lama

penerbangan dari London ke Jakarta? **b** Berapa kali anda makan nasi goréng? **c** Berapa lama kita menunggu? **d** Berapa lama dia tinggal di Indonesia? **e** Berapa kali dia menélpon? **9 a** Saya tidak pernah melihat film itu. **b** (Apa) kamu pernah (pergi) ke Medan? **c** Kami pernah makan durian. **d** Dia pernah tinggal di Amérika. **10 a** Meréka tidak tiba kemarin. **b** Ini bukan penerbangan ke Jakarta. **c** Saya tidak berbicara bahasa Arab. **d** Isteri saya bukan orang Indonesia. **e** Itu bukan orang utan. **f** Endang tidak keras kepala. **11 a** Dia tidak orang Brazil. X Dia bukan orang Brazil. **b** Dia bukan pemain sepak bola. **c** Kami tidak bahagia. **d** Saya bukan bodoh. X Saya tidak bodoh. **e** Kemarin meréka bukan datang. X Kemarin meréka tidak datang. **12 a** Apa kabar?/Bagaimana kabar anda? **b** Bagaimana dengan penerbangan anda? **c** Apa anda (kamu, Bpk, etc.) masih bujangan? **d** Siapa nama anda?/Siapa nama kamu? **e** (Apa) anda (kamu) pernah ke Miami? **f** Berapa lama meréka mau tinggal di Solo? **g** (Apa) anda (kamu) orang Indonesia (Thailand)? **13** Apa(kah) anda orang Indonesia? Apa kabar?//Maaf. Siapa nama anda?//Nama saya Stuart. Panggil saja Stu.//Jangan kuatir. Saya pernah belajar bahasa Indonesia di sekolah.//Di mana anda tinggal?//Bagaimana dengan Australia?// Berapa lama anda tinggal di Canberra?//Selamat berlibur!

Test yourself 1 Apa kabar? **2** Kabar baik, terima kasih/Baik/Séhat/ Alhamdulillah, baik. **3** A French person. **4** Bahasa Inggeris. **5** Maaf, saya tidal mengerti. **6** You use **siapa** (*who*) not **apa** (*what*). **7** **Bukan** is used with nouns and pronouns; **tidak** is used with verbs and adjectives. **8** After. **9** Tidak pernah. **10** **Selamat tinggal** is said by the person leaving; **selamat jalan** by the person staying.

UNIT 4

1 a Silahkan menyanyi! *Please sing!* **b** Silahkan berbicara! *Please stand up!* **c** Silahkan minum! *Please come in!* **d** Silahkan menari! *Please dance!* **e** Silahkan masuk! *Please drink!* **2 a** Silahkan mengemudi dengan hati-hati! **b** Silahkan menulis dengan teliti! **c** Silahkan membaca dengan tenang! **3 a** true **b** false **c** false **d** true **e** false **4** Guntur Supratna is the best choice as he speaks both English and Indonesian and he has more than five years' experience in sales. **5 a** tahun yang lalu **b** bulan depan **c** dua tahun yang lalu **d** minggu yang lalu **e** tadi siang/siang ini **6 a** Dia sudah menulis. **b** Meréka sedang mengetik. **c** Saya sedang berbicara. **d** Dia sudah membaca. **e** Kamu sedang belajar?/Apa kamu sedang belajar? **7 a** iii, **b** i, **c** ii, **d** iv, **e** wartawan **8** Saya guru bahasa.//Di sekolah bahasa Babel.//Saya punya pengalaman mengajar bahasa Inggeris dan saya bisa berbicara tiga bahasa.//Lima juta, jika memungkinkan.//Bulan depan.

Test yourself 1 Silahkan. **2** Can. **3** Mampu. **4** Use **dengan** + adjective. **5** Seorang. **6** Bulan depan *or* bulan akan dating. **7** Bésok pagi (*not* nanti pagi). **8** Use the tense marker **sedang**. **9** **Sudah** and telah. **10** Telah.

UNIT 5

1 a Dia sedang tidur, bukan? *He's sleeping, isn't he?* or *She's sleeping, isn't she?* **b** Itu salah, bukan? *That's wrong, isn't it?* **c** Meréka bukan tentara, bukan? *They aren't soldiers, are they?* **2 a** sangat gelap, gelap sekali **b** sangat luas, luas sekali **c** sangat bagus, bagus sekali **d** sangat kuat sekali **e** sangat lelah sekali **3 a** cucu perempuan **b** mertua laki-laki **c** keponakan laki-laki **d** kakak perempuan **4 a** Buku itu punya siapa?/Punya siapa buku itu? **b** Pekerjaan ini punya siapa?/Punya siapa pekerjaan ini? **c** Anak ini punya siapa?/Punya siapa anak ini? **d** Mobil itu punya siapa?/ Punya siapa mobil itu? **5 a** Buku siapa itu? **b** Pekerjaan siapa ini? **c** Anak siapa ini? **d** Mobil siapa itu? **6 a** jam tangannya **b** sekolah dasarnya **c** kebunnya **d** alat CDnya **e** Keponakan perempuannya lucu sekali **7 a** Kita/Kami (sedang) menunggu meréka **b** Dia (sudah) menélpon saya **c** Meréka (sudah) mengganggunya **d** Dia mencintainya **e** Kita/Kami (sudah) pergi dengan meréka **8 a** Umur kembar saya empat tahun. **b** Agus berumur sembilan tahun. **c** Umur yang sulang tiga tahun. **d** Cucunya berumur lima tahun. **9 a** true **b** false **c** true **d** false **e** false **f** true **g** true **10** 1 a, 2 e, 3 b, 4 c, 5 d **11 a** anak-anak – *children* (without a double plural this would mean *child*) **b** saudara perempuan **c** buku **d** film-film – *films* (without a double plural this would mean *film*) **e** tas-tas – *bags* (without a double plural it would mean *bag*) **12 a** Dengan siapa

b Dari siapa **c** Untuk siapa **d** Kepada siapa **13 a** Effendi **b** Ana
c Linda **d** Effendi **e** Taufik **f** Linda **14 a** dapur **b** kamar mandi
c ruang tamu **d** ruang makan **15 a** di sebel ah kiri **b** di belatan
c di sebelah kanan **d** di depan **e** di sebelah kanan **16** Terima
kasih. Jangan répot-répot.//Ya, betul. Saya punya dua anak.//Yang
pertama berumur tujuh tahun dan yang kedua berumur empat
tahun.//Dapur di mana?//Terima kasih. Kamar itu punya siapa?

Test yourself 1 Bukan. **2** Sangat. **3** Add **ke-** to the cardinal. **4** Yang
5 Punya and mempunyai. **6 -nya** means *his, her* or *their* and it is
attached to the noun or adjective. **7** Nama saya, saya bernama;
umur saya, saya berumur. **8** Use **dulu**. **9** Akan. **10** By doubling
the noun. **11** When the context is clear doubling the noun is
unnecessary.

UNIT 6

1 a Ada toko cinderamata. **b** Ada rumah makan tradisional.
c Tidak ada hotél. **d** Apa ada informasi? **e** Apa ada pusat kegiatan
olahraga? **f** Tidak ada balai kesenian. **2 a** film yang panjang dan
membosankan **b** anak yang antusias dan pandai **c** perjalanan yang
panjang dan melelahkan **d** tempat beristirahat yang meriah, ramai
dan mahal **e** ruang yang besar, nyaman dan unik **3 a** lima puluh
empat **b** tujuh puluh delapan **c** delapan puluh satu **d** sembilan
puluh sembilan **4 a** Jam tujuh. **b** Jam setengah lima/jam empat
léwat tiga puluh. **c** Jam sepuluh kurang lima belas/jam sembilan
léwat empat puluh lima. **d** Jam sepuluh léwat seperempat/jam
sepuluh léwat lima belas. **e** Jam dua kurang seperempat. **5 a** Hari
ini hari Jumat. **b** Bésok hari Kamis. **c** Lusa hari Jumat. **d** Bésok
hari Kamis. **6 a** rumah yang dia bangun **b** kota yang kami/kita
kunjungi **c** gadis yang dulu bekerja di sini **7 a** false **b** true **c** true
d false **e** false **8 a** iii **b** i **c** vii **d** vi **e** iv **f** viii **g** ii **h** v **9 a** Bunga apa
ini? **b** Acara apa itu? **c** Bahasa apa ini? **10 a** (Apa anda/kamu) mau
lagi? **b** Saya harus mandi lagi. **11 a** Dia bukan penari lagi. **b** Dia
tidak kaya lagi. **12 a** Dia baru saja tiba. **b** Kami baru saja makan
malam. **13 a** Kami akan pergi ke Ciater pada hari Minggu. **b** Di
Ciater ada air panas, kolam renang, rumah makan, dan lain lain.
c Dari pusat kota ke sana memakan waktu dua jam. **14 a** Jam

sebelas. **b** Jam empat belas empat puluh menit (*using the 24-hour clock*) *or* Jam tiga kurang dua puluh menit. **c** Jam dua belas léwat sepuluh menit. **d** Hari Kamis. **e** Jam setengah sembilan. **15** Ya, saya perlu beberapa informasi tentang Medan.//Apa yang bisa saya lihat di sana?//Apa ada pantai yang bagus untuk berselancar?// Dengan penerbangan apa saya bisa ke sana?//Apa termasuk makan?//Berapa harganya?// Terima kasih atas informasinya. Saya akan diskusikan lagi. **Learning tip: a** hospital **b** hot spring (also means *hot water*) **c** tears **d** fountain **e** zoo **f** perfume

Test yourself 1 Ada. **2** Use **belas**. **3** Use **puluh**. **4** Jam. **5** Jam lima léwat seperempat. **6** Pada hari Rabu (*or just* hari Rabu *in spoken Indonesian*). **7** Use them when what you say can be replaced by *what is it that* and *who is it that* respectively. **8** Pada hari apa? *or just* Hari apa? **9** In positive sentences it means *further*, *more* and *again*, and in negative sentences it means *not … any* and *not … any longer*. **10** Atas.

UNIT 7

1 a Kami ujian <u>sekelas</u>. **b** Dia <u>seumur</u> dengan saya. **2 a** Boléh saya buka jendéla? **b** Boléh kita merokok? **c** Boléh saya hidupkan radio? **3 a** Sampaikan salam saya untuknya. **b** Sampaikan salam kami untuk Sue. **c** Sampaikan salam kami untuk meréka. **d** Sampaikan salam saya sekeluarga untuk meréka. **4 a** true **b** false **c** false **d** true **e** false **f** true **g** false **5** 1 c 2 d 3 f 4 e 5 a 6 b **6 a** Meréka berdua sudah datang. **b** Kami bertiga bersahabat dengan baik. **c** Kami bersepuluh (sudah) mendaki gunung Salak. **7 a** drink **b** reply **c** toy **d** choice **e** purchase **f** entertainment **g** work **h** thought **8 a** Jalan Mawar nomor 1 – empat soré – Yenny dan rizal **b** Gedung Kartika – tujuh Juni – tujuh malam **c** Kampus Universitas Pajajaran – sembilan Juni – sepuluh pagi **d** Puncak – tiga puluh satu Désémber – Kamis – delapan malam **9** Terima kasih. Kapan?//Boléh. Saya tidak ada kerjaan bésok.//Maaf kami tidak iasa.//Terima kasih. Sampai ketemu lagi!

Test yourself 1 The same. **2** Bagaimana kalau…? **3** Boléh saya… **4** Mengapa? *or* Kenapa?, the latter being more conversational.

5 Berlim. 6 Bersama dengan. 7 Pada bulan Agustus, *or just*
bulan Agustus. 8 Nouns, verbs and adjectives. 9 It extends
the meaning of the base noun. 10 It reflects the quality of the
adjective base.

UNIT 8

1 a (Maaf, numpang tanya), bagaimana menuju ke hotel
Aryaduta? b (Maaf, numpang tanya), di mana bandara? c
(Maaf, numpang tanya), bagaimana menuju ke Cihampelas? 2
a false b false c false d true e false f true 3 a Kebun Raya Bogor
b Monumén Nasional c SMU 3 d Kebun Binatang Ragunan e
Hotél Mulia 4 a lurus, bélok, menyeberang, antara b keluar,
bélok, terus, menyeberang, belakang c keluar, bélok, sudut 5
Saya tersesat. Saya mau pergi ke kantor pos.//Apa itu di dekat
Hard Rock Café?//Bisa kamu tunjukkan di peta ini? Di mana kita
sekarang?//Terima kasih.

Test yourself 1 Di mana? Bagaimana menuju ke…? 2 Numpang
Tanya. 3 False. 4 As complete vocabulary items. 5 The r drops.
6 Me- 7 No. 8 **Mengajar** means *to teach*; **belajar** means *to learn*.
9 **Membuat** means *to make*; **berbuat** means *to do*. 10 Di antara.

UNIT 9

1 a sembilan belas ribu empat ratus tiga puluh dua b dua juta
delapan ratus enam puluh lima ribu tujuh ratus empat belas c tiga
ribu seratus sembilan puluh tujuh d delapan juta enam ratus ribu
seratus sebelas e dua puluh lima juta seratus lima puluh lima
ribu enam ratus tiga belas 2 a mendaftar kembali b mengulangi
kembali c meneliti kembali d memukul kembali 3 a true b true
c true d false e true f true 4 1st Noncik; 2nd Muhamad; 3rd Budi
(unless you win!) 5 a Beratnya 56 kilo. b Tingginya 45 séntiméter.
c Lebarnya 100 méter. d Dalamnya 2 méter. e Lamanya 7 jam.
6 a to fast b to move c to have a family/to be married 7 a to slice
b to photograph c to rob 8 a seratus sembilan puluh dua juta b dua
ribu tujuh ratus lima puluh c sembilan belas empat lima d tiga
belas juta e tiga belas ribu enam ratus enam puluh tujuh f lima

belas dua belas **g** seratus dua puluh delapan **h** tiga ribu tujuh ratus **i** dua puluh lima ribu **j** tujuh ratus tujuh puluh tujuh **k** tujuh ratus tiga puluh dua **l** seratus lima puluh ribu **m** sembilan belas sembilan dua **9** Selamat siang! Bisa saya tukar dolar ke rupiah?//Bukan. Dolar Singapura.//Berapa nilai tukar?//Seribu dolar. Saya minta beberapa uang kecil.

Test yourself 1 By using **ratus**. **2** By using **ribu**. **3** By using **juta**. **4** Se- **5** Add the numbers after **tahun**. **6** It creates expressions such as *hundreds* and *millions*. **7** It can express *the*, and it is also used with prices, fares, weights and measures. **8** In expressions where the subject is already established, and with prices, fares, weights and measures. **9** It creates a verb meaning to do what is implicit in the noun base. **10** It creates a verb meaning to do what is implicit in the noun base.

UNIT 10

1 a Berapa ongkosnya ke Medan? **b** Berapa ongkosnya dari Kupang ke Dili? **2 a** Jam berapa? **b** Berapa jam? **3 a** tujuh bulan lagi **b** lima puluh lima menit lagi **c** tiga minggu lagi **4** sehari, setahun, seabad **a** dua kali setahun **b** tiga kali sehari **c** satu kali seabad **5 a** false **b** true **c** false **d** false **e** true **f** false **6 a** vi **b** viii **c** iii **d** i **e** iv **f** ii **g** vii **h** v **7 a** tas yang mana **b** ide yang mana **8 a** yang mana **b** bisa tolong minta **c** tolong buatkan **d** tolong antarkan **e** berapa **f** bagaimana **g** ketinggalan **h** naik apa **9** Saya mau pesan tempat duduk ke Melbourne. Kelas ékonomi.//Minggu depan tanggal 15 September. Berapa ongkosnya?//Berapa lama penerbangan ke Melbourne dari Jakarta?//Baik, tolong buatkan reservasi untuk saya atas nama Daniel Johnson. Bisa saya minta duduk di dekat gang?

Test yourself 1 Ongkos. **2** Bisa saya minta…? **3** You should *not* do whatever follows **Dilarang**. **4** In. **5** **Lagi** means *in*, as in after a certain amount of time has passed, whereas **dalam waktu** refers to the time it takes to do something. **6** Once, as in *once a day*. **7** **Waktu** or **ketika** are used to express the past; **kalau** or **jika** refer to the future. **8** Naik. **9** Ber- **10** Telah.

UNIT 11

1 a *Kapan* Tuti berlibur dengan sepupunya di Lombok? b Tahun lalu *siapa yang** berlibur dengan sepupunya di Lombok? *(*Did you remember to use **yang** here? If not, turn back to Unit 6, Section 5.*) c Tahun lalu Tuti berlibur *dengan siapa* di Lombok? d Tahun lalu Tuti berlibur dengan sepupunya *di mana?* 2 1 a Does he eat? b What does he eat? 2 a Do you want to order? b What do you want to order? 3 a Do you read? b What do you read? 3 a true b false c false d true e false f false 4 a keséhatan *health* b keamanan *safety* c kebersihan *cleanliness* d kemudahan *ease* e kejelékan *ugliness* f kenyaman *pleasantness* g kebodohan *stupidity* h kesenangan *happiness* 5 a Meréka akan berangkat ke Inggeris **pada hari apa?** b Yanti pergi **ke mana** dengan Siti? c Pagelaran Ramayana mulai **jam berapa?** d Penerbangan dari Jakarta ke Bali **berapa lama?** e **Kapan** meréka akan pergi berlibur ke Medan? f Orang tuanya sudah datang **dari mana?** g Kita bisa pergi **dengan apa** ke pusat kota? h Keréta Jakarta-Surabaya ada **berapa kali** sehari? 6 Ya. Saya ingin menginap di sini untuk beberapa hari. Apa masih ada kamar yang kosong?// Berapa harganya satu malam?//Apa sudah termasuk sarapan pagi?// Sampai tanggal 10 Désémber. Bisa saya bayar dengan mata uang lain selain dolar Amérika?//Bisa. Sebentar.//Baik. Apa di sini ada sauna?// Buka jam berapa?//Terima kasih.

Test yourself 1 Apa bisa minta? *or* Apa bisa kasih? 2 To look out onto, *or* with a view of 3 It should replace the thing asked about in the corresponding statement. 4 Apa? 5 Biasa *or* terbiasa. 6 Dengan. 7 They form a noun that refers to the quality referred to in the adjective. 8 They create nouns. 9 They form another noun, sometimes referring to institutions. 10 Indonesians may seem disinterested in your problem to avoid embarrassment.

UNIT 12

1 a kedinginan – *too cold* b kepanasan – *too hot* c kepenuhan – *too full* d keasinan – *too salty* e kecepatan – *too fast* f ketinggian – *too tall* 2 a lebih daripada b lebih daripada c lebih daripada

3 a lebih baik **b** paling murah **c** paling sulit **d** lebih cantik **e** lebih ramai **f** lebih pedas **g** paling haus **h** lebih panas **i** lebih kotor **j** paling kecil **4 a** Patung itu (terbuat) dari marmer. **b** Jambang ini (terbuat) dari tanah liat. **c** Bola ini (terbuat) dari karét. **5 a** berdasi **b** bersarung tangan **c** berrok **d** berjas hujan **e** bercelana hitam **f** berkacamata gelap **g** bertopi rotan **6 a** false **b** false **c** false **d** true **e** true **f** false **7 a** keméja **b** topi **c** dasi **d** jakét **e** celana (panjang) **f** kaos kaki **g** (sepasang) sepatu **h** ikat pinggang **i** anting-anting **j** blus **k** rok **l** gelang **m** kalung **8 a** semurah **b** seberat **c** semalu **9 a** sama miskinnya dengan **b** sama botaknya dengan **c** sama genitnya dengan **10 a** embarrassing **b** pleasing **c** satisfying **d** worrying **e** boring **f** frightening **11 a** jerapah **b** kapal terbang **c** Iwan **d** Pulau Kalimantan **e** Arab Saudi **12 a** Rusia **b** Asia **c** Cina **d** Amazon **e** Jayawijaya **13 a** penuh dengan **b** kawin dengan **c** berbicara dengan **d** sama dengan **e** dengan jip **f** kenal dengan **g** terbiasa dengan **h** berteman dengan **14 a** topi – topi – Bambu **b** celana batik – 150.000 rupiah – 24 **c** cincin – Perak **d** wayang – 75.000 rupiah – Kayu **15** Saya mau membeli sesuatu untuk kakak saya.// Terbuat dari apa dasi ini?//Berapa harganya?//Apa ini harga pas?// Baiklah, saya ambil dua yang motifnya berbéda.

Test yourself 1 Terlalu and by using **ke- -an**. **2 Lebih...daripada.** **3 Paling** or **ter-**. **4** Made of/from. **5** It becomes **-ku**. **6** The verb **pakai** (or **memakai**) or the prefix **ber-** added to the clothing item. **7** Ter- **8** By adding se- to the adjective and by using **sama...-nya dengan**. **9** They create a verb that can often be translated by an -*ing* adjective in English. **10** It is a verb used to express an action carried out for someone's benefit, and it is formed with the prefix **me-** in combination with the suffix **-kan**.

UNIT 13

1 (*possible answers*) Saya mau pesan (satu porsi) nasi goréng. Bisa minta (satu porsi) és kacang. Bisa tambah lagi (satu porsi) lumpia. **2 a** false **b** true **c** true **d** true **e** false **f** false **3 Part 1** gado gado **R** rendang **A** nasi kuning **A** saté ayam **A R** lumpia **R** sambal **A R** és alpukat **R** anggur mérah **A** anggur putih **R** **Part 2 a** to have a view of the lake **b** if she could have the recipe **c** 90,000 rupiah

4 A Saya mau pesan bakso. Berapa harganya semangkuk? Jangan terlalu pedas. **B** Saya mau pesan (minuman) téh. Berapa harganya sebotol? Tolong pakai és! **C** Saya mau pesan nasi goréng. Berapa harganya sepiring? Jangan pakai telur. Tolong dibungkus! **D** Saya mau pesan saté kambing. Berapa harganya sepiring? (Bisa) minta setengah matang? **5 a** kebesaran **b** kepedasan **c** kedinginan **d** kehujanan **e** kecopetan **f** kepanasan **g** ketinggalan **6** Untuk satu orang.//Saya mau pesan mie goréng. Apa itu mengandung udang?// Bagus kalau begitu. Saya alérgi kalau makan udang.//Apa ada és campur?//Saya mau pesan és campur tanpa tapé.//Cukup itu saja. Berapa lama makanannya siap?//Tidak apa-apa. Terima kasih.

Test yourself 1 Saya mau pesan, Bisa minta…? **2** Pedas. **3** Bisa tambah lagi? **4** Berlima. **5** Beef. **6** Sepiring *or* satu piring. **7** The choice depends on what the item comes in or on. **8** It can indicate something unplanned, usually unfortunate, has happened. **9** The prefix **ter-**. **10** Cemilan.

UNIT 14

1 a sedikit kopi **b** sedikit nasi goréng **c** beberapa resép **d** sedikit pengetahuan **e** beberapa porsi nasi goréng **2 a** delapan lembar kertas **b** sebuah papaya **c** setangkai bunga mawar **d** empat ékor burung **e** tiga buah kamus **3 a** false **b** true **c** true **d** false **e** false **f** true **4 a** daging sapi, santan, cabé, bawang mérah, bawang putih, jahé, laos, seré, daun kunyit, daun salam, daun jeruk **b** 2 **c** 1 **d** tidak **e** 1 **5 a** dicari **b** diperiksa **c** ditulis **d** dikirim **e** diantar **f** dijemput **6 a** Lagu didengar dia. **b** TV ditonton meréka. **c** Obat harus diminum tiga kali sehari. **d** Pasién disuntik (oléh) doctor. **7 a** seékor **b** sebuah **c** sebutir **d** selembar **e** setangkai **f** sepucuk **8 b** Saya mau beli ikan. Berapa harganya sekilo? **c** Saya mau beli wortel. Berapa harganya sekilo? **d** Saya mau beli whiski. Berapa harganya sebotol? **e** Saya mau beli pisang. Berapa harganya sekilo? **9** Saya mau beli daging sapi.//Dua kilo. Berapa harganya?// Tolong dipotong-potong.//Terima kasih.

Test yourself 1 Sedikit can only be used for uncountable things, and **beberapa** can only be used with countable ones. **2** You can use it for countable or non-countable things. **3** Berapa banyak? **4** They are used to count objects depending on what category they belong to. **5** ékor **6** Se- **7** No. **8** Di- **9** Me- **10** Oléh.

UNIT 15

1 a olah-raga kegemaran **b** bintang film kesukaan/kesayangan **c** guru kesukaan/kesayangan **d** sandiwara kegemaran **e** binatang kesukaan/kesayangan **2 a** Pacar saya penggemar Leonardo di Caprio. **b** Meréka penggemar makanan Cina. **c** Adik (Kakak) penggemar sinétron. **d** Anda (Kamu) penggemar bola kaki, (bu) kan? **3 a** false **b** true **c** false **d** true **e** false **f** true **4 a** 2 **b** 1 **c** 1 **d** 3 **5 a** Saya (sudah) belajar pencak silat selama tiga minggu.
b Dia tertarik dengan karaté sejak dia pergi ke Jepang. **6 a** writer **b** helper **c** buyer **d** seller **e** guard **f** teacher **g** worker **h** runner **7 a** iii **b** iv **c** vii **d** xiii **e** xiv **f** viii **g** v **h** xv **i** xvii **j** xvi **k** xii **l** ix **m** vi **n** i **o** xi **p** x **q** ii (possible sentences) Saya suka sekali berenang. Saya suka sekali menyanyi. Saya suka menari. Saya suka fotografi. Saya tidak begitu suka berkebun. Saya kurang suka masak.
8 Saya paling suka membaca dan bepergian.//Buku-buku psikologi, budaya dan sejarah.//Tidak begitu, tapi novel-novel karya Agatha Christie saya sangat suka.//Negara-negara di Asia, khususnya Indonesia, Malaysia, Cina dan lain lain.//Hm, saya tidak begitu suka.//Saya juga tidak suka.

Test yourself 1 **Suka** and **gemar**. **2** It cannot be used to refer to people or animals. **3** Use **tidak begitu suka** or **kurang**. (Remember the word **benci** is harsher in Indonesian than it is in English.) **4** Use **kegemaran** or **kesukaan**. **5** Kesayangan kesukaan. **6** It also means *favourite* and its usage is unrestricted. **7** Penggemar. **8** Main.
9 **Selama** and **sejak** respectively. **10** It indicates the performer of an action.

UNIT 16

1 a Dia sakit kepala. **b** Apa anda/kamu sakit telinga? **c** Saya sakit tangan. **2 a** Keluarkan sampah! **b** Lari lebih cepat! **c** Jangan bekerja sepanjang hari! **d** Jangan membeli terlalu banyak coklat!

3 **a** true **b** false **c** true **d** false **e** true 4 1 e 2 f 3 i 4 b 5 d 6 a 7 h
8 j 9 g 10 c 5 **a** shopping mall **b** rural area **c** accommodation
d plantation **e** conversation **f** examination **g** announcement **h** fight
i experiment 6 **a** sakit gigi **b** batuk **c** demam **d** sakit tenggorokan
e sakit mata 7 Mata saya gatal dan perih.//Sudah dua hari, sejak
hari Minggu//Saya alérgi dengan debu, Dokter. Mulanya mata saya
cuma mérah, tetapi setelah itu bengkak.//Terima kasih, Dokter.

Test yourself 1 Sakit. **2** Minum *or* pakai. **3** The **me-** prefix.
4 It remains. **5** Use **jangan**. **6** It softens it. **7** The passive. **8** Time
expressions, doing something with no particular goal in mind and
for emphasis. **9** One that extends or augments the meaning of the
base. **10** Air putih.

UNIT 17

1 **a** menerjemahkan **b** mengusik **c** menyisir **d** membantah **e**
pembangunan **f** penyerang **g** penyegar **h** pengimporan 2 Selamat
pagi, bisa bicara dengan Lina?//Apa ini 769 1254?//Maaf,
terima kasih. Ini 769 1254?//Ini Julia, bisa bicara dengan Lina?//
Sampaikan saja salam saya untuk dia.//Baik, terima kasih.

Test yourself 1 Halo! **2** Banyak badai. **3** Before **c, d, j** and **t**.
4 Before **g, h, k** and vowels. **5** Before **s**, which disappears. **6** Nggak.
7 It is used for emphasis. **8** Nyokap. **9** Ya? **10** Makasih.

Listening transcripts

UNIT 1, EXERCISE 2

🔊 **CD1, TR 2, 2:08**

1 Nama saya Muhammad. Saya berasal dari Sumatra. Saya mahasiswa.
2 Nama saya Sutrisno. Saya berasal dari Jawa. Saya pengusaha.
3 Saya Tuti. Saya dari Bali. Saya penari Bali.
4 Saya Endang. Saya dari Sulawesi. Saya pelancong.

UNIT 3, EXERCISE 4

🔊 **CD1, TR 4, 1:40**

Ibu Rani	Siapa nama anda?
Interviewee	Nama saya Klaus. Klaus Van Joll.
Rani	Apakah anda berasal dari Australia?
Interviewee	Bukan, saya berasal dari Belanda, dari Amsterdam.
Rani	Anda berbicara dengan lancar dan jelas sekali. Apakah anda bisa berbicara Jerman?
Interviewee	Maaf, bisa Ibu ulangi lagi. Saya tidak mengerti. Ibu berbicara sangat cepat.
Rani	Apakah anda bisa berbicara bahasa Jerman?
Interviewee	Tidak, saya hanya berbicara bahasa Belanda, Indonesia dan Inggeris saja.

UNIT 5, EXERCISE 10

🔊 **CD1, TR 6, 2:32**

1 Nama saya Sunaryo belum menikah berasal dari keluarga besar. Ibu dan bapak saya pegawai negeri. Saya mempunyai dua kakak laki-laki dan seorang kakak perempuan. Meréka semua telah

bekerja. Adik saya dua orang, pelajar. Adik saya yang kecil berumur empat tahun, belum sekolah.

2 Saya bernama Tanti dari Surabaya. Saya sudah menikah tapi belum mempunyai anak. Saya tinggal dengan mertua saya. Suami saya montir di sebuah béngkél. Saya seorang penjahit pakaian.

3 Saya Beni, duda dengan dua orang anak. Saya sudah cerai tiga tahun yang lalu. Novi tujuh tahun dan Toni sepuluh tahun. Keduanya murid sekolah Dasar.

4 Saya bernama Anton, manajer di perusahaan swasta di Jakarta. Isteri saya seorang perancang mode di perusahaan pakaian anak-anak. Anak saya dua orang, laki-laki dan perempuan. Hadi berumur delapan tahun dan Weni berumur enam tahun.

5 Saya Indra, masih bujangan berasal dari keluarga kecil. Saya kuliah di Universitas Atmajaya di Jakarta. Saya anak tunggal. Ibu saya setiap hari sibuk bekerja di butik dan ayah saya seorang dosén.

UNIT 8, EXERCISE 3

a

> CD1, TR 9, 1:14

A   Maaf Pak, numpang tanya. Di mana Kebun Raya Bogor?
B   Sekitar dua ratus méter dari sini, dekat Istana Bogor. Jalan lurus sampai perempatan, kemudian bélok kanan.
A   Terima kasih.

b

A   Permisi, Pak. Di mana tugu Monumén Nasional?
B   Maksud Bapak Monas? Kami selalu menyebutnya Monas.
A   Ya. Maksud saya Monas.
B   Dari sini jalan lurus sampai lampu mérah, kemudian bélok kiri. Monas ada di belakang Bank BCA.

c

A	Permisi, Pak. Di mana SMU 2?
B	Tidak ada SMU 2 di sekitar sini, yang ada SMU 3 di samping lapangan sepak bola itu.
A	Terima kasih Pak, maksud saya SMU 3.

d

A	Permisi, Pak. Saya mau tanya di mana Kebun Binatang Ragunan?
B	Maaf, saya tidak tahu. Saya bukan berasal dari sini. Coba tanya ke toko di seberang jalan?
A	Terima kasih.
A	Permisi, Pak, di mana Kebun Binatang Ragunan?
C	Di ujung jalan ini. Di dekat SMU Ragunan.

e

A	Permisi, Pak. Bagaimana caranya ke hotel Sahid?
B	Apa? Sahid Jaya?
A	Ya, Sahid Jaya. Sebentar Pak, saya salah. Maksud saya hotel Mulia…
B	Hotel Mulia? Lurus saja, ikuti jalan ini sampai bertemu dengan bundaran, kemudian bélok kanan. Hotel Mulia ada setelah Plaza Senayan.

UNIT 9, EXERCISE 4

🔊 **CD2, TR 2, 1.28**

The numbers called out in the lottery game are: 47, 18, 56, 13, 6, 69, 43, 85, 50, 16, 63, 94, 61, 30, 28, 72, 9, 11, 83, 24, 58, 77, 38, 20, 59, 41, 12, 22, 34, 17, 29, 10, 98, 70, 32, 79, 37, 91, 7, 36, 21, 87, 3, 52, 60, 99, 93, 25, 66, 45.

UNIT 13, EXERCISE 3

CD2, TR 6, 2.00

Pelayan	Selamat malam. Méja untuk berdua?
Agus	Ya. Bisa méja di dekat jendéla? Saya suka pemandangan danau.
Pelayan	Tentu, Pak. Silahkan ikut saya. Ini daftar makanannya. Satu untuk Ibu dan ini untuk Bapak. Saya kembali lagi kalau bapak dan ibu sudah siap.
Ratih	Wow! Saya lapar sekali.
Agus	Saya juga. Saya berseléra untuk makan.
Ratih	Mudah-mudahan meréka punya saté kambing. Eh lihat, meréka punya. Saya dengar saté kambing di sini terkenal.
Pelayan	Apa ibu dan bapak sudah siap?
Agus	Kamu sudah ada yang dipesan?
Ratih	Ya.
Agus	Bisa saya pesan saté ayam dan nasi kuning? Hm… tunggu sebentar. Bisa saya pesan rendang juga?
Pelayan	Saté ayam, nasi kuning, rendang daging dan untuk ibu?
Ratih	Hm, saya mau saté kambing dan e…
Pelayan	Oh maaf, Bu. Saté kambingnya sudah habis, tapi kami ada saté ayam. Lezat sekali. Kami punya resep sendiri.
Ratih	Sayang sekali. Saya benar-benar kepingin saté kambing, tetapi tidak apa-apa. Saya yakin saté ayam juga énak.
Pelayan	Satu porsi saté ayam, dan yang lain?
Ratih	Ya, saya mau gado-gado.
Pelayan	Saté ayam, gado-gado. Itu saja?
Ratih	Um, saya juga mau lumpia.
Pelayan	Baik, jadi saté ayam, gado-gado dan lumpia.
Agus	Apa makanannya diberi sambal?
Pelayan	Maaf harus dipesan terpisah.
Agus	Tolong sambal untuk dua orang.
Pelayan	Baik. Mau pesan minuman apa?
Agus	Ya, segelas red wine untuk saya dan bagaimana dengan kamu, Sayang?
Ratih	Saya juga, sama.

Pelayan	Baik, jadi dua gelas red wine.
Ratih	Tunggu, saya berubah pikiran. Bisa segelas white wine untuk saya?
Pelayan	Tidak masalah. Satu gelas white wine… Bagaimana makanannya Pak, Bu?
Ratih	Lezat sekali, terima kasih, khususnya saté ayam. Saya belum pernah merasakan saté ayam yang selezat ini. Apa resépnya?
Pelayan	Maaf, Bu. Saya tidak bisa memberitahu. Itu rahasia koki. Apa mau makanan penutup?
Agus	Saya kenyang sekali. Apa kamu mau coba satu?
Ratih	Ya. Punya és alpukat?
Pelayan	Ya, kami punya. Satu és alpukat?
Ratih	Ya.
Agus	Bisa minta bonnya?
Pelayan	Tentu Pak. Ini.
Ratih	Berapa semuanya?
Agus	90.000 rupiah.
Ratih	Sangat murat, ya?

Indonesian–English vocabulary

abu-abu   *grey*
acara   *programme*
acara pernikahan   *wedding ceremony*
Ada apa?   *What's wrong?*
Ada gula ada semut.   *Where there is sugar there are ants.*
adat   *tradition, custom*
ahli   *expert*
ahli hukum   *lawyer.*
air   *water*
air mancur   *fountain*
air panas   *hot spring, hot water*
air putih   *drinking water*
akademi   *academy.*
akan   *will/shall*
akhir pekan   *weekend*
akutansi   *accounting*
alamat   *address*
alat CD   *CD player*
alérgi   *allergy*
alérgi dengan   *allergic to*
alérgik   *allergic*
aman   *safe*
ambil   *take*
Amérika   *America*
anak-anak   *children*
anak laki-laki   *son*
anak muda   *young people*
anak perempuan   *daughter*
anak tunggal   *only child*
anéh   *weird*
anggap   *to consider*
Anggap saja rumah sendiri!   *Make yourself at home!*
anggur   *wine*

angklung   *a West Javanese bamboo instrument*
angkot   *public city transport*
angkot yang berwarna coklat   *the brown-coloured angkot*
anjing   *dog*
antar   *to take (someone, somewhere)*
Antarkan saya ke…   *Take me to…*
antusias   *enthusiastic*
apa/apakah   *question marker*
apoték   *pharmacy*
arsitektur   *architecture*
asam   *sour*
asaman (asam, a)   *pickles*
asap   *smoke, fumes*
asin   *salty*
asli   *original*
atas   *on, for*
atas nama   *under the name of*
aula   *auditorium, hall*
aula sekolah   *school hall*
Australia   *Australia*
Awas!   *Watch out!*
ayam   *chicken*
ayam goréng   *fried chicken*
Ayo!   *Come on!*

baca   *to read*
Bagaimana?   *How?*
Bagaimana kabar anda?   *How are you?*
Bagaimana menuju ke…?   *How do I get to…?*

Bagaimana rasanya? *What does it taste like?*

bagi *for*

bagian *part, section*

bagus *good, nice*

Bagus kalau begitu. *That's fine.*

bahagia *happy*

bahan *material*

bahasa *language*

Bahasa Indonesia *Indonesian (language)*

baik *well, good, fine*

baiklah *all right*

Baiklah kalau begitu. *That's fine.*

baju *dress, outer clothes*

bakar *to grill*

bakmi *noodles*

bakso/baso *meatball soup with noodles*

bala-bala *fried vegetables with flour*

balai *public building*

balét *ballet*

balik arah *U turn*

bambu *bamboo*

bandara (bandar udara) *airport*

bangun *to get up, to wake up, to build*

bantu *to help*

bantuan (bantu, v) *help*

banyak *a lot, many*

Bapak *Mr*

bar *bar*

baru *new*

baru sampai *just arrived*

baso *meatball*

bau *to smell bad*

bawah tanah *underground*

bawang bombay *onion*

bawang mérah *shallot/red onion*

bawang putih *garlic*

bayam *spinach*

bayar *to pay*

beberapa *some, a few*

bekerja (kerja, v) *to work*

belajar (ajar, v) *to learn, to study*

belakang *behind*

Belanda *Dutch*

belanja *shopping*

beli *to buy*

belian (beli, v) *a purchase, purchased item(s)*

bélok *to turn*

bélokan (bélok, v) *turning*

belum *not yet*

benci *to hate*

béngkél *workshop, garage*

bepergian (pergi, v) *travelling*

berada *to be*

berangkat (angkat, v) *to leave for, to set out*

Berapa? *How many?, How much?*

berasal dari *to come from*

berat *heavy*

beratnya *it weighs*

berbéda (béda, n) *different*

berbelanja (belanja, n) *to go shopping*

berbicara (bicara, v) *to speak*

bercanda (canda, v) *to kid*

berdebar (debar, v) *to beat*

berdiri (diri, n) *to stand up*

berdua *two person(s), in a pair*

berenang (renang) *to swim*

bergaul (gaul, v) *to socialize*

berhasil (hasil, n) *succeed*

berhenti (henti, v) *to stop*

berhitung (hitung, v) to count
berhubungan (hubung, a) to be in contact with
beri to give
berjalan (jalan, v) to walk
berjalan kaki go on foot
berjemur (jemur, v) to sunbathe
berkebun (kebun, n) to do gardening
berkeluarga (keluarga, n) married
berkemah (kemah, v) to go camping
berkomunikasi (komunikasi, v) to communicate
berkunjung (kunjung, v) to visit
berlaku (laku, n) to be valid
berlari (lari, v) to run
berlibur (libur, n) to be on holiday
bermacam-macam many different kinds of
bernafas (nafas, n) to breathe
bernostalgia (nostalgia, n) to be nostalgic
berpakaian (pakai, v) to get dressed
berpakaian rapi dress well
bersejarah (sejarah, n) historical
berselancar (lancar, a) to go surfing
berseléra (seléra, n) to have an appetite
bersenang-senang to have a good time
bersih clean
bertanya (tanya, n) to ask
bertemu (temu, v) to meet
bertiga (tiga) three persons, as a three

beruntung (untung, n) to be lucky
betah to feel at home, to feel comfortable
betul that's correct
biasanya usually
biaya cost
bidang field
bingung confused
biologi biology
bioskop movie theatre, cinema
biro perjalanan travel agency
biru blue
biru muda light blue
bisa can, to be able to
biskuit biscuit
bisnis business
bisnis manajemen business management
bistik steak
bodoh stupid
bola kaki football, soccer
bola voli volleyball
boléh may
bon bill
bosan to get bored
botak bald
brosur brochure
buat to make, to do
buatan tangan hand made
bubur ayam rice porridge with chicken, tofu and celery
bubur kacang hijau mung bean porridge
bubur ketan hitam sticky rice sweet with coconut milk
bujangan single, bachelor
buka open
bukan no
buku book

bulan *month*
bumbu-bumbu *spices*
bundaran *roundabout*
bunga *flower*
burung *bird*
buta *blind*
butah *necessity*
butik *boutique, shop*

cabé *chilli*
campur *mix, mixed*
cantik *beautiful*
cap *printed*
capai *to reach*
capcai *stir-fried vegetables*
capek *tired*
cara *way, method*
cari *look for*
cék-in *check in*
celana *trousers*
celana panjang *trousers*
cepat *fast*
Cepat! *Hurry up!*
cerai *divorced*
céréwet *talkative*
ceritakan (cerita, v) *to tell*
Cina *China*
cinderamata *souvenir*
cita-cita *goals, ambitions, dreams*
coba *to try*
coklat *brown*
coklat tua *dark brown*
corak *pattern*
cuaca *weather*
cuci *to wash*
cukup *enough*
cuma *just, only*

daérah *area*
daftar *list*

daftar makanan *menu*
daging *meat*
dalam *inside*
dalang *puppeteer, dalang*
damai *peaceful*
dan *and*
danau *lake*
dangdut *dangdut, folk singing and dancing*
dari *from*
dari mana? *where from?*
dasar *basic, typical*
datang *to come*
datanglah (datang, v) *please come*
daun *leaf*
daun jeruk *lemon leaves*
dekat *near*
delapan *eight*
demam *feverish*
dengan *with*
dengan baik sekali *very well*
dengan lambat *slowly*
dengan lancar *fluently*
di *in*
di antara *in between*
di belakang *at the back*
di depan *in front*
Di jalan apa? *On what street?*
di luar *outside*
di samping *next to*
di sana *there*
di sebelah kanan *on the right*
di sebelah kiri *on the left*
di seberang jalan *across the road*
di sini *here*
dibungkus *to take out, to take away, wrapped up (food)*
digabung (gabung, n) *to be combined*

dihabiskan (habis, v)   to be spent on
diisi (isi, v)   to be filled in
dijual (jual, v)   to be sold
dikemas (kemas, v)   to be packed
dikunjugi (kunjung, v)   to be visited
dilarang (larang, v)   to be probibited, No...
dinding   wall
diperas (peras, v)   to be extracted
diskon   discount
diskusikan (diskusi, n)   to be discussed
ditimbang (timbang, v)   to be weighed
dodol   an Indonesian sweet
dokter   doctor
dokter gigi   dentist
dolar   dollar
dosen   lecturer
drama   drama
dua   two
dua hari yang lalu   the day before yesterday
duda   widow
duduk   to sit down, seat
duduk di dekat jendéla   a window seat
dulu   a long time ago, previously
dunia   world
durian   a spikey kind of fruit

éja   to spell
ékononi   economy
enam   six
érobik   aerobics
és   ice

fasilitas   facility
favorit   favourite
film   film
foto   photo
fotografi   photography

gadis   young lady, girl
gado-gado   cooked vegetables with peanut dressing
gajah   elephant
gaji   salary
gambar   picture
gambaran (gambar, n)   description
gamelan   Indonesian orchestra
ganteng   handsome
garpu   fork
gayung   scoop
gedung   building
gelang   bracelet
gelap   dark
gembira   happy
genit   flirtatious, coquettish
géografi   geography
giat   energetic, active
gula   sugar
gulai   Indonesian-style curry
gunung   mountain
guru   teacher
guru besar   senior lecturer

hadap   front
hadiah   present
Halo!   Hello! (on the phone)
halte   bus stop
hampir   almost
hanya   only
harap   to hope
harapkan (harap, v)   to expect
harga   price
harga pas   fixed price

hari day
hari ini today
hari libur holiday
harum fragrance
harus must, have to
hati-hati careful
haus thirsty
hiasan decoration
hiasan dinding wall decoration
hiburan entertainment
hidup life
hijau green
hitam black
hitung to count
hobi hobby
hotél hotel
hubungan masyarakat sociology
Hujan deras. It's raining heavily.
hukum law

ibu rumah tangga housewife
ide idea
ikan fish
iklan advertisement
ikut to follow
ikuti (ikut, v) to follow
ilmu knowledge, science
ilmu kedokteran medicine (as a subject)
ilmu lingkungan environmental studies
ilmu sastra humanities
ilmu wisata tourism
ilmuwan scientist
impor import
indah beautiful (of places)
informasi information
Inggeris England
ingin to want
ini this, this is

inspirasi inspiration
Irlandia Irland
isteri wife
istirahat rest, stay
itu that, that is

jadi so
jahé ginger
jaipongan traditional music from West Java
jalan to walk, street
jalanan (jalan, n) road
jalan-jalan take a leisurly walk, hang around
jam hour, time
jam tangan watch
jangan don't
jangan kuatir don't worry
Jangan repot-repot. Don't trouble yourself too much.
janji appointment
jantung heart
jarang rarely
jauh far
jawaban (jawab, n) answer
jelas clear
jelék ugly
jendéla window
Jepang Japan
Jerman Germany
jeruk orange, citrus fruit
jika if
jika memungkinkan if possible
joging jogging
juga too, also
Jumat Friday
juru foto/juru potrét photographer
juru masak chef
juta million
jutawan millionaire

kabar news
kacamata spectacles
kacang peanut
kadang-kadang sometimes
kain sarung sarong
kakak elder sister/brother
kakék grandfather
kalau if
kaléng can
kalung necklace
kamar room
kamar kosong vacancies
kamar mandi bathroom
kamar tidur bedroom
kambuh lagi to come back
  (of an illness)
kaméra camera
kami we
Kamis Thursday
kampus campus
kamu you (informal)
kamus dictionary
Kanada Canada
kantor office
kantor polisi police station
kapal vessel, boat
kapan when
kapan-kapan sometimes
karaoké karaoke
karaté karate
karena because
kari curry
kartu krédit credit card
kartu nama name card
kasih to give
kasir cashier
kawin married
kaya rich
ke mana where to?
keahlian (ahli, n) skill
keahlian teknik engineering

keasinan too salty
kebaikan goodness, too good
keberangkatan (berangkat, v)
  departure
kebesaran too big
kebetulan by chance, by
  accident
kebudayaan (budaya, n) culture
kebun garden
kecak a Balinese dance
  accompanied by ritual chanting
kécap manis sweet soya sauce
kecelakaan (celaka, a) accident
kedinginan too cold
kedua second
keduanya both of them
kegiatan (giat, a) activity
kehabisan to run out of
kehausan (haus, a) very thirsty
kehidupan (hidup, n) way of life
keindahan (indah, a) beauty
kekecilan (kecil, a) too small
kelapa coconut
kelapa muda young coconut
kelas class
kelepon sweet, green rice ball
kelihatan (lihat, v) to look, seem
keluhan (keluh, v) complaint,
  symptom
kelupaan (lupa, v) to forget
kemahalan (mahal, a) too
  expensive
kemana-mana everywhere
kemarin yesterday
kemarin soré yesterday
  afternoon
kembali to return, to come back,
  to do something again
Kembali! Don't mention it!
kembar twins
keméja shirt

kemudian *then*
Kenalkan, saya... *Let me introduce myself, I'm...*
kentang *potato*
kepala *head*
kepala sekolah *head teacher*
kepanasan (panas, *a*) *too hot*
kepanjangan (panjang, *a*) *too long*
kepéndékan (péndék, *a*) *too short*
kerajinan (rajin, *a*) *diligence, handicraft*
kerajinan tangan *handicraft*
keran *tap*
keras *hard, loud*
keréta *train*
kerjaan (kerja, *v*) *job*
kerjakan (kerja, *v*) *to do*
kerupuk *cracker*
kerupuk kentang *chips*
kesenian (seni, *n*) *art*
kesulitan (sulit, *a*) *difficulty*
ketinggian (tinggi, *a*) *too tall*
ketrampilan (trampil, *a*) *skill*
keuangan (uang, *n*) *finance*
khusus *special*
kimia *chemistry*
kipas *fan*
kira *to estimate, to guess*
kira-kira *around, about, approximately*
kirim *to send*
klasik *classic*
klub malam *nightclub*
kode *code*
kolam renang *swimming pool*
komedi *comedy*
komputer *computer*
kontan *cash*
kopi *coffee*

kopor *luggage*
koran *newspaper*
kosong *empty*
kotoran (kotor, *a*) *rubbish, trash*
kuat *strong (physically)*
kuatir *worry*
kucing *cat*
kué *cake*
kuliah *university lecturer*
kumpul *to assemble, to gather*
kunci *key*
kuning *yellow*
kunjung *to visit*
kunyit *turmeric*
kupon *coupon*
kurang yakin *not sure*
kurangi (kurang, *n*) *to reduce*
kursus *course*
kwetiau *flat, thick noodles*

laboratorium *laboratory*
lagi *again*
lagu *song*
lain *another*
lakukan *to do*
lambat *slow*
lampu *lamp*
lampu mérah *traffic light*
lancar *fluent*
langganan (langgan, *v*) *customer*
langsing *slim*
langsung *direct*
lantai *floor, storey*
lantai atas *upstairs*
lantai bawah *downstairs*
laos *galangal*
lapangan *field*
lapangan terbang *airport*
larang *to forbid*
lapar *hungry*

latihan (latih, *v*) *to practise, to train*
lautan (laut, *n*) *ocean*
layak *decent, fair, worth it*
lebih *better, more*
lebih suka *to prefer*
lelah *tired*
lemari *cupboard*
lemari és *fridge*
lemas *weak*
léwat *past*
lezat *delicious*
liburan (libur, *n*) *holiday*
lihat *to see*
Lihat! *Look!*
lima *five*
lodéh *vegetables cooked in coconut milk*
lokét *ticket window*
luar negeri *foreign country*
luas *wide, broad*
lucu *cute*
lumpia *spring roll*
lupa *forget*
lurus *straight on*
lusa *the day after tomorrow*

Maaf! *Excuse me, I am sorry!*
maafkan (maaf, *v*) *to forgive*
Maafkan saya. *I'm sorry.*
mabuk *drunk*
macet luar biasa *a big traffic jam*
mahal *expensive*
mahasiswa/i *student*
main *to play*
mainan (main, *v*) *toy*
makan malam *dinner*
makan pagi *breakfast*
makan siang *lunch*
makanan (makan, *v*) *food*

makanan ringan *snack*
Malaysia *Malaysia*
malu *shy*
mampu *capable*
mandi *to take a shower, to take a bath*
mandi uap *steam bath*
manis *sweet (to the taste)*
manisan (manis, *a*) *sweets*
marah *angry*
margarin *margarine*
mari *let, allow*
marun *maroon*
masa *period, phase*
masa berlaku *validity*
masak *to cook*
masakan (masak, *v*) *cuisine*
masih *still*
masuk *to enter*
masukkan (masuk, *v*) *put in*
matématika *mathematics*
mau *to want, will*
méja *table*
melelahkan (lelah, *a*) *tiring*
memasak (masak, *v*) *to cook*
membaca (baca, *v*) *to read*
membantu (bantu, *v*) *to help*
membawa (bawa, *v*) *bring, take*
membeli (beli, *v*) *to buy*
membelikan (beli, *v*) *to buy (for someone)*
memberi (beri, *v*) *to give*
memberi kabar *to inform, to let know*
membuang (buang, *v*) *to throw*
membuang sampah *to litter*
membuat (buat, *v*) *to make*
memeriksa (periksa, *v*) *to examine*
memerlukan (perlu, *v*) *to need*
memesan (pesan, *v*) *to order*

menari (tari, *v*) *to dance*
menarik (tarik, *v*) *interesting, to pul*
menarik uang *to withdraw money*
menawarkan (tawar, *v*) *to offer*
mencampuri (campur, *v*) *to interfere*
mencari (cari, *v*) *to look for*
mencintai (cinta, *v*) *to love*
menderita (derita, *n*) *to suffer*
menélpon (télpon, *n*) *to telephone*
menerima (terima, *v*) *to accept, to receive*
mengajak (ajak, *v*) *to invite*
mengajar (ajar, *v*) *to teach*
mengajari (ajar, *v*) *to educate, to teach*
mengambil (ambil, *v*) *to take*
mengantar (antar, *v*) *to take (someone somewhere)*
mengapa? *why?*
mengawasi (awas, *v*) *to watch over*
mengemudi (kemudi, *v*) *to drive*
mengenai *about*
mengenal (kenal, *v*) *to know*
mengerjakan (kerja, *v*) *to do, to carry out*
mengerti (erti, *v*) *to understand*
mengetik (ketik, *v*) *to type*
mengganggu (ganggu, *v*) *to disturb*
menggigil (gigil, *v*) *shivering*
menggunakan (guna, *v*) *to use*
menghadap (hadap, *v*) *to face*
menghadiri (hadir, *v*) *to attend*
menghubungi (hubung, *v*) *to contact*
menginap (inap, *v*) *to stay, to spend the night*

mengingat (ingat, *v*) *to remember*
mengkilap (kilap, *v*) *to shine, to be shiny*
mengkonfirmasikan (konfirmasi, *v*) *to confirm*
mengundang (undang, *v*) *to invite*
mengundang seléra *to make one's mouth water*
mengurus (urus, *v*) *to look after*
menikah (nikah, *n*) *married*
menikmati (nikmat, *n*) *to enjoy*
meninggal (tinggal, *v*) *to die*
menit *minute*
menjadi (jadi, *v*) *to become*
menjaga (jaga, *v*) *to look after*
menjelaskan (jelas, *a*) *to explain*
menjemput (jemput, *v*) *to pick up*
menjual (jual, *v*) *to sell*
menonton (tonton, *v*) *to watch*
mentah *raw, undercooked*
menteri *minister*
menulis (tulis, *v*) *to write*
menunggu (tunggu, *v*) *to wait*
menunjukkan (tunjuk, *v*) *to show*
menyanyi (nyanyi, *v*) *to sing*
menyediakan (sedia, *a*) *to provide*
menyelam (selam, *v*) *to dive*
menyelesaikan (selesai, *v*) *to finish*
menyenangkan (senang, *a*) *pleasant*
menyéwa (séwa, *v*) *to rent*
menyiapkan (siap, *a*) *to prepare*
menyuntik (suntik, *v*) *to inject*
mérah *red*
mérah jambu *pink*

merancang (rancang, *v*)
  to design
merayakan (raya, *a*)   to celebrate
merépotkan (répot, *a*)   to bother
meriah   lively
merica   pepper
merokok (rokok, *n*)   to smoke
mertua   parent-in-law
mesin   machine
mesin ATM   ATM machine
mesin fax   fax machine
méter   meter
mie   noodles
minggu   week
minggu depan   next week
minta   to ask for, to request
minum   to drink
minuman (minum, *v*)   drink
minuman keras   alcoholic
  drink(s)
misalnya   for example
miskin   poor
mobil   car
modern   stylish
montir   mechanic
monumén   monument
mual   to feel like vomiting
mudah   easy
mudah-mudahan   hopefully
mulai   to start
mungkin   maybe
muntah terus   to vomit
murah   cheap
murid   pupil, student in the lower
  grades
musik   music
musium   museum

naik   to go up, to ride
nama   name
nanti   later
nanti malam   tonight

nasi   rice
nasi goréng   fried rice
nasi kuning   steamed yellow rice
nasi uduk   steamed rice with
  coconut and herbs
nasihat   advice
negara   state
nelayan   fisherman
nénék   grandmother
nilai tukar   rate
nomor   number
nonton   to watch, to see
novel   novel
Numpang tanya...   May I ask...
nyaman   pleasant

O, ya...   By the way...
obat   medicine
olahraga   sport
oléh-oléh   present from a trip,
  souvenir
ongkos   cost
orang   person, people
orang Brazil   Brazilian (person)
orang Inggeris   Englishman
orang tua   parents

pabrik   factory
pacar   boyfriend, girlfriend
pahit   bitter
pakai   to use, to wear
pakaian   clothes
pakét   parcel, package
pakét wisata   package tour
paling   the most
pandai   clever
pandang   look, glance
panggil   to call
panjang   long
pantai   beach
pantas   it's no wonder
panti pijat   massage parlour

papa *father*
parkir *to park*
paruh *half, part*
paruh waktu *part time*
pasar *market*
paspor *passport*
pasti *of course, definite*
patah *broken*
pecel lélé *fried catfish with chilli sauce*
pecinta (cinta, *n*) *lover*
pecinta alam *nature lover*
pedas *spicy*
pegawai *employee*
pegawai negeri *public servant*
pegelaran (gelar, *n*)
  performance
pekerja (kerja, *v*) *worker*
pekerjaan (kerja, *v*) *job*
pelabuhan (labuh, *v*) *port*
pelajaran (ajar, *v*) *lesson*
pelancong *tourist*
pelari (lari, *v*) *runner*
pelayan *waiter*
pelukis (lukis, *v*) *painter*
pemain (main, *v*) *player*
pemain piano *pianist*
pemalu (malu, *a*) *a shy person*
pemandangan (pandang, *n*)
  scenery, landscape
pemasaran (pasar, *n*) *marketing*
pembantu (bantu, *v*) *maid*
pembayaran (bayar, *v*)
  payment
pembeli (beli, *v*) *buyer*
pembuat (buat, *v*) *maker*
pembuat program komputer
  computer programmer
pémpék *fried or boiled sago with a special sauce*
pemusik (musik, *n*) *musician*

penari (tari, *v*) *dancer*
penari balét *ballet dancer*
penari Bali *Balinese dancer*
pencuci (cuci, *v*) *launderer, cleaning agent*
pencuci mulut *dessert*
péndék *short*
péndét *a Balinese religious dance*
pendidikan (didik, *v*) *education*
penduduk (duduk, *v*) *population*
penerbangan (terbang, *v*) *flight*
pengajar (ajar, *v*) *teacher*
pengajaran (ajar, *v*) *teaching*
pengalaman (alam, *n*)
  experience
pengalaman kerja *work experience*
pengganti (ganti, *v*) *to replace, instead (of)*
pengusaha (usaha, *v*)
  businessman
penjaga (jaga, *v*) *guard*
penjaga toko *shop assistant*
penjahit pakain *tailor*
penjual (jual, *v*) *seller*
pénsil *pencil*
pensiun *retired*
penuh *full*
penuh waktu *full time*
penulis (tulis, *v*) *writer*
penyakit (sakit, *a*) *illness*
penyanyi (nyanyi, *v*) *singer*
pérak *silver*
perancang (rancang, *n*)
  planner, designer
perancang mode *fashion designer*
Perancis *French*
perapatan *crossroads*
peraturan *regulation, restriction*

perawat (rawat, v) *nurse*
perbankan (bank, n) *banking*
percaya *to believe*
perempatan *crossroads*
perempuan *girl*
periklanan (iklan, n) *advertising*
periksa *to check, to examine*
perjalanan (jalan, n) *journey*
perkantoran (kantor, n) *office complex*
perkebunan (kebun, n) *plantation*
perlu *to need*
permisi *excuse me*
pernah *ever*
pernikahan (nikah, v) *wedding*
perpustakaan (pustaka, n) *library*
pertama *first*
pertandingan (tanding, v) *competition, contest*
pertandingan bola kaki *football game*
pertanian (tani, n) *agriculture*
pertimbangkan (timbang, v) *to consider*
pertunjukan (tunjuk, v) *performance*
pertunjukan kesenian *performing art show*
perusahaan (usaha, v) *company*
perusahaan swasta *private company*
pesan *to order, to reserve*
pesawat *plane, machine*
pésta *party*
peta *map*
petani (tani, n) *farmer*
petualangan (tualang, v) *adventure*
pinjam *to borrow*

pijat *massage*
pikir *to think*
pikiran (pikir, v) *thought*
pilih *to choose*
pilihan (pilih, v) *option, choice*
pimpinan/manajer *manager*
pinjamkan (pinjam, v) *to lend*
pintar *clever*
pisang *banana*
plastik *plastic*
porsi *portion*
potong *piece*
potongan (potong, n) *discount*
potongan harga *discount*
pramugara *air steward*
pramugari *air hostess, stewardess*
présidén *president*
produk *product*
program *programme*
propinsi *province*
pucat *pale*
pukis *crescent-shaped cake*
punya *to have*
punya siapa? *whose?*
pura *temple*
pusat *centre*
pusat industri *industrial centre*
pusat kebugaran *fitness centre*
pusat kota *city centre*
pusat perbelanjaan *shopping centre*
pusing *dizzy*
pustakawan/pustakawati *librarian*
putih *white*

Rabu *Wednesday*
ramah *friendly*
ramai *crowded*
rambutan *a type of hairy fruit*

rapat *meeting*
rapat karyawan *staff meeting*
rapi *neatly*
rasa *taste*
rasanya *it tastes like*
raya *great, large*
rebus *boiled*
rékoméndasi *recommend*
rencana *plans*
rendang *a dish made with meat, spices and coconut milk*
répot *busy, occupied*
riwayat *story, biography*
riwayat hidup *curriculum vitae*
rokok *cigarette*
romantis *romantic*
ruang *room, space*
ruang kelas *classroom*
ruang keluarga *living room*
ruang makan *dining room*
ruang tamu *guest room*
rugi *bankrupt/lose out*
rujak *fruit salad in spicy sauce*
rumah *house*
rumah makan *restaurant*
rumah sakit *hospital*
rute *route*

sabar *patient, patience*
Sabtu *Saturday*
saja *just, only*
sakit *sick, ill*
Sakit apa? *What seems to be the trouble?*
salah *wrong*
salah makan *to eat something that disagrees with you*
salam *regards*
sama *with, and*
sama dengan *equal to, the same as*

sambal *chilli sauce*
sambil *while*
Sambil menyelam minum air. *To kill two birds with one stone.*
Sampai bertemu lagi! *See you again!*
sambung *to dial, to be connected, to continue*
sampaikan (sampai, v) *to pass on, to convey*
Sampaikan salam saya untuk... *Give my regards to...*
sangat *very*
santan *coconut milk*
saos *sauce*
saos kacang *peanut sauce*
saos tiram *oyster sauce*
sarapan pagi *breakfast*
sarjana *master's degree*
saté *grilled meat on skewers with peanut sauce*
saudara *you, brother, sister*
saudara laki-laki *brother*
saudara perempuan *sister*
sauna *sauna*
saya *I, I am*
Saya kira tidak. *I don't think so.*
Saya kurang suka *I don't really like*
Saya tersesat. *I am lost.*
Sayang! *What a shame!, darling*
sayang sekali *unfortunately*
sayur *vegetable*
sebagai *as*
sebelum *before*
sebelumnya *formerly, previously*
Sebentar! *Just a moment!*
secepatnya *as soon as possible*
sedang *now*
sedikit *a little*

Sedikit-sedikit lama lama menjadi bukit. *Take it one step at a time.*

segar *fresh*

séhat *healthy*

sehingga *until, up to, so that*

seikat *a bundle*

sejarah *history*

sejuk *cool*

sekali *very, once*

sekarang *now*

sekitar *around*

sekolah dasar *elementary school*

sekretaris *secretary*

séksi *sexy*

selalu *always*

Selamat datang! *Welcome!*

Selamat jalan! *Goodbye!*

Selamat malam! *Good evening!*

Selamat pagi! *Good morning!*

Selamat siang! *Good afternoon!/good day!*

Selamat soré! *Good afternoon!*

Selamat tidur! *Good night!*

Selamat tinggal! *Goodbye!*

Selamat ulang tahun! *Happy birthday!*

Sélandia Baru *New Zealand*

Selasa *Tuesday*

selatan *south*

seluruh *all*

semangat *motivation*

sembuh *to get better, recover (from an illness)*

semenanjung *peninsula*

semua *all (this)*

semur daging *beef cooked in sweet sauce*

semut *ant*

senam *aerobics*

senang *happy*

sendiri *alone, oneself*

séndok *spoon*

seni *art*

Senin *Monday*

sepatu *shoe(s)*

seperti *like*

sepi *quiet*

sepupu *cousin*

seragam *uniform*

seré *lemon grass*

sering *often*

sesak nafas *asthma*

seseorang (orang, n) *someone*

sesuatu *something*

setelah *after*

setengah *half*

setiap *every*

siap *ready*

siapa? *who?*

siapkan (siap, v) *to prepare*

sibuk *busy*

silahkan *please*

simpan *to keep*

Singapura *Singapore*

sisanya (sisa, n) *the rest*

Skotlandia *Scotland*

snorkling *snorkeling*

sopan *polite*

soré *afternoon*

soto *soup*

Spanyol *Spain*

standar *standard*

stasiun *station*

suami *husband*

sudah *already*

Sudah bérés. *Everything's in order.*

suka *to like*

sulit *difficult*

sumbangkan (tumbang, v) *to make fall down*

sumberdaya manusia *human resources*
sumpit *chopstick(s)*
sungai *river*
supir *driver*
surat *letter*
surat-menyurat *to handle correspondence*
susah *difficult*

tahu *to know*
tahu isi tofu *filled with vegetables*
tahun baru *new year*
taksi *taxi*
tambah *to add*
tambah lagi *to have some more*
tanda tangan *signature*
tanpa *without*
tapé *fermented cassava*
tari topeng *masked dance*
tarian (tari, v) *dancing*
tari-tarian *dancing*
tas *bag*
tawar *bargain*
téh *tea*
téh jahé *tea with ginger*
tekanan (tekon, n) *pressure*
tekanan darah *blood pressure*
teliti *accurate*
télpon *telephone*
telur *egg*
telur dadar *omelette*
telur mata sapi *fried egg*
teman *friend*
tembakau *tobacco*
tempat *place*
tempat beristirahat (istirahat, n) *holiday resort*
tempat parkir *car park*

tempat tukar uang *money changer, bureau de change*
témperatur *temperature*
tenang *quiet, calm*
ténis méja *ping-pong*
tentang *about*
tentara *soldier(s)*
tentu *sure*
tentu saja *of course*
tepat *exact*
tepat sekali *exactly*
tepat waktu *on time, punctual*
tepi *edge, border*
tepi pantai *beach front*
tepung *flour*
terbang *to fly*
terbiasa *to be used to*
terbuat *to be made of*
Terbuat dari apa? *What is it made of?*
tercapai (capai, v) *to be reached*
terhadup (hadup, n) *to toward*
terima *to receive*
terima kasih *thank you*
terisi (isi, v) *to be occupied*
terjebak (jebak, v) *trapped, stuck*
terkenal (kenal, v) *famous*
terlalu *too*
terlambat (lambat, a) *late*
termasuk (masok, v) *included*
Terserah kamu. *It's up to you.*
tersesat (sesat, v) *lost*
tertarik (tarik, v) *interested*
teruskan (terus, a) *to go straight on*
terutama *especially*
tetapi *but*
tiba *to arrive*
Tidak apa apa. *That's all right.*
tidak pernah *never*

tidak termasuk   *not included*
Tidak usah.   *It's not necessary.*
Tidak, terima kasih.   *No,
  thank you.*
tidur   *to sleep*
tiga   *three*
tikét   *ticket*
tikét pesawat   *air ticket*
tikét pulang pergi   *return ticket*
tikét satu jalan   *one-way ticket*
tikus   *mouse*
tikus besar   *rat*
tinggal   *to stay*
tinggi   *high, tall*
tiram   *oyster*
titip   *to entrust*
titip pesan   *to leave a message*
toge   *bean sprouts*
toko   *shop*
tolong   *please*
topeng   *mask*
traktir   *to treat*
tukar   *to change*
tulis   *to write*
tuliskan (tulis, v)   *to write down*
tunda   *to delay, to put off*
tunggu   *to wait*
tunjukkkan (tunjuk, v)   *to show*
turis   *tourist*
tur   *tour*
turun   *to get off, to get down*
tutup   *close*
TV   *(pronounce as in English) TV*

uang   *money*
ubah   *difference*
udang   *shrimp*

udara   *air*
ukuran (ukur, n)   *size*
ulangi   *to repeat*
umur   *age*
undang   *to invite*
ungu   *purple*
unik   *unique, special*
untuk   *for, to, in order to*
urusan (urus, n)   *affairs, business*
usaha   *to manage, to organize*

vétsin   *monosodium glutamate*
vidéo   *video*

waktu   *time*
waktu luang   *free time*
walaupun   *although*
Wales   *Wales*
warga   *citizen, member*
warga negara   *nationality*
warna   *colour*
wartawan/wartawati   *journalist*
wayang   *puppet*
wayang golék   *wooden puppet
  performance in Java and
  Bali*
wayang kulit   *leather shadow
  puppet performance*
wayang orang   *traditional drama
  performance*
wisata   *tour*
wisuda   *graduation*
wortel   *carrot*

ya   *yes*
yakin   *sure, convinced*
yang mana?   *which one?*

English–Indonesian vocabulary

This list is designed as a reference to supplement the language you have learnt in the course, especially while travelling. For this reason, many of the words are those you may need to find quickly in situations such as accidents, emergencies etc.

above **di atas**
abroad **luar negeri**
accept **menerima/terima**
accident **kecelakaan**
accommodation **penginapan/ akomodasi**
across **seberang**
address **alamat**
adult **déwasa**
advertising **periklanan**
after **setelah/sesudah**
afternoon **siang/soré**
again **lagi**
age **umur**
ago **yang lalu**
air **udara**
airplane **pesawat udara**
airport **bandar udara/lapangan terbang**
alarm clock **jam wéker**
all **semua**
allergic **alérgik**
always **selalu**
and **dan**
angry **marah**
animal **héwan/binatang**
answer **menjawab/jawab**
antiseptic **penangkal inféksi**
anything **apa saja**
apple **apel**

appointment **janji**
arrival **kedatangan**
arrive **tiba/sampai**
autumn **musim gugur**

back **di belakang/punggung** *(of body)*
bag **tas**
bakery **toko roti**
banana **pisang**
bandage **perban/pembalut**
bank **bank**
banknote **uang kertas**
barber **tukang cukur**
bath **mandi**
bathroom **kamar mandi**
battery **baterai**
beach **pantai**
beautiful **indah/cantik**
bed **tempat tidur**
bedroom **kamar tidur**
beef **daging sapi**
before **sebelum**
begin **mulai**
behind **di belakang**
between **di antara**
big **besar**
bird **burung**
blanket **selimut**
blood **darah**

body **badan/tubuh**
border **tepi**
boring **bosan**
bottle **botol**

broken **patah**
brown **coklat**
building **bangunan**
busy **sibuk, répot**
bus stop **halte**
buy **membeli/beli**

camera **kaméra**
campsite **tempat ténda/tempat perkémahan**
careful **hati-hati**
centimetre **séntiméter**
change **mengganti/ganti/ menukar/tukar** *(money)*
cheap **murah**
check-in **cék in**
cheese **kéju**
cheque **cék**
chest **dada**
chicken **ayam**
child **anak**
choose **memilih/pilih**
cinema **bioskop**
city **kota**
class **kelas**
clean **bersih**
clock **jam**
closed **tutup**
coconut **kelapa**
coffee **kopi**
cold **dingin**
colour **warna**
come **datang**
comfortable **nyaman**
country **negara**
crab **kepiting**
credit card **kartu krédit**

crossroads **perempatan/ perapatan**
cup **mangkuk**

daily **harian/setiap hari**
dance (verb) **menari/tari** *(noun)* **tarian**
dangerous **bahaya**
dark **gelap**
date (calendar) **tanggal** *(romantic)* **janji**
date of birth **tanggal lahir**
daughter **anak perempuan**
day **hari**
delicious **lezat/énak**
dentist **dokter gigi**
depart **berangkat**
departure **keberangkatan**
destination **tujuan**
develop a film **mencétak film**
diarrhoea **diaré**
dictionary **kamus**
different (from) **berbéda**
difficult **sulit**
dinner **makan malam**
direct **langsung**
dirty **kotor**
disco **diskotik**
dive **menyelam**
doctor **dokter**
dog **anjing**
door **pintu**
drink **minum**
drive (verb) **mengemudi**
dry **kering**

each **tiap/tiap-tiap**
ear **telinga/kuping**
early **pagi-pagi/duluan**
east **timur**
easy **mudah/gampang**

eat **makan**
egg **telur**
electricity **listrik**
embassy **kedutaan besar**
emergency **gawat darurat**
empty **kosong**
engine **mesin**
engineer **insinyur**
English **bahasa Inggeris**
enough **cukup**
enter **masuk**
entertainment **hiburan**
entrance **pintu masuk**
envelope **amplop**
equipment **peralatan**
evening **malam**
every **setiap**
everything **segala sesuatu**
excellent **istiméwa/bagus sekali**
exchange **pertukaran**
exchange rate **nilai tukar/kurs**
exhibition **paméran**
exit **pintu keluar**
expensive **mahal**
express **eksprés/cepat**
eye **mata**

face **wajah/muka**
fall **jatuh**
family **keluarga**
famous **terkenal**
far **jauh**
farmer **petani**
fast **cepat**
father **ayah/bapak/papa**
faulty **cacat**
feel **merasa/rasa**
festival **perayaan/pésta**
fever **demam**
field **bidang/ladang**
film **film**

fine **baik**
finger **jari**
fire **api**
first **pertama**
first aid **pertolongan pertama**
first class **tingkat pertama**
fish **ikan**
fisherman **nelayan**
flight **penerbangan**
floor **lantai**
flower **bunga/kembang**
food **makanan**
foot **kaki**
for **untuk**

game **pertandingan/
permainan**
garage **gerasi**
garbage **sampah**
garden **kebun**
gardening **berkebun**
garlic **bawang putih**
gift **hadiah**
girl **anak perempuan**
give **memberi/beri**
glass **gelas**
glasses **kacamata**
go **pergi**
goat **kambing**
gold **emas**
good **bagus/baik**
government **pemerintahan**
grape **anggur**
green **hijau**
greengrocer **penjual sayuran
dan buah-buahan**
grey **abu-abu**
guide **petunjuk**

hair **rambut**
half **setengah, separuh**

ham   **daging babi**
hand   **tangan**
hand made   **buatan tangan**
hand phone   **télépon genggam**
handbag   **tas tangan**
handicraft   **kerajinan**
happy   **bahagia/gembira**
hard   **keras**
hat   **topi**
head   **kepala**
headache   **sakit kepala**
health   **keséhatan**
hear   **mendengar**
heart   **hati**
heater   **pemanas**
heavy   **berat**
help (verb)   **membantu/**
  bantu *(noun)* **pertolongan**
  (exclamation) **Tolong!**
herbs   **ramuan**
here   **di sini**
high   **tinggi**
hike   **sepéda**
hill   **bukit**
hire   **menyéwa/séwa**
hitchhike   **menggoncéng/**
  goncéng
hobby   **hobi**
holiday   **liburan**
honey   **madu**
honeymoon   **bulan madu**
horrible   **mengerikan**
horse   **kuda**
hospital   **rumah sakit**
hot   **panas**
hotel   **hotél**
hour   **jam**
house   **rumah**
humid   **lembab**
hungry   **marah**
husband   **suami**

I   **saya**
ice   **és**
ice cream   **és krim**
I.D.   **Tanda Pengenal/**
  surat keterangan
I.D. card   **KTP/Kartu**
  Tanda Pengenal
ill   **sakit**
immigration   **imigrasi**
important   **penting**
included   **termasuk**
indigestion   **salah cerna**
infection   **inféksi**
in front of   **di depan**
information   **informasi/**
  keterangan
injection   **suntikan**
insect   **serangga**
inside   **di dalam**
insurance   **asuransi**
interesting   **menarik**
island   **pulau**
itinerary   **rencana perjalanan**

jacket   **jakét**
jackfruit   **buah nangka**
jail   **penjara**
jeep   **jip**
jewellery   **perhiasan**
job   **pekerjaan**
journalist   **wartawan**
journey   **perjalanan**
juice   **jus**
jumper   **sweater/baju hangat**

key   **kunci**
kill   **membunuh/bunuh**
kilogram   **kilogram**
kilometre   **kilométer**
kiosk   **kios**
kitchen   **dapur**

knee	**lutut**
knife	**pisau**
know	**tahu/kenal**
lace	**renda**
lake	**danau**
land (verb)	**mendarat/darat**
language	**bahasa**
large	**besar**
last	**terakhir**
late	**terlambat**
later	**nanti**
laundry	**binatu**
laxative	**obat usus**
lazy	**malas**
leak	**lemah**
learn	**belajar**
leather	**kulit**
left (direction)	**kiri**
leg	**kaki**
lemon	**jeruk nipis**
letter	**surat**
library	**perpustakaan**
lift	**lift**
light	**lampu**
like	**suka**
lips	**bibir**
listen	**mendengar/dengar**
little	**kecil/sedikit**
live	**tinggal**
long	**panjang**
long distance	**interlokal**
look	**melihat**
lose	**hilang**
lost	**tersesat**
lotion	**salep/krim**
loud	**keras/kencang**
low	**rendah**
luggage	**barang-barang/ bagasi**
lunch	**makan siang**

machine	**mesin**
made of	**dibuat dari**
magazine	**majalah**
mail	**surat/pos**
main	**utama**
make	**membuat**
malaria	**malaria**
man	**orang laki-laki/pria**
manager	**pimpinan, manajer**
many	**banyak**
map	**peta**
market	**pasar**
massage (verb)	**memijit/pijit**
(noun)	**pijit**
material	**bahan baju**
mattress	**kasur**
maybe	**mungkin**
mayor	**mayor**
mechanic	**montir**
medicine	**obat-obatan**
meet	**bertemu**
meeting	**pertemuan/rapat**
menstruation	**datang bulan/ haid/ménstruasi**
menu	**daftar makanan**
message	**pesan**
metal	**logam**
metre	**méter**
midnight	**tengah malam**
migraine	**sakit kepala berat**
milk	**susu**
millimetre	**miliméter**
million	**juta**
mineral water	**air mineral**
minute	**menit**
money	**uang**
monkey	**monyét**
month	**bulan**
monument	**monumén**
morning	**pagi**
mosque	**mesjid**

mosquito **nyamuk**
mother **ibu/mama**
motorcycle **motor**
mountain **gunung**
mountain climbing **mendaki gunung/naik gunung**
mouse **tikus**
mouth **mulut**
museum **musium**
music **musik**
Muslim **muslim**
must **harus**

name **nama**
nappy **popok**
nationality **warga negara/kebangsaan**
nature **alam**
near **dekat**
necessary **perlu/penting**
necklace **kalung**
needle **jarum**
neighbour **tetangga**
net **jaring/jala**
new **baru**
news **berita**
newspaper **surat kabar/koran**
next **selanjutnya/di samping**
nice **bagus, baik**
night **malam**
noisy **ribut**
noodles **mie (**pronounced **mi)**
north **utara**
nose **hidung**
now **sekarang**
number **nomor/angka**
nurse **perawat**
nut **kacang**

occupation **pekerjaan**
ocean **samudera/lautan**

offer **menawarkan/tawar**
office **kantor**
often **sering**
oil **minyak**
old **tua**
one **satu**
one way **satu arah**
onion **bawang mérah**
only **hanya**
open **membuka/buka**
operation **operasi**
opposite **berlawanan/lawan**
or **atau**
orange **jeruk**
order **perintah**
original **asli**
other **yang lain**
outside **di luar**
owner **pemilik**

packet **pakét**
pain **sakit**
painful **menyakitkan**
painkiller **penawar sakit**
paint **melukis**
painter **pelukis**
palace **istana**
paper **kertas**
parcel **parsel/bingkisan**
parent **orang tua**
park **taman**
party **pésta**
pass (verb) **melewati/lewat** (noun) **kartu**
passenger **penumpang**
passport **paspor**
pay **membayar**
payment **bayaran**
peaceful **damai**
peanut **kacang**
pen **péna**

pencil **pénsil**
pepper **merica**
perfect **sempurna**
performance **pertunjukan,
pegelaran**
perhaps **barangkali**
permission **izin**
permit **izin**
person **orang**
petrol **bénsin**
pharmacy **apotik**
phone (verb) **menélpon**
phone booth **gardu télpon**
phone card **kartu télpon**
photograph **foto**
photographer **tukang foto/
tukang potrét**
photography **fotografi**
pick up **menjemput**
pickpocketed **kecopétan**
picture **gambar**
piece **potong/lembar**
pig **babi**
pill **pil**
pillow **bantal**
pillow case **sarung bantal**
pineapple **nanas**
pink **mérah jambu**
place **tempat**
place of birth **tempat lahir**
plan **rencana**
plant **tanaman**
plate **piring**
platform **péron**
play **membayar/bayar**
plug **stéker**
poisonous **beracun**
police **polisi**
pool **kolam**
poor **miskin**
popular **terkenal**

pork **daging babi**
port **pelabuhan**
post (verb) **mengirim surat**
(noun) **surat**
post office **kantor pos**
postcard **kartu pos**
potato **kentang**
pottery **tembikar**
pregnant **hamil**
prepare **menyiapkan**
prescription **resép**
present **kado/hadiah**
pretty **cantik**
price **harga**
print **mencétak**
prison **penjara**
private **pribadi**
problem **masalah**
profession **profési/pekerjaan**
pull **menarik, penuh**
puncture **kebocoran/pecah**
purple **ungu**
purse **dompt**
push **mendorong/dorong**

quality **kualitas/mutu**
quantity **jumlah**
quarantine **karantina**
quarter **seperempat**
question **pertanyaan**
queue **antri**
quick **cepat**
quiet **sepi/tenang**

radiator **radiator**
railway **jalan keréta**
railway station **stasiun keréta**
rain **hujan**
rare **jarang**
rash **kudis/ruam**
rat **tikus besar**

rate **tarif/kurs**	*roof* **atap**
raw **mentah**	*room* **kamar**
razor **alat cukur**	*rotten* **busuk/rusak**
razor blade(s) **pisau cukur**	*round* **bundar bulat**
read **membaca/baca**	*rubbish* **sampah**
ready **siap**	*rules* **peraturan**
receipt **kwitansi**	*run* **lari**
receive **menerima/terima**	
recently **baru-baru ini**	*sad* **sedih**
recommend **menasihati/**	*safe* **aman**
nasihat	*salary* **gaji**
red **mérah**	*sale* **obral**
refrigerator **kulkas/lemari és**	*salt* **garam**
refund **pembayaran kembali**	*salty* **asin**
region **wilayah**	*sand* **pasir**
relax **bersantai/santai**	*sandal(s)* **sandal**
religion **agama**	*sanitary towels* **pembalut**
remember **mengingat**	*say* **berkata/bilang**
rent (verb) **menyéwa/séwa**	*scarf* **seléndang/syal**
(noun) **séwa**	*scenery* **pemandangan**
repair **memperbaiki/perbaiki**	*school* **sekolah**
repeat **mengulangi/ulangi**	*scissors* **gunting**
reply **membalas**	*sea* **laut**
request **meminta**	*seaside* **tepi laut**
reservation **réservasi**	*season* **musim**
reserve **memesan/pesan**	*seat* **kursi/tempat duduk**
rest **istirahat**	*seat belt* **sabuk pengaman**
restaurant **rumah makan,**	*second* **kedua**
restoran	*see* **melihat**
retired **pensiun**	*self-service* **pelayanan sendiri**
return **kembali**	*sell* **menjual**
return ticket **tikét pulang pergi**	*send* **mengirim**
rice **beras/nasi**	*servant* **pembantu**
rich **kaya**	*serve* **melayani/layan**
ride **mengemudikan/naik**	*service* **pelayanan/jasa**
right **kanan**	*several* **beberapa**
ring **cincin**	*sew* **menjahit/jahit**
ripe **matang**	*shampoo* **sampo**
river **sungai**	*shave* **mencukur**
road **jalan**	*sheep* **domba**
rob **merampok/rampok**	*sheet* **sepréi**

ship **kapal laut**	*something* **sesuatu**
shirt **keméja**	*sometimes* **kadang-kadang**
shoe(s) **sepatu**	*son* **anak laki-laki**
shop **toko**	*soon* **segera**
shopping **berbelanja**	*south* **selatan**
short **péndék**	*souvenir* **oléh-oléh/cinderamata**
shorts **celana péndék**	*soy sauce* **kécap asin**
shoulders **bahu**	*speak* **berbicara/bicara**
show **pertunjukan**	*special* **spésial/khusus**
shower **mandi**	*spoon* **séndok**
shrimp **udang**	*sport* **olahraga**
shrine **tempat suci/pura**	*spring* **musim semi**
shut **menutup**	*stairs* **tangga**
sick **sakit**	*stamp* **perangko**
sickness **penyakit**	*starfruit* **belimbing**
sign **tanda**	*start* **mulai**
signature **tanda tangan**	*station* **stasiun**
silk **sutera**	*stay* **tinggal/menginap**
silver **pérak**	*steak* **bistik**
simple **sederhana**	*steal* **mencuri**
sing **menyanyi**	*stomach* **perut**
single **bujangan**	*stop* **berhenti**
single room **kamar untuk satu orang**	*storm* **badai**
	street **jalan**
sister **saudara perempuan**	*strong* **kuat**
sit **duduk**	*student* **pelajar/mahasiswa**
size **ukuran**	*stupid* **bodoh**
ski **ski**	*sugar* **gula**
skin **kulit**	*suitcase* **kopor**
sleep **tidur**	*summer* **musim panas**
sleeping bag **tas tidur**	*sun* **matahari**
sleepy **ngantuk**	*sunglasses* **kacamata hitam**
slice **potong/mengiris/iris**	*sunny* **cerah**
slow **lambat**	*suntan lotion* **salep untuk melindungi kulit dari matahari**
small **kecil**	
smoke **merokok**	*supermarket* **pasar swalayan**
snake **ular**	*surf* **berselancar**
soap **sabun**	*surname* **nama keluarga**
sock(s) **kaos kaki**	*sweet* **manis**
soft **lembut**	*swim* **berenang**
somebody **seseorang**	*swimming pool* **kolam renang**

table **méja**	*travel agency* **biro perjalanan**
tablet **tablét**	*travellers' cheques* **cék turis**
take **mengambil/ambil**	*travel sickness* **mabuk jalan**
talk **bercakap-cakap/berbicara**	*trip* **perjalanan**
tall **tinggi**	*trousers* **celana panjang**
tasty **énak**	*true* **benar**
tea **téh**	*turn* **bélok**
teacher **guru**	*twins* **kembar**
telegram **telegram/surat kawat**	*tyre* **ban**
telephone **télpon**	
temperature **suhu udara**	*umbrella* **payung**
tennis **ténis**	*under* **di bawah**
theatre **téater**	*understand* **mengerti**
thief **pencuri**	*underwear* **celana dalam**
think **berpikir**	*university* **universitas**
thirsty **haus**	*urgent* **penting/mendesak**
throat **tenggorokan**	*useful* **berguna**
ticket **tikét**	
ticket office **lokét**	*vacant* **kosong**
tiger **harimau**	*vacation* **liburan**
tight **erat**	*vaccination* **vaksinasi**
time **waktu**	*valuable* **berharga**
timetable **jadwal**	*value* **nilai**
tin **kaléng**	*vegetables* **sayur-sayuran**
tip **tip**	*vegetarian* **végétarian**
tired **lelah/capék**	*very* **sangat**
today **hari ini**	*village* **désa/kampung**
together **bersama-sama**	*visa* **visa**
toilet paper **kertas klosét**	*visit* **berkunjung**
toilet **kamar kecil**	*volcano* **gunung berapi**
tomorrow **bésok**	*vomit* **muntah**
tonight **malam ini**	
tooth/teeth **gigi**	*wait* **menunggu/tungu**
toothache **sakit gigi**	*waiter* **pelayan**
toothpaste **odol/pasta gigi**	*waiting room* **ruang tamu**
tour **berkeliling/tur/wisata**	*wake up* **bangun**
tourist **pelancong**	*walk* **berjalan**
towel **handuk**	*wall* **dinding**
traffic **lalu lintas**	*want* **ingin**
traffic lights **lampu lalu lintas**	*wardrobe* **lemari**
train **keréta api**	*warm* **hangat**

wash	**mencuci**	*without*	**tanpa**
watch	**menonton/nonton**	*woman*	**perempuan, wanita**
water	**air**	*wonderful*	**bagus sekali**
watermelon	**semangka**	*wood*	**kayu**
weak	**lemah**	*woodcarving*	**ukiran kayu**
wear	**memakai/pakai**	*woollen*	**terbuat dari wol**
weather	**cuaca**	*work*	**bekerja**
week	**minggu**	*world*	**dunia**
weekend	**akhir pekan**	*write*	**menulis/tulis**
weight	**berat**	*wrong*	**salah**
west	**barat**		
wet	**basah**	*year*	**tahun**
wheel	**roda**	*yellow*	**kuning**
wheelchair	**kursi roda**	*yesterday*	**kemarin**
white	**putih**	*young*	**muda**
wife	**istri**	*youth*	**remaja**
window	**jendéla**	*youth hostel*	**losmén pemuda**
windy	**berangin**		
wine	**anggur**	*zoo*	**kebun binatang**
winter	**musim dingin**		